ROADMAP™ C1-C2

STUDENT'S BOOK

with digital resources and mobile app

Jonathan Bygrave, Jeremy Day, Lindsay Warwick and Damian Williams

Contents

FAST-TRACK ROUTE

EXTENDED ROUTE

MASTER YOUR SKILLS LESSON	GOAL	FOCUS
1A Master your writing page 126	write a blog post	using hyperbole to enhance impact
1B Master your reading page 106	understand short anecdotes in an article	recognising cohesive devices in a text
1C Master your listening page 96	understand a persuasive speech	recognising persuasive language
2A Master your reading page 108	understand a newspaper article	recognising scepticism
2B Master your listening page 97	understanding an informal explanation	recognising understatement
2C Master your writing page 128	write project communications	rejecting ideas and asking for changes
3A Master your reading page 110	understand business articles	evaluating the effectiveness of an argument
3B Master your writing page 130	write a proposal	using persuasive language
3C Master your listening page 98	understand a formal talk and informal conversation on the same topic	recognising differences in formality
4A Master your reading page 112	understand a narrative or biography	recognising foreshadowing of events
4B Master your writing page 132	write a letter of application for an internship	putting a positive spin on limited experience and skills
4C Master your listening page 99	understand a group discussion	recognising references to common expressions
5A Master your listening page 100	understand a narrative	understanding colloquial language
5B Master you reading page 114	understand a story	distinguishing between literal and allegorical meaning
5C Master your writing page 134	write an essay	synthesising information from a number of sources

Contents

FAST-TRACK ROUTE

EXTENDED ROUTE

1A Team building

- Goal: give feedback on an event
- Language focus: present, past and future perfect
- Vocabulary: phrases with delexical verbs

A

Reading

1 Work in pairs and discuss the questions.

1 What are the people doing in the photos? Why?
2 Have you ever taken part in activities like these? What happened?
3 What are the benefits of team-building activities?

2 Read the article. Which team-building activity/activities does each statement refer to?

1 The first team to finish is the winner.
2 You can do it in your workplace with no preparation or equipment.
3 There are two stages: making something and doing something with it.
4 It involves a lot of walking.
5 It forces people to ask and answer questions.
6 It's best to make a plan before you start construction.

6 quick but powerful team-building activities

Let's face it, most of us prefer to work alone. But if we make the effort to break down the barriers between us, it unleashes boundless potential in each of us. Whether you're a business leader or an educator, you need to give your people a nudge to push them beyond their comfort zones. Let's take a look at six of the best ways to do some priceless team building.

Scavenger hunt: Each team has a list of objects to find, such as a snail shell or a golf ball. At the end of the time limit, the team with the most objects is the winner. Alternative versions include photo scavenger hunts (where teams have to photograph items on the list) and data hunts (where they go on a search for information, like dates on buildings). A fun way to get some exercise in the fresh air!

Tell the truth: Team members take turns to share quirky facts about themselves. The others ask questions to work out if they're lying or telling the truth. A great way to get to know your colleagues' hidden sides!

Raft building: Divide your people into teams and give them 30 minutes to design and construct a raft from plastic drums, planks of wood and rope. Afterwards, they use the rafts to hold an exhilarating race across a river.

Get in line: Divide the group into two teams. The teams then race to organise themselves into lines based on questions like 'How many countries have you visited?' A great way of getting people talking – and listening to each other.

Marshmallow challenge: Give each team a packet of spaghetti and some marshmallows, and set a time limit. At the end, the team with the tallest tower is the winner. This activity encourages design thinking as much as teamwork: it's much better to plan your structure before making a start.

Out and about: Why not simply go for a long hike together? Sometimes all it takes to integrate a team is a change of scenery and the time to have a good old-fashioned chat.

3 Work in pairs and discuss the questions.

1 Which activities in the article sound like fun? Which wouldn't you enjoy?
2 Which do you think would be the most successful at enhancing team spirit?

Vocabulary

4 a Underline phrases in the article that match phrases 1–9. Which words replace the verbs in bold?

1 if we **try** to break down the barriers
make the effort
2 you need to **nudge** your people
3 Let's **look** at six of the best ways
4 to **build** teams, which is priceless
5 they **search** for information
6 to **exercise** in the fresh air
7 to **race** across a river, which is exhilarating
8 Why not simply **hike** a long way
9 the time to **chat** in a good old-fashioned way

b Look at the answers in Exercise 4a. Which part of the phrase helps you understand the meaning in each case? What is a 'delexical verb'?

5 a Complete the phrases with the delexical verbs in the box.

do get give go have hold make take

1 _______ a lie-down/a well-earned rest/a sit down
2 _______ for a run/on a teambuilding course/for a stroll
3 _______ someone help/someone a break/someone a warm welcome
4 _______ some fresh air/people talking/the benefits of something
5 _______ a welcome meeting/a singing competition/a feedback session
6 _______ a contribution/a success of something/a statement
7 _______ some rock-climbing/plenty of preparation/someone good
8 _______ the initiative/the lead during an activity/something into consideration

b Work in pairs. Think of how some of the phrases in Exercise 5a might relate to team building.

*At the start of a team building day, the organisers might **give people a warm welcome**.*

Go to your app for more vocabulary and practice.

C

D

Language focus

6 1.1 **Listen to some people organising an event. Answer the questions.**

1. What was wrong with last year's event?
2. What was good about it?
3. What do they decide to do differently this year?

7 a 1.2 **Choose the most natural alternative to complete the extracts. Then listen and check.**

1. We've *talked/ been talking* about this a lot recently and we've *come/ been coming* to the conclusion that it was a bit of a waste of time.
2. Everyone just worked with people they'd already *known/ been knowing* for years.
3. People will be in teams with people from other departments, so they won't have *met/ been meeting* most of them before.
4. They were exhausted because they'd *travelled/ been travelling* for hours.
5. We spent a week hiking in the mountains, and by the third day we *have had/ had had* enough of each other!

b Read the language focus box and check your answers.

Present, past and future perfect

Present perfect simple and continuous

1 Measuring time up to now: Use the simple form for states and the continuous form for actions.

*We**'ve known** each other for years.*
*I**'ve been waiting** here since 10 o'clock.*

2 Present results: Use the simple form to talk about the present result of completed events and the continuous form to talk about the results of processes.

*I'm worried because I**'ve lost** my keys.*
*I'm tired because I**'ve been running**.*

3 Experiences up to now: Almost always use the simple form, even for repeated events.

*I**'ve** already **seen** this film ten times.*

4 Recent events and trends: Use the simple form for recent events and the continuous form for trends.

*I**'ve** just **been** to the park. I**'ve been reading** a lot recently.*

Past and future perfect simple and continuous

We use these forms for the same reasons as the present perfect simple and continuous, but with a focus on 'then' instead of 'now'.

*I'm tired **now** because I**'ve been running**.*
*I was tired **then** because I**'d been running**.*
*I'll be tired **then** because I**'ll have been running**.*

8 a 1.3 **How do you think *have/ had* is pronounced in these sentences? Listen and check.**

1. We'd been doing activities all day.
2. By then, they'll have been travelling for two days.
3. We've been taking regular breaks.

b Listen again and practise.

9 Complete the sentences with the most natural perfect form of the verb in brackets.

1. They'll be tired when the activity finishes – they ______________ non-stop for two hours. (hike)
2. I was bored in the training session because I ______________ the same information dozens of times over the years. (already/hear)
3. Recently, people ______________ tired of all these silly games during team-building events. (get)
4. Please let me know as soon as you ______________ where you want the group to go. (decide)

Go to page 146 or your app for more information and practice.

Speaking

PREPARE

10 **You're going to give feedback on an event. Turn to page 176.**

SPEAK

11 **Work in pairs. Take turns being the event organiser and an attendee. Attendee: Give feedback on the event. Organiser: Respond to the attendee's feedback, justifying your decisions.**

Master your writing page 126

1B Online/Offline

› **Goal:** describe your reaction to a situation
› **Language focus:** subject raising
› **Vocabulary:** idioms for expressing and controlling emotions

Reading

1 Work in pairs and discuss the questions.

1. What things irritate you when you're online? What about when you're offline?
2. Is there a difference between the way you (and other people) handle frustrating situations online and offline? Why?

2 a Work in pairs. Think of reasons why people's behaviours might change when they go online.

They might not think they're talking to a real person.

b Read the article. Which of the ideas you discussed are mentioned?

Language focus

3 a Underline the ways ideas 1–6 are expressed in the article.

1. It turns out the person we're abusing isn't the evil CEO …
   the person we're abusing turns out not to be the evil CEO …
2. It happens by chance that we see a member of our own community …
3. It might appear that the respondent is blanking you deliberately.
4. It appears that the writer is actively trying to humiliate us individually.
5. It turns out that the writer had a completely different target in mind.
6. It seems that some genuinely unpleasant people enjoy causing trouble …

b Work in pairs. How are the two versions in Exercise 3a different grammatically? Think about the subjects and what comes after the verbs.

6 reasons why people change when they go online

Have you ever noticed how lovely people turn into monsters when they're online? Here are six reasons why everyone seems so angry on the internet.

Lack of feedback clues: In normal life, we get irritated all the time. But we calm down quickly when we see the other person's facial expression or hear the tone of their voice and realise they feel bad about making an honest mistake. But online, that information is missing and our anger quickly gets out of hand.

Lack of empathy: Most of us hate upsetting others. But online, it's easy to forget that the object of our abuse is a real person with feelings. When we're communicating with large corporations, we assume they're impervious to normal emotions, so we unleash our fury on them. But the person we're abusing turns out not to be the evil CEO but rather some low-paid temp simply trying to help.

Herd mentality: We naturally organise ourselves into online communities with people of similar opinions. So when we happen to see a member of our own community engaged in a conflict with an 'outsider', it's hard to resist the temptation to defend your own 'side'. As more and more people wade in, a simple disagreement can quickly spiral out of control.

Knee jerk reactions: When you post a complaint on a company's social media feed, you naturally expect an instant response. If you have to wait more than a few minutes, the respondent might appear to be blanking you deliberately, which quickly transforms your mild irritation into intense fury.

Egocentric assumptions: Whenever we read general criticisms from our social circle, such as 'I hate people who do X', we tend to take them personally. The writer appears to be actively trying to humiliate us individually, because we once did X. So we take offence, even if, as is often the case, the writer turns out to have had a completely different target in mind.

Lack of punishment: The final reason is actually much less powerful than most people assume. It's true that there are rarely repercussions for bad online behaviour. It's also true that some genuinely unpleasant people seem to enjoy causing trouble simply because they can. But the vast majority of online rage and abuse is committed by normal people who wouldn't dream of upsetting others in real life. In other words, people like me, people like you.

4 **Read the language focus box to check your answers to Exercise 3b.**

Subject raising

With a small number of verbs (e.g. *seem, appear, turn out*), it is possible to express the same idea in two different ways:

1 *it* + verb + *that*-clause

*It seems that **you**'re right.*

2 subject + verb + *to*-infinitive

__You__ seem to be right.

A range of *to*-infinitive structures are possible:

1 *It appears that they're lying.* →
2 *They appear **to be lying**.*

1 *It turned out that they'd left.* →
2 *They turned out **to have left**.*

1 *It seems that they were misbehaving.* →
2 *They seem **to have been misbehaving**.*

Version 1 is useful if you want to avoid a complicated *to*-infinitive structure. In most other cases, version 2 is preferred because it's shorter and there's no need for a meaningless subject (*it*).

Two versions are also possible with the verb *happen*, but version 2 suggests that the event was unplanned/unexpected. Version 1 is quite rare.

1 *It happened that Joe came to visit yesterday* →
2 *Joe happened to come to visit yesterday.*
(= I wasn't planning/expecting him to visit.)

5 a 1.4 **Listen to three sentences. In which sentence is *it* pronounced most clearly? Why?**

1 It seems that you want to leave.
2 It turned out that the solution was simple.
3 It appeared that somebody was watching us.

b **Practise saying the three sentences as naturally as possible.**

6 **Rewrite the sentences so they start with the subject in bold.**

1 It seems that **nobody** understood the rules.
Nobody seems to have understood the rules.
2 It turned out that **she**'d been reading a text when she crashed her car.
3 It happened that **my video** went viral.
4 It appears that **somebody** has been trying to contact me for days.
5 It turned out that **the abusive post** had been written by a 14-year-old boy.
6 Did it happen that **you** noticed who broke the window?

7 **Work in pairs. Complete the sentences so that they are true for you. Then ask questions about your partner's stories.**

1 The other day, I happened to …
2 ____________ (Somebody/Something) turned out to be/to have been a lot more … than I expected.
3 ____________ (Somebody/Something) appears to have been ____________ (doing what?)
4 I'm not sure, but ____________ (somebody) seems to be ____________ (doing what?) at the moment.

Go to page 146 or your app for more information and practice.

Vocabulary

8 a **Read sentences 1–8 below. Which phrases are about:**

a feeling strong emotions?
b expressing your emotions?
c controlling your emotions?

1 I don't mind a little honest criticism – I've got a pretty **thick skin**.
2 It really **drives me up the wall** when people leave all the windows open.
3 I often want to scream at people, but I usually decide to **bite my tongue**.
4 Nasty online comments really **get under my skin**. Sometimes I think about them for days.
5 If I'm angry, I **let off steam** by kicking a tree rather than **lashing out** at other people.
6 I sometimes **bottle up** my emotions and **put a brave face on** things, but in the end it makes me more stressed.
7 I didn't want to **make a scene**, but I needed to **get something off my chest**. I knew he was lying to me.
8 Whenever I'm feeling annoyed, I try to remember to **take a step back** and look at the bigger picture. It really helps me to **put things into perspective**.

b **Work in pairs. Tell your partner which of the sentences in Exercise 8a are true for you. Why?**

Go to page 166 or your app for more vocabulary and practice.

Speaking

PREPARE

9 1.5 **Listen to three people talking about conflicts. Answer the questions. Who:**

1 had a bad experience which helped him/her avoid a worse experience?
2 blamed themselves for allowing the conflict to spiral out of control?
3 changed their opinion after seeing somebody face-to-face?

10 **You're going to tell a story about a good or bad experience where you expressed or controlled strong emotions. Use the questions below to help you.**

- What happened? Why? How did it make you feel?
- What did you do? What happened as a result?

SPEAK

11 **Work in pairs. Take turns to tell your stories. Work out some general advice for how to avoid and deal with conflict.**

Master your reading page 106

1C Kidfluencers

- **Goal:** justify a point of view
- **Language focus:** infinitive phrases
- **Vocabulary:** connotation 1

Reading

influencer (n)
a person who uses social media sites (e.g. YouTube, Instagram) to promote or recommend products and services to followers. Also: *social media influencer*
kidfluencer (n)
a social media influencer who is still a baby or child

1 Work in pairs. Read the definitions and discuss the questions.
1. Do you know any influencers or kidfluencers? What do you know about them?
2. What sort of people are influenced by influencers and kidfluencers? Have you ever been influenced by them?
3. Would you like to be an influencer/kidfluencer? Why/ Why not?

2 Read the article quickly. Is it generally positive or negative about kidfluencers? Underline words and phrases that helped you decide.

Kidfluencers

One of the biggest trends of the internet age has been the rise of social media influencers – people who share their advice and recommendations with subscribers on their YouTube channels, or followers on their Instagram accounts. The most successful influencers have audiences of millions, all hungry to learn what's hot and what's not.

Needless to say, where there's influence, there's money. Marketers were quick to realise that a glowing recommendation from a top influencer can be far more powerful than a traditional marketing campaign. As a result, influencers can make outrageous sums of money in exchange for a few not-so-subtle recommendations. **To be sure**, many influencers started out with modest ambitions, by giving genuine recommendations based on their expertise, but later, once their audiences have grown and the marketers start offering money, the temptation to give paid-for recommendations can be overwhelming.

Of course, it wasn't long before a few pushy parents spotted the potential for turning their babies and toddlers into child influencers – or kidfluencers, **to give them their proper title**. After all, what better way to sell tacky toys and sugary snacks to children than to get other children to do the selling? Marketers have long known that their most powerful allies are children, who have the ability to manipulate their parents into spending money on junk, **not to put too fine a point on it**. And the best way to drive those kids crazy with the urge to spend their parents' money is to show them other cooler kids using the same products.

In many countries, there are tight restrictions on advertising to – and with the help of – children. But because kidfluencing isn't exactly advertising, the kidfluencers (or, **to be more precise**, the marketers pulling the strings) are able to exploit loopholes in the restrictions and make a fortune.

And so we see toddlers making millions from unboxing videos before they can walk, pre-schoolers launching their own branded product lines before they can read and write, and pre-teens with larger followings of adoring fans than A-list pop and film stars. This creates all kinds of ethical problems, **to put it mildly**, but as long as the money keeps flowing, the rise of kidfluencers is only likely to continue.

3 Work in pairs and discuss the questions.
1. Where might you see an article like this? What is the writer's purpose in writing it?
2. Do you think the writer is being reasonable in their assertions and opinions?

Vocabulary

4 a Match adjectives 1–7 with nouns a–g.

1 pushy	a fans
2 tacky	b recommendation
3 glowing	c sums of money
4 modest	d parents
5 sugary	e toys
6 adoring	f snacks
7 outrageous	g ambitions

b Work in pairs. Which adjectives in Exercise 4a have a positive (+) connotation? Which have a negative (–) connotation?

c Here are some more adjectives that go with the nouns in Exercise 4a. Do they have positive (+) or negative (–) connotations?
1. die-hard/obsessive/screaming fans
2. lukewarm/gushing/informed recommendations
3. meagre/moderate/phenomenal sums of money
4. firm/doting/supportive parents
5. educational/flimsy/durable toys
6. nutritious/bite-size/processed snacks
7. blind/driving/consuming ambition

5 Add adjectives from Exercise 4 to this sentence to make it as positive as possible and then as negative as possible.

Kidfluencers make sums of money by making recommendations to their fans and persuading their parents to buy snacks and toys.

Go to page 166 or your app for more vocabulary and practice.

Language focus

6 a Match functions 1–6 with the phrases in bold in the article in Exercise 2.

1 to clarify something you just said
to be more precise
2 to provide the official name for something
3 to point out that you're using delicate language, although you want to say something stronger
4 to admit that you're going to say something that the listener/reader probably already knows
5 to admit that you're not really using delicate language
6 to admit that your statement might contradict your previous argument

b Read the language focus box and choose the correct alternatives.

Infinitive phrases

Infinitive phrases [1]*always/usually* start with a *to*-infinitive (e.g. ***to tell** the truth*), but some have a negative word before the *to* infinitive (e.g. ***needless** to say*).

We often use them to show how we feel about [2]*an action/a whole statement* or to explain why we're making it.

To come back to my earlier point, I think we should …

They can come at the beginning or end of a statement and are usually separated from the rest of the statement by [3]*commas/full stops* or brackets (in writing) or pauses (in speaking).

To be honest, I'm not sure./I'm not sure, to be honest.

Many infinitive phrases are fixed expressions (i.e. you [4]*can/can't* usually change the words).

7 Complete the infinitive phrases in bold with the verbs in the box.

add be begin cap cut make name put

1 You spend far too much time on social media. You're going to lose all your friends soon if you're not careful, **to ______ it bluntly**.
2 I don't like social media. **To ______ with**, everyone's so negative, and in addition there's so much false information.
3 I've had a terrible day. And **to ______ it all**, I've been locked out of my social media account.
4 I use loads of social networking sites: Facebook, Twitter and Instagram, **to ______ but a few**.
5 He didn't reply to my invite. Then, **to ______ insult to injury**, he planned something for the same day.
6 **To ______ perfectly honest**, if you post strong opinions on social media, you'll probably regret it ten or twenty years from now.
7 They started the network as a homework project as students and, **to ______ a long story short**, 20 years later it has grown into one of the biggest in the world.
8 I accidentally upset someone on Twitter today – I was trying to be funny but it didn't work. Then, **to ______ matters worse**, I tried to send a smiley emoticon but I sent an angry one by mistake.

8 Work in pairs. What do the infinitive phrases in Exercise 7 mean? Write another example sentence for each one.

9 a Work in pairs. How does the comma/pause change the meaning in each pair of sentences?

1 a It's not a good idea to be brutally honest.
b It's not a good idea, to be brutally honest.
2 a She tried her best to be fair.
b She tried her best, to be fair.
3 a I'm not keen to say the least.
b I'm not keen, to say the least.

b 1.6 Listen. Which version do you hear, a or b?

Go to page 146 or your app for more information and practice.

Speaking

PREPARE

10 1.7 Listen to Ann and Jordan discussing kidfluencers. Who expresses these opinions, Ann (A) or Jordan (J)?

a Parents have selfish motives regarding their children becoming kidfluencers.
b Some kids may want to be kidfluencers.
c Their argument won't be resolved.

11 Work in pairs. Think of arguments for and against each statement below.

1 Social media platforms should be responsible for the content that users post on them.
2 It shouldn't be possible to post anonymous comments on the internet.
3 Influencers provide a valuable public service – sometimes it's good to be told what to think.
4 It's reasonable for 'free' websites and apps to make money from advertisers.

SPEAK

12 Work with a different partner. Discuss the statements in Exercise 11. Try to disagree with your partner – but always justify your opinions.

Master your listening page 96

1D English in action

› **Goal:** join a conversation already in progress
› **Vocabulary:** socialising

Vocabulary

1 Work in pairs and discuss the questions.

1 Have you ever attended a face-to-face networking event (e.g. a conference)? Why were you there?
2 Why do you think some people don't like networking events?

2 a Complete the comments with the words in the box.

acquaintance	blank	brains	breaker	frosty
hover	ice	mingle	mutual	pleasantries	small

1 Whenever I go to networking events, I prefer to ______ on the edge of conversations without saying anything.
2 I'm quite good at making ______ talk with strangers, but I find it hard to move on to more serious topics.
3 I set myself a target at events like this – I need to make the ______ of at least twenty new people.
4 There can be a rather ______ atmosphere at first, but once you break the ______, everybody is more talkative.
5 When I meet new people, my mind goes ______ after we've exchanged a few ______, and I never know what to say next.
6 My favourite trick for making conversation is to pick somebody's ______ about their area of expertise – asking for advice is a great ice-______.
7 It's much easier to meet new people when you have a ______ acquaintance who can introduce you.
8 I like to ______ at large social gatherings – I just wander around the room having brief conversations with lots of people.

b Work in pairs. Which comments in Exercise 2a do you agree with? Can you think of any advice for the people who made the comments?

Listening 1

3 a 1.12 Listen to a conversation between three people at a networking event for local businesspeople. Which person: Jagruti (J), Martin (M) or Tahira (T) does the following:

1 ______ apologises a lot.
2 ______ has a clear idea of why they are at the event.
3 ______ checks and practises other people's names.
4 ______ complains and is negative.
5 ______ makes assumptions about another person.
6 ______ talks a lot about themselves.
7 ______ seems reluctant to say much about themselves.

b Work in pairs. Which things in Exercise 3a should you avoid doing? Why? What should you do instead?

4 Look at the Useful phrases 1 box. Match the phrases with tips 1–5. Some phrases match more than one tip.

Tips for joining a conversation

1 Check it's OK to join (and continue) a conversation – but you don't need to apologise for it.
2 Ask simple, open-ended questions to get the other person talking.
3 Stay positive and enthusiastic about what the other person says – even if you're not really interested.
4 Make sure everyone in the group is involved. If necessary, put one speaker 'on hold' while you bring in another speaker. You can invite them to talk again later.
5 Learn everyone's names and other important details, and use them regularly during the conversation.

Useful phrases 1

Do you mind if I join you? ______
So, how's the conference for you so far? ______
Would you like me to leave you in peace? __1__
So what do you do? ______
I'd love to listen in on your advice, if that's OK. ______
So I'd love to pick your brains in a moment, Martin – I'm sure 'The Sands' is an amazing golf course. ______
And you are? ______
Sorry, I'm not very good with names. Can you say it again? ______
So, Jagruti, what brings you to this event? ______
So, Martin. We're all ears. Tell us your tips for … ______

5 a 1.13 **Listen again to Tahira's introduction. Match parts 1–4 with techniques a–d.**

1 Well, I'm Tahira, and I'm an interior designer.
2 I've recently quit my job to 'follow my dreams' and become my own boss.
3 I'm here to pick up some tips and meet some like-minded people.
4 So I'd love to listen in on your advice, if that's OK.

a Throw in some unusual information that others can ask you about later.
b Make it clear you're not planning to take over the conversation.
c Present your name and (if appropriate) your job clearly, succinctly and confidently.
d Explain your purpose.

b Work in pairs. Imagine you're at a networking event for students and local businesspeople. Plan your own introductions based on Tahira's model. Then practise them so they sound confident and natural.

6 a 1.14 **Listen to some extracts from the conversation. Which speakers sound enthusiastic (E)? Which sound unenthusiastic (U)?**

1 No, that's fine. Go ahead.
2 Aha. Nice to meet you.
3 Right. Nice to meet you.
4 Hah, I know what you mean.
5 Oh, right.
6 Er … OK.
7 It's lovely to meet you.
8 Woah! That's impressive!

b Work in pairs. Practise saying the phrases in Exercise 6a as enthusiastically as possible.

7 **Work in groups. Stand up. Introduce yourself to one or two other members of the group. Listen carefully to each other's introductions and respond enthusiastically.**

Listening 2

8 1.15 **Listen to part of a radio interview about networking skills. Answer the questions.**

1 How do most people feel about networking events?
2 What does Giorgio mean by 'Be curious'?
3 What's the best way to join a group that is already in conversation?
4 How can you then get involved in the conversation?
5 Why should participants prepare a story?
6 In what situations does Giorgio suggest that showing sensitivity is important?

9 **Add headings A–D to the Useful phrases 2 box.**

A Reacting to stories
B Telling an anecdote
C Showing sensitivity
D Relating your experience to other people's

Useful phrases 2

1 ______
Please carry on.
Don't mind me – I'm just listening.
But that's a different story. Do carry on.
Don't let me interrupt you.
Do you mind if I join you?

2 ______
Wow! That's a great story!
Oh, that's so unlucky!
That's unbelievable.

3 ______
A similar thing happened to me.
I had a rather different experience.
That reminds me of the time when I …
That's exactly what happened to me.

4 ______
I once lost a car in a forest.
I'm ashamed to say it, but I once travelled 500 km to a conference, but realised when I got there that I'd got the dates mixed up.
I had the good luck to meet my all-time hero.

Speaking

PREPARE

10 **Work in pairs.** **Turn to page 177** **and plan some stories together in preparation for the conference.**

SPEAK

11 a **Work in groups to tell your stories – without sounding like a bore!**

b **When you're ready, leave your group and join a different group. Try to break into their conversation.**

Go online for the Roadmap video.

2A Changes

- **Goal:** give a presentation on past, current and future trends
- **Language focus:** the continuous aspect
- **Vocabulary:** trends

Vocabulary

1 **Work in pairs and discuss the questions.**

1 What are some recent trends in these areas?

education   health   sport   technology   the environment   transport

2 Do you think these developments have been good or bad? Why? Do you agree with your partner?

2 **Look at the phrases in bold in sentences 1–10 and guess their meanings.**

1 Due to environmental concerns, there has been **a downward trend** in air travel.
2 Environmental problems are reaching **a tipping point** from which it won't be possible to save the planet.
3 Government campaigns are a good way to **reverse the trend** in unhealthy eating.
4 Electric cars are becoming popular in my country, and this trend **looks set to continue**.
5 When I hit 20 years, I felt like I'd **passed a milestone** in my career.
6 The development of flexible touchscreens **marks the start of a new era** in mobile devices.
7 The use of clean-air technology is definitely **on the up**.
8 More sports teams are **reverting to** traditional tactics.
9 The innovative public transport system in my city is **setting the trend** for other cities around the world.
10 In general, the future of cancer treatment **looks promising**.

3 **Work in pairs and discuss the following:**

- something which is on the up in your country
- an upward or downward trend among people your age
- an area of industry or commerce which looks promising
- a recent technological development which marked the start of a new era

Go to your app for more vocabulary and practice.

Reading

4 a **Work in pairs and discuss the questions.**

1 How much of the news is made up of negative and positive stories? Why do you think this is?
2 What reasons are there to be positive about the future?

b **Read the article quickly. Does it mention any of your ideas in Exercise 4a?**

Are things looking up?

It's hard to be optimistic about the future sometimes, when you see everything that's happening in the news. But good news stories don't always get reported, so here are some you may have missed.

The environment is being restored
Gao trees are thriving in and around Niger. These trees help support the environment by drawing nitrogen from the air into the soil. And this is not some grand project backed by an international organisation, this change is being pushed forward by small-scale farmers who see the benefits it has on their crops. This growth seems to have been having a positive effect on climate change, too, as the trees absorb carbon dioxide from the air.

People are smoking less
A million people in a year have quit in France, and the number of people smoking in the US has been falling steadily to the lowest point since records began. The fall seems to be happening because of a range of measures, including photos on cigarette packets. Changing attitudes among young people against smoking are also driving the downward trend.

The downward trend in inequality
For the first time since agriculture-based civilisation began – some 10,000 years ago – the number of people considered 'middle-class' or 'rich' has reached over 50%. This represents a tipping point, since it's the first time the number of people living in poverty has been lower than 50%.

The way we move is changing
The first Electronic Vehicles (EVs) that appeared had issues with performance and battery life. Car manufacturers have been making massive strides since then and, as EVs become more efficient and cheaper to buy and run, they're becoming an increasingly popular option for car buyers. With several countries announcing bans on petrol-driven cars by 2030, it's hoped that everyone will be driving them in the future.

The sea is getting cleaner
Over five trillion pieces of plastic are currently floating in the oceans, and the largest accumulation of these is known as the Great Pacific Garbage Patch (GPGP), a huge island of plastic litter which had been growing at an alarming rate, until one charity decided to do something about it. They've created a 600-metre long boom which is using natural oceanic forces to clean it up. The work seems to be going well, with the team behind it predicting a clean up of half the GPGP in just a few years.

5 **Work in pairs. Which of the stories in the article do you find the most positive? Why?**

Language focus

6 a **Work in pairs. Look at extracts a–f from the article and answer questions 1–3 below.**

a The sea is getting cleaner.
b The number of people smoking in the US has been falling steadily.
c Car manafacturers have been making massive strides since then.
d The environment is being restored.
e It's hoped that everyone will be driving them in the future.
f The fall seems to be happening because of a range of measures.

1 What structure do they have in common?
2 Does each extract refer to the past, present or future?
3 Are the activities described complete or in progress?

b **Read the language focus box and check your answers.**

The continuous aspect

We use the continuous aspect (*be* + verb + *ing*) to describe an activity that we see as unfinished or in progress.

This could be because we want to emphasise that:

- the activity is temporary

Over five trillion pieces of plastic ***are*** *currently* ***floating*** *in the oceans.*
The work seems ***to be going*** *well.*

- we're describing 'part' of an activity, not the finished whole (i.e. there's more to come)

Car makers ***have been making*** *massive strides.*
This change ***is being pushed*** *forward by farmers.*

- it's a repeated or changing action

They're becoming *an increasingly popular option.*
It's hoped that everyone ***will be driving*** *them in the future.*

- we're describing trends

The way we move ***is changing.***
The growth seems ***to have been having*** *a positive effect on climate change.*

When we use the continuous aspect, we are usually more interested in the action itself than a result.

They've been working *hard to clean up the plastic.*
(We're more interested in what they've been doing.)
They've cleaned *up half the plastic in this area.*
(We're more interested in the result.)

7 a **Look at sentences 1–3. How are the words in bold pronounced when spoken quickly?**

1 People appear **to have** been getting the message.
2 The movement seems **to have** been slowly gaining acceptance.
3 These things seem **to have** been happening more often these days.

b 2.1 **Listen and check.**

8 **Work in pairs. Discuss why the continuous aspect is used in the second sentence in each pair.**

1 a The children have planted twenty trees.
b The children have been planting trees.
2 a She seems to find it difficult.
b She seems to be finding it difficult.
3 a The number of gorillas in the wild has risen.
b The number of gorillas in the wild has been rising.
4 a The measures seem to have had an effect.
b The measures seem to have been having an effect.
5 a Marsha will get the bus to work tomorrow.
b Marsha will be getting the bus to work from now on.

9 a **Complete each prompt using the continuous aspect and your own ideas.**

1 In the future, most people will …
2 People are generally … (more/less) …
3 People seem to be becoming …
4 Technology is being …

b **Work in pairs and share your ideas.**

Go to page 148 or your app for more information and practice.

Speaking

PREPARE

10 **Work in pairs. You're going to give a presentation on past, current and future trends. First, turn to page 176 and choose one of the topics you want to present or choose your own.**

11 **Plan how to give your presentation. Decide who will present what.**

SPEAK

12 **Work with another pair who worked with a different topic. Take turns to give your presentations to each other. Ask questions to find out more information.**

Master your reading
page 108

2B Work, work, work

- **Goal:** speculate about work situations
- **Language focus:** probability
- **Vocabulary:** agreement and disagreement

Listening

1 Work in pairs and discuss the questions.

1 Think back to when you were eight years old. What job did you want to do when you were older?

2 What job do you do/want to do now? Is it the same or different?

2 a 2.2 Listen to a podcast about working practices and job titles. What did Chris and Elaine want to be when they were eight years old?

b Listen again. Decide if the sentences are true (T), false (F) or not given (N).

1 Elaine's job pays well.

2 Elaine asks Chris about his childhood ambitions in order to make a point about future jobs.

3 Chris thinks modern job titles are necessary.

4 Elaine says some modern job titles are necessary.

5 Companies give employees glamorous-sounding job titles so they can pay them less.

6 Elaine says current trends in job titles are likely to continue in the future.

7 Chris is able to give simplified job titles for all four jobs Elaine describes.

8 The title 'Rockstar' doesn't always refer to music.

3 Work in pairs. Come up with job titles for the following people to make their jobs sound cooler.

1 traffic wardens

2 boxers

3 tax inspectors

Language focus

4 Read the language focus box and choose the correct alternatives.

Probability

There are a number of ways to express probability.

There are a small number of [1] *verbs/adjectives* (*sure, certain, likely* and *unlikely*) describing probability where we can change the word order to emphasise different things.

To emphasise the [2] *probability/subject*, start the sentence with 'it' as the subject.

***It was highly unlikely** that they knew about it.*

***It's highly likely** that the jobs our children do in the future don't exist yet.*

To emphasise the [3] *probability/subject*, bring it to the start of the sentence and use an infinitive.

***They** were highly unlikely **to have known** about it.*

***The jobs our children do in the future** are highly unlikely **to exist** yet.*

5 a 2.3 Listen to the sentences. What happens to the *k* in *(un)likely*?

1 They're likely to have been delayed in the traffic.

2 It's unlikely that you could have done anything.

3 He's likely to step down after the election.

4 You're unlikely to be promoted.

5 It's unlikely that they'll make it in time.

b Listen again and repeat.

6 a Put the words in the correct order to make sentences.

1 promoted / You're / to / next / likely / week / be
You're likely to be promoted next week.
2 the / received / unlikely / that / documents / yet / It's / they've
3 this / is / Maisy / certain / have / about / known / to
4 to / discussing / likely / be / the / now / They're / matter
5 Raj / the / certain / to / in / meeting / have / is / been
6 next / taken / to / highly / that / we're / It's / going / be / over / likely / year
7 given / unlikely / have / The / this / thought / much / CEO / is / to
8 We / doing / the / that / robots / be / be / can / our / in / future / certain / will / jobs

b Rewrite the sentences in Exercise 6a using a *-that* clause or an infinitive.

1 It's likely that you'll be promoted next week.

7 a Complete the sentences so that they are true for you.

1 I'm highly unlikely ...
2 It's certain ...
3 This year is likely ...
4 My parents are sure ...

b Work in pairs. Compare your sentences and give more information.

Go to page 148 or your app for more information and practice.

Vocabulary

8 Read the conversations and decide if the words in bold describe agreement (A) or disagreement (D).

1 **A:** Do you think people are likely to **get on board with** the idea of accepting a better job title instead of a pay rise?
B: Definitely not. They'll hate the idea.

2 **A:** How do you feel about hot-desking in order to save some space?
B: I'd **be willing** to accept the idea if it means I can work from home a couple of days a week. I can imagine a few others in the office might **be at odds with** the idea though.

3 **A:** If we close the school canteen, we're likely to **receive some pushback** from both students and teachers alike.
B: I agree. We'll definitely **come up against some resistance.**

4 **A:** I think most students **are open to** the idea of sharing resources.
B: Do you reckon? I think most will **take issue with** it. Personally, I'd **be loath to** share mine.

5 **A:** I think staff are likely to **go along with** the proposals for flexible working hours.
B: I agree. I think we can be pretty certain that most people will like the idea.
C: I'm not sure. Given how settled they are now, I think it's likely to be **met with a lukewarm response**.

9 a Complete the questions with the missing words.

1 Would you be ______ to the idea of working fewer hours for less pay?
2 Are there any changes in your place of work/study that would be met with a ______ response? What would they be?
3 Have you ever suggested a great idea that ______ up against some resistance? What happened?
4 What are you ______ to do to succeed in your career?
5 What approaches to work or study are at ______ with the way you like to do things?

b Work in groups and discuss the questions.

Go to page 167 or your app for more vocabulary and practice.

Speaking

PREPARE

10 a 2.4 Listen to Anya and Jitesh discussing some proposed changes to their workplace. Tick the things they mention.

1 moving to a different premises
2 working longer hours in exchange for longer holidays
3 more working from home
4 having a day a week to work on personal projects.
5 closing the on-site canteen
6 having larger teams with fewer managers
7 swapping round managers more frequently

b Listen again and answer the questions. Which proposal do they:

a both think is a bad idea?
b decide to change?
c decide to implement on a trial basis?

11 Think about the place where you work or study. How popular do you think each measure in Exercise 10a would be? Make notes on the advantages and disadvantages of each proposal.

SPEAK

12 Work in groups. Discuss each of the proposals in Exercise 10a in relation to your place of work or study. Agree on two proposals to implement.

13 Share your ideas and reasons with the class.

Master your listening page 97

2C Local issues

› **Goal:** discuss a proposal

› **Language focus:** cleft sentences

› **Vocabulary:** connotation 2

A

B

Vocabulary

1 **Work in pairs. What issues might people have with their local area relating to the things shown in the photos?**

2 a **Read the letter to a local newspaper and answer the questions.**

> Why oh why doesn't the council improve our public transport system?! It's one of the biggest [1]**problems** facing our local area at the moment, yet it's paid scant attention by those who can do something about it. The buses are [2]**archaic**, and they never run on time – the whole system is [3]**chaotic**. And don't get me started on local trains. They're non-existent! It makes life really [4]**difficult** for people like me, who don't own a car. It's high time the council stopped being so [5]**penny-pinching** and actually spent some money on the system. It's the 21st Century!

1 Which of the issues in the photos is the writer complaining about?

2 How would you describe the tone of the letter?

b **Match the words in bold in the letter with more positive words a–e.**

a vintage
b relaxed
c economical
d challenging
e issues

3 **Work in pairs. What is the difference in meaning between the pairs of sentences? Which has a more positive connotation?**

1 a The company **exploits** staff with few qualifications or experience.
  b The company **employs** staff with few qualifications or experience.

2 a My town gets very **lively** on Friday nights.
  b My town gets very **rowdy** on Friday nights.

3 a The old town is a **charming** area of the city.
  b The old town is a **run-down** area of the city.

4 a A large **mob** of people were outside the council offices, protesting the building plans.
  b A large **group** of people were outside the council offices, protesting the building plans.

5 a Red Farm Park is an area of **cheap** housing.
  b Red Farm Park is an area of **affordable** housing.

6 a The council is taking **firm** measures to prevent people driving in cycle lanes.
  b The council is taking **harsh** measures to prevent people driving in cycle lanes.

4 **Work in pairs. Which words in Exercises 2 and 3 would you use to describe these things?**

- the public transport system in your town/city
- always buying the cheapest version of something
- a teacher who corrects you all the time
- the old part of your town/city
- traditional clothes/costumes from your country
- fashion

A: *I think the old part of our town is charming.*
B: *Really? I think a lot of the buildings are run-down.*

Go to page 167 or your app for more vocabulary and practice.

Listening

5 2.8 **Listen to a radio interview with a local councillor. What two local issues does the interviewer ask about?**

6 **Listen again and answer the questions.**

1 Why is Elaine Miller cautious about spending money on public transport?

2 What measure does she say they're introducing for young people in the city?

3 What change is happening with refuse collection?

4 How does she say she feels about making the cuts?

5 How does the councillor justify the change to refuse collection?

Language focus

7 a 2.9 **Listen to extracts from the interview and complete the second version of each sentence.**

1 We looked at ways of making sure any extra investment actually works.
_______ we _______ to look at making sure any extra investment actually works.

2 I'm saying that we have to invest sensibly and carefully.
_______ I'm saying _______ we have to invest sensibly and carefully.

3 My colleague made that statement.
_______ was my colleague _______ made that statement.

4 I can't stand having to make cuts.
_______ I can't stand _______ having to make cuts.

C

D

b **Work in pairs. Why do you think the speakers used the second version of each sentence? Read the language focus box and check your ideas.**

Cleft sentences

Cleft sentences are used to connect what the speaker and listener already know, or are already discussing to what is new information. There are two main types:

In cleft sentences that begin with *it*, the *it*- clause emphasises the new information, and the following clause links it to what is already known.

A: *Everyone is suffering financially these days.*

B: *Yes, but it's the unemployed who are the worst off.*

(We're already discussing financial problems, and the unemployed is the 'new information'.)

In cleft sentences beginning with *what*, the *what*- clause refers to the 'known' information, and the following clause introduces the new information.

What I'm saying is that it's important to plan ahead.

(I've already given this opinion before, but here's what you missed/need to focus on.)

When we substitute the main verb with *did*, we use a *to* infinitive.

What we ***did was to set up*** *an investigation.*

If the main verb is followed by a gerund, then the cleft is also followed by a gerund.

What I ***hate*** *is* ***being ignored***.

We can also follow the *what*- clause with a noun.

What I don't like is ***disorganisation***.

Replace *what* with *all* to emphasise one thing above everything else.

All *we want is cheaper homes.*

8 a 2.10 **Listen to the sentences and notice the weak form of *that*.**

1 What I'm saying is that it's not easy.
2 It's the people at the top that matter.
3 What I love about this idea is that it's cheap to implement.
4 All we're saying is that you'll have to wait a bit longer.
5 It's the retail sector that will suffer most.

b **Listen again and repeat.**

9 Rewrite the sentences using the prompts.

1 It's not feasible to increase the number of buses.
What I'm saying ...
2 We discussed regulations for dog walkers at the last meeting.
It was at the last meeting ...
3 We discussed the policy at length.
What we did ...
4 We'd like to install speed bumps on Clarence Road.
It's on Clarence Road ...
5 Many residents enjoy cycling to work.
What ...
6 We don't know how people will react.
What ...

10 a **Complete the prompts to make sentences that are true for you.**

1 What I love most about ...
2 What annoys me most about where I live ...
3 It's the lack of ...

b **Work in pairs. Compare your sentences and give each other more information.**

Go to page 148 or your app for more information and practice.

Speaking

PREPARE

11 **Work in two groups. You're going to have a city council meeting. Turn to page 177.**

SPEAK

12 a **Work in groups of four, with two Student As and two Student Bs. Discuss each proposal in Exercise 11 and try to reach agreement.**

b **Report back to the class. Did you agree on any of the proposals?**

Master your writing page 128

2D English in action

> Goal: manage a fast-paced conversation
> Vocabulary: conversation

Vocabulary

1 Work in pairs. Think about speaking in English and discuss the questions.

1 Do you prefer speaking to one person or in a group?
2 How easy do you find speaking in a group of English speakers?
3 What do you do when you don't understand something in a conversation?
4 What do you do to keep a conversation going?

2 a Match comments 1–8 with replies a–h.

1 Can I just **butt in** here? I think those figures need checking.
2 I need to have a **heart-to-heart** with Chris about his problems at home.
3 I can't believe he said that to me!
4 Speaking of Sally, she said a really funny thing to me the other …
5 So did you have a **chit chat** with Chiara at the party?
6 Let me **reiterate**. This needs to be sorted by Friday before the orders go out.
7 Great party, isn't it? So what did you think of Marcus's presentation?
8 What was Angela **going on about** with you?

a Sorry to interrupt you, I'm sure what Sally said was funny, but you're **going off on a tangent** again. Can you save it for later? We really need to discuss the project now.
b Agreed. We'll **thrash it out** this afternoon and get something to you by tomorrow lunchtime, OK?
c Let's not **talk shop**. We're supposed to be having fun!
d I tried, but I get so nervous around her, I just seem to **clam up** and not say anything.
e Ha, it's just **banter**, don't take it personally.
f Yes, but you need to **broach the subject** carefully.
g Hmm yes, maybe you're right. Let me **confer with** Jackie in finance and double-check them.
h Oh nothing really, she was just gossiping about the people in her team.

b Work in pairs. Who do you think the people in the conversations in Exercise 2 are? Where do you think they are?

3 a Choose the correct alternatives to complete the sentences.

1 I hate it when people *reiterate/butt in* when I'm in the middle of saying something.
2 I'm terrible at telling anecdotes. I'm forever *going off on a tangent/bantering* and then forgetting where I was in the story!
3 My mates always make fun of each other. It's not serious though, it's just *banter/reiteration*.
4 I don't always agree with my team. When this happens we just have to *butt in/thrash it out* until we come up with a compromise.
5 It's difficult to *talk shop about/broach the subject of* politics with my dad, as we have such opposing opinions about what's right.
6 I always *go on about something with/confer with* my colleagues before making an important decision at work.
7 I hate public speaking. I just seem to *clam up/go on about something* and not know what to say.
8 I had a really bad history teacher at school. He just used to *have a heart-to-heart about/go on about* his life and didn't notice that nobody was listening.

b Choose four of the sentences in Exercise 3a and change them so that they are true for you.

c Work in pairs. Share your sentences and give more information.

Listening 1

4 2.11 **Listen to three conversations. Where do you think the people are in each one?**

5 a Listen again. Which of these techniques do the speakers use to keep the conversation going?

- a using interesting comparisons
- b active listening (phrases to show you're listening)
- c getting back to what you were saying
- d pressing for more details
- e keeping your turn

b Complete the Useful phrases 1 box with four of the techniques in Exercise 5a.

Useful phrases 1

1 ___________
How rude!
Right.
The cheek of it!
No way!
2 ___________
Do tell!
How so?
Go on.
So what was going on?
3 ___________
Let me finish.
Hang on, there's more.
4 ___________
So as I was saying …
Getting back to …

c Add these phrases to the Useful phrases 1 box. Can you think of any more phrases to add to each section?

- a Wait, hear me out.
- b Really?
- c What I was trying to say was …
- d What happened then?

6 a Choose a phrase from each section in the Useful phrases 1 box and think of what someone might say before it.

A: It was all a bit mysterious.
B: So what was going on?

b Work in pairs. Show your dialogues to your partner. Your partner will add the next line. Practise the conversations.

Listening 2

7 a 2.12 **Listen to the end of the three conversations in Exercise 4. What does each person say to show they want to end the conversation?**

b Listen again and complete the phrases in the Useful phrases 2 box with one, two or three words.

Useful phrases 2

Ending a conversation
I'll [1]___________ back to work.
Anyway, [2]___________ late.
I'd [3]___________ off.
Oh, hey, sorry Ella, but I've [4]___________ seen someone…
It [5]___________ meet you.
I might have to [6]___________, too.

c How do the speakers use their intonation to show that they want to finish a conversation?

8 Work in groups and discuss the questions.

1. Have you ever been in a conversation which you found difficult to leave? Why?
2. How do you usually finish a conversation?

Speaking

PREPARE

9 You're going to practise maintaining a conversation. First, pick one of the topics and make notes on what to say. Try to think of as many ideas as possible.

- gossip about someone you know
- a recent unusual experience
- an issue at work
- ideas for what to do at the weekend
- something silly you've posted online

SPEAK

10 a Work in groups of three. Student A: Turn to page 176. Student B: Turn to page 179. Student C: Turn to page 177.

b Tell your group about the topic you made notes on. Use the Useful phrases 1 box to keep the conversation going as long as possible. When you have finished, end the conversation in a polite way.

Go online for the Roadmap video.

Check and reflect: Units 1 and 2

1 a Complete the sentences with the correct form of the verbs in the box.

do get give go make take

1 After criticism of the company in the press, the CEO was forced to ______ a statement.
2 I'm exhausted. I think I'll ______ for a quick lie-down.
3 If you complain about poor service in a restaurant, it might ______ the owner some good.
4 Do you prefer to ______ the lead during meetings and group discussions?
5 Can you come back in an hour or so and ______ me a break?
6 I hate it when everybody's sitting in silence. What's a good way to ______ people talking?

b Work in pairs. Discuss questions 3, 4 and 6. Ask follow-up questions.

2 Find the four sentences with a mistake and correct them.

1 Everyone will be cold by the end of the treasure hunt. They'll have walked around for hours.
2 I was covered in grass because I've been cutting the lawn.
3 We've been having a few problems with our TV lately.
4 I'll phone you when we'll have finished our meal.
5 We tried to sail in the boats that we'd made the previous day.
6 They're my favourite band. I've been seeing them in concert five times.

3 Put the words in the correct order to make sentences.

1 be / music / louder / seems / The / getting / to
2 a lot / be / exam / out / we'd / turned / to / harder / than / expected / The
3 see / her to / If / call / Jenny, / tell / happen / me / you / to / please
4 been / seems / earlier / to / a / There / misunderstanding / have
5 eating / have / Somebody / desk / at / appears / been / their lunch / my / to

4 Match the sentence halves.

1 I know you're angry, but there's no need
2 I'm sorry I shouted at you – I just needed
3 Thinking about your long-term goals can help you
4 You get a lot of verbal abuse in this job so it's vital
5 Even if you're disappointed about losing, try
6 Instead of yelling at them, it may be better

a to have a thick skin.
b to put things into perspective.
c to put a brave face on it.
d to lash out at me.
e to bite your tongue.
f to let off steam.

5 a Do the words in bold have a positive (+) or negative (–) connotation?

1 Should restaurants serve only **modest** portions?
2 Do you ever buy **tacky** souvenirs?
3 Have you ever posted a **lukewarm** review?
4 What's your favourite **nutritious** snack?
5 Why do some people receive a **meagre** salary for important work?
6 Is it good for kids to have **doting** parents?
7 Is it OK for kids to have **sugary** drinks and food sometimes?
8 Can you trust **gushing** recommendations?

b Work in pairs. Discuss three of the questions in Exercise 5a.

6 Complete the sentences with one word.

1 We were disappointed to finish last, to put it ______.
2 I forgot to lock my bike. ______ to say, it got stolen.
3 I feel sorry for you but, to be ______ it's your own fault.
4 We tried our best but, to cut a long story ______, it didn't work out for us.
5 She ate all my sandwiches and then, to add insult to ______, complained about them.
6 I know they're your friends but, not to put too fine a ______ on it, they're a bad influence on you.

7 Choose the correct alternatives.

1 Recent changes in the composition of the workforce look *set/promising* to continue.
2 There has definitely been a *reverse the/downward* trend in the number of people having large families.
3 The melting of the Arctic ice could be a significant tipping *milestone/point* for climate change.
4 It is hoped the new product range will *reverse/rise* the trend of a declining industry.
5 The use of public transport in the city is definitely *at/on* the up.
6 Many farmers are *reverting/marking* to more traditional agricultural practices.

8 a Complete the sentences with the correct continuous form of the verbs in brackets.

1 Electric cars in my country ______ (become) more and more popular.
2 In ten years' time, most people ______ (work) from home.
3 This time next year I ______ (learn) English for ten years.
4 I ______ (not do) much exercise lately.
5 The economy of my country seems ______ (get) better at the moment.
6 I ______ (living) with my parents at the moment until I can get a place of my own.

b Change the sentences in Exercise 8a so that they are true for you.

9 **Match the sentence halves.**

1 It's highly likely
2 We're unlikely
3 I'm sure that
4 He's likely
5 It's highly unlikely that

a she won't have seen your message yet.
b that there will be job losses after the company merger.
c to have submitted the application already.
d to see many changes in the short term.
e they know about our plans yet.

10 **Put the words in bold in the correct order to complete the sentences. There is one word missing in each phrase.**

1 Do you think they're likely to **with** / **board** / **get** the idea? Or simply reject it outright?
2 We can definitely **along** / **go** the idea of flexible working hours.
3 Most teachers **open** / **are** trying out new methodologies.
4 Sarah's ideas were met with **response** / **lukewarm** during the presentation.
5 The new plans are somewhat **odds** / **at** the government's overall policy.
6 It's not popular, and we're likely to **resistance** / **against** / **come** / **some**.

11 a **Choose the option, a–c, which does not complete the sentences.**

1 The area where I live is very ______ at night.
   a lively
   b harsh
   c rowdy
2 I find English prepositions very ______ .
   a difficult
   b challenging
   c firm
3 There are lots of ______ places in my country.
   a vintage
   b charming
   c run-down
4 In my job/studies, I face many ______ every day.
   a problems
   b mobs
   c issues
5 I think people who always buy the cheapest versions of things are ______ .
   a relaxed
   b penny-pinching
   c economical

b **Use the correct options in Exercise 11a to make sentences that are true for you.**

12 **Match the sentence halves.**

1 It was Craig
2 All I'm saying is
3 It's people talking about each other that
4 What we need is
5 What we do
6 It's the people in Sales

a I really hate.
b who ate your biscuits, not me.
c who have the highest expenses.
d that we need to invest more in education.
e more affordable housing.
f is to look at how we can save more time.

13 **Complete each useful phrase with one word.**

1 Putting a speaker 'on hold': So I'd love to ______ your brains in a moment. But first, …
2 Starting a conversation: What ______ you to this conference?
3 Hovering before joining a conversation: Don't ______ me – I'm just listening.
4 Relating your experience to other people's: A ______ thing happened to me.
5 Eliciting more information: So what was ______ on?
6 Getting back to what you were saying: So, ______ I was saying, …
7 Leaving a conversation: Anyway, it's getting late. I'd ______ be off.
8 Leaving a conversation: I might have to make a ______ .

Reflect

How confident do you feel about the statements below? Write 1–5 (1 = not very confident, 5 = very confident).

- I can give feedback on an event.
- I can describe my reaction to a situation.
- I can justify a point of view.
- I can join a conversation already in progress.
- I can give a clear presentation on past, current and future trends.
- I can speculate about work situations.
- I can discuss a proposal.
- I can manage a fast-paced conversation.

For more practice go to your Workbook or app.

3A Ideas

- **Goal:** use brainstorming techniques
- **Language focus:** question forms
- **Vocabulary:** ideas

A

B

C

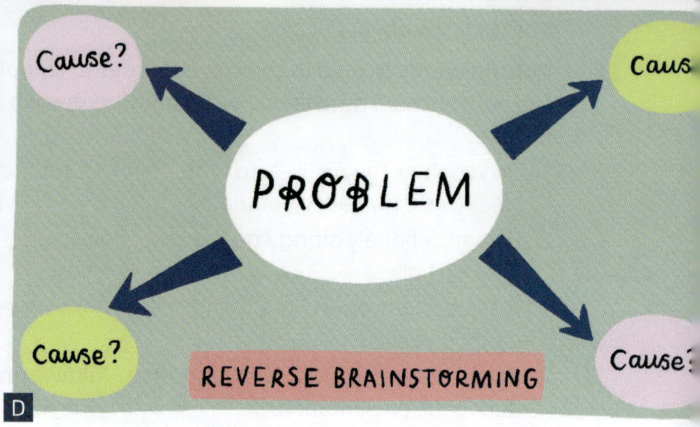

D

Listening

1 **Work in pairs. Look at the pictures of ways of generating ideas and discuss the questions.**

1 What do you think is involved in each process?
2 In what situations do you need to generate ideas?
3 What techniques do you use to generate ideas?

2 **3.1 Listen to an interview about brainstorming techniques. Put activities A–D in the order you hear them.**

3 **Work in pairs and discuss the questions.**

1 Which of the techniques the professor mentioned sounds most interesting to you?
2 Can you think of situations in which each technique would be most useful?

Language focus

4 **Complete the language focus box with questions a–f.**

a You're going to talk to us about brainstorming today, aren't you?
b Isn't brainstorming basically just people thinking of ideas together?
c You call it what?
d What exactly is it that makes them so loyal?
e You mean you ask people to think of how to *cause* a problem?
f I wonder if you could tell our listeners what they should do in that situation?

Question forms

There are lots of different ways of asking questions in spoken English. For example:

- Negative questions which include a negative auxiliary. These are usually fairly loaded (i.e. the speaker assumes an answer) and can be used to check understanding of something you already believe.

***Don't** we start with the five questions?*

or to try and elicit agreement:

1 ______________________________

- Statement + question word to show surprise.

*We go **where**?*

2 ______________________________

- *You mean/So you're saying* + statement to check or confirm information, or to show we've understood a point.

*So **you mean** with this data we can present our findings to the board?*

***So you're saying** we don't need to leave yet?*

3 ______________________________

- Indirect questions. These are often used with questions which are difficult to ask, or to sound more polite.

Could it be argued that it's a waste of time and money?

Would it be ridiculous if we refused to go?

4 ______________________________

- Question tags to check or confirm information.

***You don't mean** in the current climate though, **do you**?*

5 ______________________________

Be aware of less common question tags.

***Let's** think about the first issues, **shall we**?*

***Everybody/Everyone** likes chips, don't **they**?*

- Question word + *is it* (cleft questions) to add emphasis.

*What **is it** that you're trying to do?*

6 ______________________________

5 a 3.2 **Listen to the sentences. Does the intonation rise or fall at the end of each one?**

1 We do it how many times?
2 You've been here for how long?
3 We need to leave at what time?

b Listen again and repeat.

6 Work in pairs. Discuss how the meaning changes in the second version of each question.

1 **a** How much is this going to cost?
b This is going to cost how much?
2 **a** Is their credit history the most important factor?
b You mean their credit history is the most important factor?
3 **a** How much did we lose, exactly?
b Could you tell me how much we lost?
4 **a** Why do they always take so long to respond?
b Why is it that they always take so long to respond?
5 **a** Don't you think he's strange?
b Do you think he's strange?
6 **a** Could you have done this better?
b Is it fair to say that you could have done this better?
7 **a** Is it important to read it first?
b Isn't it important to read it first?

7 a Use the prompts to write questions to ask someone about their job or studies.

1 Isn't it …?
2 Don't you …?
3 You don't … do you?
4 Why is it that …?
5 You've … for how long?
6 Could you tell me …?

b Work in pairs. Ask and answer your questions. Give more information.

Go to page 150 or your app for more information and practice.

Vocabulary

8 Work in pairs. Discuss the meaning of the phrases in bold.

1 It **occurs to me** that we should get out of town for the day.
2 I've been thinking but nothing **springs to mind**.
3 Something's just **dawned on me** – we've forgotten about Martin!
4 I think we should **bounce a few ideas around** and see what we come up with.
5 I've had **a bright idea** – let's take our shoes off!
6 OK, relax, we don't do it – it was **just a passing thought**.
7 I'm afraid I'm **out of ideas** for now.
8 Seeing that amazing film has **given me an idea** – let's go shark diving!
9 Donny had **a brainwave** about how to get the funding. Listen up.

9 a Complete the sentences with one word.

1 I much prefer ______ ideas around in a group than trying to think of them myself.
2 When I think of my childhood, the first thing that ______ to mind is football.
3 I'd been feeling very tired till it ______ to me that I was working too hard.
4 I kept doing it until one day it ______ on me that I didn't really enjoy it any more.
5 I was recently thinking about what to do when I suddenly had a ______.
6 I'd love to make a big change to my life but at the moment I'm out of ______.

b Work in pairs. Which of the sentences in Exercise 9a are true for you? Why?

Go to page 168 or your app for more vocabulary and practice.

Speaking

PREPARE

10 a Work in groups. You're going to use some brainstorming techniques. Choose a situation to brainstorm about and decide which technique to use.

- Your school needs a new logo. What can it be?
- You'd like to celebrate the end of the course with your class. What can you do?
- A friend or family member is looking for a job. What advice can you give them?
- What advice can you give to someone learning a language?

b Work individually. Think of some ideas and make notes on the situation your group has chosen.

SPEAK

11 a Work in your group. Carry out your brainstorming using your chosen technique.

b Report back to the class. What solution(s) did you come up with?

Master your reading
page 110

3B Problems, problems

› **Goal:** solve a problem
› **Language focus:** reason clauses
› **Vocabulary:** problems and solutions

Vocabulary

1 a Work in pairs. Try to solve the puzzles.

b Discuss the questions.

1 How did you try to solve the puzzles? Did you use any specific techniques?
2 Do you prefer solving problems alone or working with other people? Why?
3 What problem-solving techniques do you know of?

2 Read the blog post. Does it mention any of the techniques you discussed in Exercise 1b?

6 problem-solving techniques that work

1 Take a deep breath
It might sound blatantly obvious, but it's easy to let a problem overwhelm you. Step back, **take stock** and calm down. Write down what the problem is. This will help you **pin it down** in practical terms.

2 Unleash your inner five-year-old
Children are naturally curious, and – often much to our chagrin – will relentlessly ask 'Why?' about the simplest things. If we do this, we can establish the **root cause(s)** of a problem more carefully, especially by framing our questions with phrases like *What if …? Can I …? Why not …?*

3 Context, not content
Try to look at the wider context related to a problem. Instead of **mulling over** the problems, think about your lifestyle: *Are you watching TV just before bed? Drinking coffee in the afternoon?*

4 Try on a new hat
In 1985, Edward de Bono devised a system called *Six Thinking Hats*. The idea is that you approach a problem in six different ways, or 'hats', each a different colour. These include, for example, a white 'hat' which deals with information – what are the facts? What do we know for sure? This can help avoid **misinterpreting** key information. Conversely, the red 'hat' deals with emotion and **intuitive** thinking, i.e. what's your gut feeling?
This is a useful technique for a group of people at work, with each person adopting one of the roles. Alternatively, you can revisit a problem in your life six times, with each of the hats.

5 Brainstorm
A useful technique for coming up with possible solutions in groups. The important thing to remember is that all ideas should be accepted at first, and that it's important to keep a record of all ideas.

6 Walk away
Never **underestimate** the power of taking a break. Sometimes when you've been **wrestling with** a problem for ages you get so **befuddled** that you just **go round in circles**. Go for a walk, clean the kitchen, get some fresh air. You might find that you have a brainwave when you least expect it.

A

3 a Look at the words and phrases in bold in the blog post. What can you guess about their meaning?
So, 'take stock' is a verb, and it's between 'step back' and 'calm down' – maybe it means 'think about things'?

b Match five of the words and phrases in bold in the blog post with the groups of words in 1–5 below with similar meanings.

1 perplexed baffled
2 deliberate ruminate ponder
3 zero in on shed light on
4 misconstrue misread
5 rack your brains grapple with

4 Choose the correct alternatives.

1 We don't seem to be making any progress with this, we're just *going round in circles/zeroing in on*.
2 I think you *perplexed/misinterpreted* what she was saying. She was talking about the national situation, not the local one.
3 I need some time to *underestimate/grapple with* the situation, it's very complex.
4 Let's have a break so we can *take stock of/misconstrue* what we know so far.
5 I have no idea how to solve this one, I'm absolutely *baffled/intuitive*.

5 a Look at the words in the box. What sound does each of them have in the final syllable?

grapple	baffle	befuddle

b 3.3 **Listen and practise saying the words.**

Go to your app for more vocabulary and practice.

B

Language focus

6 3.4 **Listen to three conversations about problems. Which techniques from the blog in Exercise 2 are recommended for each situation?**

7 a Look at the extracts from the conversations in Exercise 6. Underline the words and phrases that introduce reasons.

a I guess I haven't tried anything new for fear of failing at that, too.
b Seeing as none of the things you've tried seem to work
c Since this isn't the first time this has happened, I think we need to seriously consider changing distributor.
d We get a really good deal with that distributor, in that they give us an extra 10% off orders over 50,000.
e I don't think we should stick with a bad supplier for fear of losing a few quid in the short term.
f As we don't know all the facts yet, let's wait until we do before we make the final decision.

b Read the language focus box and check your answers.

Reason clauses

There are several words and phrases we can use to introduce reasons.

Since, As **and** ***Seeing as*** **+ clause** refer to reasons that the listener already knows, or are common knowledge between the speaker and listener.

Since *Alicia isn't here, let's leave the discussion until later, when she is.*

As *you've already contacted them, let's wait and see what they say.*

Seeing as *we agree on this point, we should move on to the next one.*

In that **+ clause** is used to justify a comment or reason.

This isn't a very popular product, ***in that*** *it hasn't sold very well at all.*

For fear of/At the risk of **+ object + *-ing*** is used to describe possible outcomes.

We can't change the design now ***for fear of it affecting*** *our deadline.*

At the risk of sounding stupid*, how does this technique work?*

We can also use *-ing* clauses to express reasons.

Being *short of cash, I didn't go with the others.*

8 Use the information to write reason clauses with the words and phrases in brackets. More than one word order may be possible.

1 They might not know the address. Text it to them. (in case)
Text them the address in case they don't know it.
2 I was lucky. I had friends to help. (in that)
3 I wasn't having a good time. I went home early. (as)
4 You already know Julian. I won't introduce you. (since)
5 I didn't want to be the first one at the party. I arrived late. (not wanting)
6 I haven't confronted him because I'm scared I'll lose my job. (fear)

9 a Think of possible reasons for these situations. Use reason clauses from the language focus box.

1 We should speak only English.
2 Let's stay at home tomorrow.
3 I called all of my friends last night.
4 Let's discuss this later.
5 I decided not to go there again.

b Work in pairs. Compare your sentences.

Go to page 150 or your app for more information and practice.

Speaking

PREPARE

10 a You're going to solve a problem. Choose one of the following problems:

- you suspect someone you know may be a criminal, but you're not sure
- your boss is making your life at work really difficult
- two people in your family are not talking to each other
- your own idea

b Invent the details of the problem. Think about the following:

- what happened leading up to the problem/what are/were the causes
- who was involved
- what you've already tried to solve it
- possible consequences of the problem

SPEAK

11 a Work in pairs. Share your problem, then work together to try to solve it.

b Report back to the class. Summarise your partner's problem and possible solutions. Did you find a solution to your problems?

Master your writing page 130

3C Fact or fiction?

Goal: discuss how to fact-check news stories

Language focus: ways of modifying adjectives

Vocabulary: the news and reporting

Reading

1 Work in pairs and discuss the questions.

1 Do you think it's important to check the news regularly?

2 Where do you usually get your news from?

2 Read the article about fake news and match headings a–e with paragraphs 1–5.

a The wrong image
b A cause for concern
c Looking elsewhere
d Check your source
e + fake

FAKE NEWS!

1 ______

'Fake news' is a term commonly used by both politicians and ordinary people alike that is directed at any news stories slanted in a way that goes against their opinion. But fake news is a real thing, and something to be concerned about. A 2018 study into the spread of true and false news online discovered the **rather alarming** fact that true stories took six times longer to spread than false ones, and that fake stories in the study were 70% more likely to be shared. So how can we fact-check what we read?

2 ______

One **really useful** thing you can do to prevent yourself falling for a fake story is to check precisely where it has come from. The very first thing to look at when you see an unusual story is the URL or web address of the site it's been shared from. While our first impressions of what the address sounds like can give us a vital clue as to its credibility, we can also look it up on a list. Melissa Zimdars, author of the book *Fake News: Understanding Media and Misinformation in the Digital Age*, has created a useful, open-source online list of untrustworthy websites, which includes categories such as 'conspiracy' and 'junksci' (junk science).

3 ______

It is **perfectly straightforward** to search the title of the suspect story and add the word 'fake' to the search. This often throws up a whole host of results which reveal that it was a hoax. Which brings us to the next measure – using fact-checking websites. A multitude of these exist online. These are invaluable resources as you know the stories they credit will have been verified professionally, and are not just **utterly ridiculous** inventions.

4 ______

One technique which has been used extensively to spread (sometimes **completely**) **misleading** information is using a misrepresented photo. The originator of the story takes an image, then claims it shows something that it doesn't, though at first glance it seems **perfectly credible**. A reverse image search (where you search for stories using the image rather than words) can show the real source of the photo.

5 ______

A final practical fact-checking measure, once you think you've found a credible story, is to look for extra sources. Find at least two other sources stating the same claims, and you're likely to be able to claim it as fact.

3 Work in pairs and discuss the questions.

1 Can you think of any recent news stories which turned out to have been false?

2 What do you think of the fact-checking techniques outlined in the article? How do you think you might use them in the future?

3 What are your most trusted news sources? Which sources are famous for being inaccurate or very biased?

Language focus

4 a Work in pairs. Look at the adverbs + adjectives in bold in the article in Exercise 2 then answer the question.

Is each adverb used with:

- only gradable adjectives (like, *good* or *hot*)?
- only ungradable adjectives (like *excellent* or *boiling*)?
- both?

b Read the language focus box and check your answers.

Ways of modifying adjectives

There are various ways we can modify adjectives using adverbs. The adverb we use depends on:

1 whether the adjective is gradable or ungradable. Some adverbs can only be used to modify gradable adjectives (e.g. *barely, bitterly, deeply, extremely, fairly, perfectly, rather, somewhat, seriously, very*)

*I'm **pretty hopeful** we'll meet the deadline.*

*The exam was **extremely difficult**.*

Some adverbs can only be used to modify ungradable adjectives (e.g. *absolutely, completely, essentially, nearly, totally, utterly, virtually*)

*This story is **utterly ridiculous**.*

*I was **absolutely terrified** throughout that film.*

Really, pretty and *quite* can be used with both gradable and ungradable adjectives.

However, with gradable adjectives *quite* means *fairly*, whereas with ungradable adjectives it means *absolutely*.

*The text was **quite difficult** to follow, but I managed it in the end.*

*The text was **quite impossible** to follow! I didn't understand a word!*

2 whether the adjective forms part of a collocation. Some modifying adverbs collocate with certain adjectives (e.g. *bitterly cold/disappointed; completely open/honest; deeply serious/sorry; perfectly capable/straightforward; seriously alarming/hurt*)

*It was **bitterly cold** outside this morning.*

*To be **completely honest**, I don't really like the idea.*

5 a **Look at sentences 1–5 and decide which words carry the most stress.**

1 People are perfectly capable of working it out themselves.
2 They're deeply sorry for the distress they've caused you.
3 They were pretty annoyed with the press coverage.
4 It's utterly ridiculous, how could people believe it?
5 I'm fairly sure this is a fake.

b 3.5 **Listen and check.**

6 **Choose the option which is NOT possible.**

1 a You should speak to Sergio. He's deeply sorry for what he said to you.
  b You should speak to Sergio. He's perfectly sorry for what he said to you.
  c You should speak to Sergio. He's really sorry for what he said to you.
2 a Ugh, this tastes very awful!
  b Ugh, this tastes absolutely awful!
  c Ugh, this tastes quite awful!
3 a I'm bitterly disappointed with your behaviour.
  b I'm somewhat disappointed with your behaviour.
  c I'm nearly disappointed with your behaviour.
4 a This story seems fairly credible to me.
  b This story seems perfectly credible to me.
  c This story seems utterly credible to me.

7 **Work in pairs. Think of an adjective for each of the adverbs in the language focus box which describes something in your life.**

I was bitterly cold this morning.

Go to page 150 or your app for more information and practice.

Vocabulary

8 **Choose the correct alternatives.**

1 Very few newspapers are *impartial/realistic*, although they all claim they offer an objective representation.
2 The press should never *open/disclose* sensitive information about ongoing police investigations.
3 There's too much sensationalism in the news at the moment. A lot of the stories we're seeing are full of *unsubstantiated/insubstantial* claims which only end up misrepresenting the facts.
4 I'm sure I could recognise fake *footage/filming* of a news event if I saw it on TV.
5 Many stories about politicians are full of personal attacks and character *murders/assassinations* from journalists with opposing views.
6 Creators of news want to find an angle to a story that people are interested in, even if it means *breaking/bending* the truth.
7 Most fake news posts are very *credible/creditable*, but some are just ridiculous.
8 Fake news posts and articles are usually just ludicrous publicity *actions/stunts*, they're not really dangerous.
9 A lot of what people call fake news could be true – it's just a question of *interpretation/interplay* of the facts.

9 **Work in pairs. Discuss which of the statements in Exercise 8 you agree with. Give reasons.**

Go to page 168 or your app for more vocabulary and practice.

Speaking

PREPARE

10 3.6 **Listen to Matt and Trina discussing a news story. Answer the questions.**

1 What was the story about?
2 Why did Matt think it was real?
3 Why did Trina think it was fake at first?
4 Which of the fact-checking techniques in the article in Exercise 2 do they mention?

11 **Turn to page 178 and read the news stories. Make notes on the following:**

- your first impression (real or fake?) and why
- which techniques would be most suitable to fact-check the story

SPEAK

12 **Work in pairs. Explain whether you think the stories are true or fake and why. Discuss what you think are the best techniques to fact-check each one.**

Master your listening page 98

3D English in action

› **Goal:** summarise information

› **Vocabulary:** idioms related to clarity

Vocabulary

1 a Choose one of the topics and try to summarise it in exactly eight words.

- your last weekend
- your school days
- the plot of a book/film you like
- the best way to learn English

b Work in pairs. Share your summary with your partner.

2 a Match statements 1–6 with responses a–f.

1 I'm more confused now than I was before he gave that summary.
2 I hope that's all clear.
3 I wouldn't trust the figures she gave in her summary.
4 That was **as clear as day**, thanks.
5 I'm sorry, but I don't understand all this jargon.
6 There's something not right here, but I **can't quite put my finger on it**.

a **Crystal clear**, thanks.
b OK, let me give it to you **in plain English**.
c I know. It was **as clear as mud**!
d Oh good. I tried to make it as clear as possible for you.
e Well, it looks OK to me.
f I know what you mean. She seems to have a bit of **a hidden agenda**.

b Match the idioms in bold in Exercise 2a with the definitions.

1 100% clear (two idioms)
2 confusing/unclear
3 a secret motive for doing something
4 using simple language
5 not able to identify something exactly

3 a Think of an example of each of the following:

- a time you couldn't quite put your finger on something that was wrong
- some instructions that were clear as mud for you
- someone whose pronunciation in English is crystal clear
- a time you felt someone had a hidden agenda

b Work in pairs. Share your information.

Reading

4 a Work in pairs and discuss the questions.

1 What kind of information do you need to summarise in these situations:
  - at school/university?
  - at work?
  - socially?

2 What techniques can you use to help you summarise?

b Read the text about summarising strategies. Did it mention any of your ideas? What kind of things would each strategy work for (e.g. a story, a film, an academic paper)?

How to summarise clearly and effectively

Being able to summarise effectively is a useful skill whether it's an academic article, news article or a film or book. It's important to be able to get the key information across succinctly and clearly. Here are some useful summarising strategies you can use.

3 - 2 -1

A useful technique for summarising a lecture or lesson. Start with 3 of the most important facts you learnt, then 2 interesting things you found out, and finally note down 1 thing you'd like to find out more about.

Somebody - Wanted - But - So

This is useful for summarising news stories or fictional stories, such as in films. The four key words provide the structure for the main points:

Somebody: Who is the main person in the story?

Wanted: What did they want?

But: What problem did they come up against?

So: How did they solve it?

4 Ws, 1H (or Five Questions)

This technique uses different question words to form the basis of your notes for summarising: Who (is the text about?), What (happened?), When (did it happen?), Why (did they do what they did)? How (did they do it?).

First, Then, Finally

This is a useful technique for a basic summary. You simply make notes on what happened in the text in chronological order, starting with the background/main information, then the events of the story or article, and finishing by saying how it ended.

The Cornell Method

A useful technique for summarising factual information. On a blank piece of paper, you draw a line down the middle. In the left-hand column you list the main facts, then next to each one in the right-hand column you add any supporting details which are important. These then guide your summary.

Twenty words

A final technique you can use to summarise is to try and get the main points of the text down to no more than twenty words, which act as reminders of the main points of the text, to help you remember each step in the summary.

Listening

5 a 3.10 **Read the article on page 179. Then listen to three people summarising the information it contains. Answer the questions.**

1 Which techniques from the article do the professor and Clara use?

2 Who doesn't summarise well? Why not?

b 3.11 **Listen to the first speaker again and tick the Useful phrases he uses.**

Useful phrases

Summarising

The main points are as follows …
What they did was …
The gist of it is that …
In a nutshell, …
The first thing you need to know is…

Referring to information

The former … / the latter …
Not only that, but …
In the previous/following section, …
So what happened was …
Going back to what I said at the beginning, …
In that case …

6 a 3.12 **Listen to two sentences. What happens to the letters in bold?**

1 The mai**n** points are as follows.

2 In tha**t** case, the results were exceptional.

b Listen again and repeat.

7 Match 1–6 with a–f.

1 In a nutshell,
2 The main points are as follows.
3 Not only that, but
4 In the previous section
5 The former was a generic study.
6 What they did was

a Firstly, they wanted to do tests on cheese. Secondly, …
b they also found out that different music had different effects.
c set up an experiment with six rolls of common cheese.
d it's a story about love and happiness.
e The latter was much more specific.
f the author describes the background to the research.

8 Work in pairs. Use the Useful phrases to summarise the situation you summarised in only eight words in Exercise 1. Try to give more information this time.

Speaking

PREPARE

9 You are going to summarise a text. Work in pairs. Student A: Turn to page 180. Student B: Turn to page 179. Choose one of the techniques in Exercise 4b to summarise your text. Make notes.

SPEAK

10 a Read your summary to your partner. Use your notes from Exercise 9 and the Useful phrases in Exercise 5b. Which text did you like best?

b Give your partner feedback on their summary, using the questions below.

- Did they include the main points?
- Which of the Useful phrases did they use?
- Is there anything else you'd like to find out?

Go online for the Roadmap video.

4A High emotion

A

- **Goal:** talk about personal experiences
- **Language focus:** non-future uses of *will*
- **Vocabulary:** anxiety and excitement

Reading

1 Work in pairs. Look at the photos and discuss the questions.

1 What might cause fear in each situation?
2 What makes you scared or anxious? Why?
3 Do you ever enjoy being scared? Why/Why not?

2 Read the article quickly and answer the questions.

1 What's the difference between a fear and a phobia?
2 Why are some people scared of certain foods?
3 Why do many people hate giving presentations?
4 How can you alter your emotions?
5 Why do some people like being scared?
6 Which phrase can help you harness the power of your fears?

How to conquer your anxiety

1 On the whole, fear is a good thing. If we weren't afraid of fires, heights and venomous snakes, we would never survive. But sometimes our fears do more harm than good, holding us back from doing what we want to do. They can also become self-reinforcing: if the sight of a spider once gave you a terrifying **panic attack**, you'll now be scared not just of spiders but also of more panic attacks. In other words, you've become afraid of fear itself, and your simple fear has become a complex phobia.

2 We can categorise fears and phobias into two types. The first type is the fear of death or injury. To give a simple example, arachibutyrophobia is the fear of peanut butter, which may come from a **traumatic** experience of having a sticky substance blocking your throat and being unable to breathe. If you experienced this as a child, it'll be no surprise if the thought of peanut butter **brings you out in a cold sweat**.

3 The second type of fear and phobia involves social embarrassment – basically, looking foolish in front of others. Again, these may originate from traumatic childhood experiences, when social pressure can be at its strongest. For many people, speaking to a large audience can be **a daunting prospect**. Even the sight of a microphone can cause your stomach to **churn**, your knees to go weak and your heart rate to soar – which can be **debilitating** if your job requires you to give presentations.

4 Luckily, there's a simple trick to overcoming fears: convince yourself that you're excited. According to the scientific consensus, our emotions consist of two elements: the physical symptoms we feel and our conscious analysis of what those symptoms mean. This suggests that it's possible to change the emotions simply by changing your interpretation, a process called 'emotional reappraisal'.

5 Emotional reappraisal explains why so many people enjoy bungee-jumping or scary films: they've trained themselves to interpret the physical symptoms of fear as signs of excitement. And it shows why some people report **getting a buzz out of** performing in public: the **rush** of adrenaline and cortisol can create a feeling of **exhilaration**.

6 So if your fears are holding you back, try to transform your anxieties into **thrills**. Just repeat these three simple words: 'I am excited.'

Vocabulary

3 Read the article again. Match the words and phrases in bold with definitions 1–10.

1 so bad that it prevents you from doing what you want/need to do
2 exciting experiences
3 a sudden large quantity of something (e.g. hormones)
4 a sudden and intense feeling of uncontrollable fear and discomfort
5 to twist and turn unpleasantly
6 feeling excited because of
7 extremely unpleasant with long-term effects
8 something scary in the future
9 extreme excitement
10 makes you feel very anxious

4 Work in pairs and discuss the questions. Use the words and phrases in Exercise 3. Then compare your ideas with the explanations on page 180.

1 What bad experiences might lead to chorophobia (the fear of dancing)?
2 What's the connection between sports and emotional reappraisal? What other everyday activities might involve emotional reappraisal?

Go to page 169 or your app for more vocabulary and practice.

Language focus

5 a 4.1 Listen to a conversation between Rickie and Ula.

1 Who has a hidden talent?
2 Who often uses emotional reappraisal?
3 Who developed a phobia from other people's reactions?
4 Who often wears the same item of clothing?
5 Who shares a fear with a famous person?
6 Who changes their mind during the conversation?

b Work in pairs. What do you think of the 'I'm excited' technique? Would it work for everybody?

B

C

6 a Look at extracts 1–7 from the conversation. Why are *will* and *would* used in each case?

1 They'**ll** probably all be having the same conversation as us right now, ...
2 When I'm alone in the car, I'**ll** happily sing along to the radio.
3 You'**ll** probably have wondered why I always wear T-shirts and pullovers.
4 When I was a child, my parents **would** freak out every time I touched a button.
5 I **won't** wear any clothes with buttons – I **won't** even touch them.
6 You'**ll** remember, I'm sure, that he always wore pullovers, just like me.
7 Near the beginning of his career, he **wouldn't** even touch the multi-button computer mouse ...

b Read the language focus box and check your ideas.

Non-future uses of *will*

Predictions

We can use *will/won't* to make predictions about the present as well as the future. Use the future continuous to make predictions about events in progress now, and the future perfect to make inferences about the past.

You'll be wondering why I'm wearing this hat, I bet.
(= You're probably wondering.)
Don't phone Kim now. He'll be in a lecture at the moment. (= He's probably there.)
You won't have heard this joke before.
(= I predict that you haven't heard it.)

Habits

We can use *will/won't* to talk about present habits (i.e. repeated actions) and *would* for past habits.

My son will sit for hours playing with his toy cars.
(= He often does this.)
When I was younger, I'd often watch scary movies with my parents. (= I used to watch them.)

Refusals

We can use *won't* and *wouldn't* to talk about a refusal to do something in the present or past.

Daniela's angry with me but she won't tell me why.
(= She refuses.)
I asked him to help but he wouldn't even listen to me.
(= He refused to listen.)

We often use *will/would* to pretend that the weather/an object refuses to do something.

Why won't it stop raining?
(= Why does the rain refuse to stop?)
Sorry I'm late – my car wouldn't start.
(= It decided it didn't want to start.)

7 Rewrite the parts of these sentences in bold, using *will* or *would*.

1 Whenever he sees a spider, **he tends to scream** and run out of the room.
2 Ah, you teach at the local school, do you? In that case, **I'm sure you know my son**, Frank.
3 She suffers from a terrible fear of public speaking but **she refuses to tell her boss** – she's too embarrassed.
4 When I was a child, **I used to dance all the time**. But now **I usually just watch** other people dancing.
5 **I'm sure you've heard of claustrophobia** and other well-known phobias.
6 What's wrong with my phone? **It's buzzing all the time and it doesn't want to stop**.
7 You should call them to say you'll be late. **They're probably getting worried** about you.
8 We got lost on the way but **Greg refused to stop** and ask for directions.

8 a 4.2 Listen to two sentences. In which sentence is *will/won't* stressed? Why?

b Practise saying sentences with stressed and unstressed *will/won't*.

9 Work in pairs and discuss the questions using *will* or *would*.

1 What things do you refuse to do? Why?
2 Is there anything that you refused to eat as a child but you eat now?
3 Do you know anybody with an annoying habit?
4 Did you have any unusual habits as a child/teenager?

Go to page 152 or your app for more information and practice.

Speaking

PREPARE

10 4.3 Listen to part of a radio interview with a person who suffers from asymmetriphobia. Answer the questions.

1 What is Artur afraid of?
2 What probably caused the phobia?
3 What causes Artur to have panic attacks?
4 How sympathetic are Artur's colleagues?

SPEAK

11 You are going to tell a story about a phobia. Turn to page 181.

12 Work in groups. Tell your stories, using language from this lesson. Guess whether each story is real or made up.

Master your reading page 112

4B Volunteering

A

- **Goal:** discuss political or social issues
- **Language focus:** real conditionals
- **Vocabulary:** adjective + noun collocations

Reading

1 Work in pairs. Look at the photos and discuss the questions.

1 What types of volunteering can you see? What other jobs do people volunteer for?

2 Have you ever worked as a volunteer? If so, what happened? If not, would you like to?

3 What are the benefits of volunteering? What does the volunteer get out of it?

2 Read the article quickly and answer the questions.

1 What are the benefits of intergenerational volunteering for the two groups of people?

2 What are the benefits for society as a whole?

Bridging the age gap

For many retired people, the greatest threats to their health and well-being are loneliness, isolation and lack of purpose. Studies have shown that when they have a strong sense of purpose, they live longer, healthier lives. At the other end of the spectrum, teenagers and young adults face daunting challenges of their own. In some cases, young people may experience peer pressure to join gangs, commit crimes or simply drift away from education and employment. They may face the challenge of finding a job without prior work experience or practical skills. Or they may wish to live independently but be unable to pay the exorbitant rents in their area.

Intergenerational volunteering can provide a solution to these problems. It involves bringing older and younger people together for mutual support. After all, 'the aged' represent a huge untapped resource: they include retired engineers, doctors, teachers and businesspeople with years of accumulated experience and expertise. Young people, too, have valuable skills to share, most obviously their up-to-date knowledge of technology.

In some schemes, retired people help out in primary schools, to hear the children read and offer them individual support. Similar schemes are run in secondary schools and even universities. Other projects involve sending children and teenagers into old people's homes on a regular basis to teach them 'twenty-first century skills', to entertain them or simply to befriend them and listen to their stories and advice. Elsewhere, there are schemes that match university students with more affluent elderly people who have spare rooms. The student can either live rent-free in exchange for household chores and support for the homeowner, or they can pay a reduced rent in exchange for chatting with the older person regularly and keeping an eye on their health and well-being.

Intergenerational volunteering projects have had a truly profound impact on both demographics. By bringing together people of different generations and socioeconomic backgrounds, they have fostered trust, respect and friendship, which are essential for the fabric of society.

3 Work in pairs and discuss the questions.

1 Do you think intergenerational volunteering exists where you live? If not, would it work?

2 Can you think of any challenges or risks arising from projects like this?

Vocabulary

4 a Choose the adjectives that collocate with the nouns in bold. Then find the collocations in the article to check.

1 I have a very *high/ rich/ strong* **sense** of duty towards society.

2 Applicants must have at least two years' *foregoing/ preceding/ prior* **work experience**.

3 I can't afford the *exorbitant/ extravagant/ inflated* **rent** on my flat – I need to find something cheaper.

4 I like studying with friends because we can offer each other *mutual/ reciprocal/ shared* **support**.

5 The island's unspoilt beaches represent an *intact/ untapped/ untested* **resource** which could encourage tourism.

6 You should practise on a *frequent/ persistent/ regular* **basis**, not just every now and then.

7 My elderly grandfather can no longer cope with all his *household/ homely/ indoor* **chores**.

8 My year as a volunteer had a *changeable/ metamorphic/ profound* **impact** on my outlook on life.

b Find at least three more adjective + noun collocations in the article.

Go to your app for more vocabulary and practice.

Language focus

5 4.4 Listen to part of a meeting. Choose the correct alternatives.

1 The main purpose of the project is to *encourage intergenerational communication/ improve buildings and natural environments.*

2 The main challenge facing the project is that *some participants steal from others/ there's a shortage of mentors.*

3 Alison agrees to provide *the full amount to fund the project/ a document containing a provisional offer.*

6 a Look at five extracts from the meeting. In what way are they different from regular zero and 1st conditional sentences?

1 If you'd like to come in and sit down, we can start when you're ready.
2 If they didn't have children, then at least they had a network of friends and relatives living nearby.
3 It'll really help our negotiations if we've already got 50% from you.
4 If they won't help, then you'll have to find another partner.
5 If it'll help your negotiations, we'd be happy to put up the 50%.

b Read the language focus box. Why are these different structures used?

Real conditionals

Real conditionals refer to real or likely situations. Two very common patterns are:
the zero conditional, which is often used to describe something that is always true (*if* + present, present).
*If people **have** a strong sense of duty to each other, society **improves**.*
the first conditional, to describe possible future events (*if* + present, will).
*If you **set** something up, people **will definitely help**.*
However, many other verb forms are also possible with these structures, e.g.:
Zero conditional for something that was always true in the past.
*If you **had** a problem, people **helped you**/**would help** you.*
First conditional featuring a past action with present/future result.
*If they'**ve worked** with older people before, they'**ll know** how to help.*
We usually don't use *if* and *will* in the same clause. However, we can use *if* + *will* to talk about promises, predictions and willingness/refusals.
If you'll give us the money, we'll run the project by ourselves.
If you won't help me, I don't know who will. (= if you refuse to help me)
In real conditionals, *if* + *would* is mainly used for polite requests and offers (e.g. if you'd like/if you wouldn't mind).
If you'd like to follow me, I'll show you your room. (= if you want)

7 a 4.5 Listen to three more extracts from the meeting and answer questions a–d.

1 So, if you'd like to tell us more about your project ...
2 If you could say a few words about why they're so isolated from society ...
3 If you'll just bear with me a moment, ...

a Are the phrases offers or requests?
b What do you notice about their intonation?
c Why doesn't the speaker finish the sentences?
d What would be a suitable reply?

b Work in pairs. Practise saying and responding to the extracts.

8 a Rewrite the sentences using the word(s) in brackets.

1 I can't help you if you refuse to tell me your name. (won't)
2 Maybe he has had a bad experience, and he doesn't want to try again. (If)
3 When I was a child, my grandfather used to fix anything that was broken in our house. (if anything/would)
4 I can lend you my car but you need to promise to take care of it. (you'll)
5 Would you like to cook? If so, we can stay at home. (you'd)

b Work in pairs. Think of reasons for the situations and possible consequences.

1 young people who refuse to go to school
If they had a bad time at school, they ...
If they won't go to school, they ...
2 older people who are isolated in society
3 young people who can't find work

Go to page 152 or your app for more information and practice.

Speaking

PREPARE

9 Work in groups. You're going to plan a project to help people in your community. Discuss the questions.

1 Who will you try to help?
2 What challenges do these people face? How might your project help them?
3 What do you need from the council? What benefits can you offer to the community?
4 What will happen if the council refuses to help?

SPEAK

10 Work in different groups. You are going to take part in a meeting with a committee of the local council. Try to persuade them to support your project (e.g. by providing money).

Master your writing page 132

4C The mind's eye

Goal: answer questions about abstract topics

Language focus: giving impressions

Vocabulary: the senses

Aphantasia and hyperphantasia

In 2005, Professor Adam Zeman was approached by a man who claimed to have lost the ability to visualise, as if his mind's eye had gone blind. Dr Zeman was unable to find any similar cases, so he researched it himself. When he published his research in 2010, the reaction from most quarters was fairly **muted**. But a handful of readers were astonished – people who had never been able to visualise since birth, but never realised that they were different from the rest of the population. The revelation that most other people could form genuinely **vibrant** mental images in **rich** detail was truly stunning ... and a little disorienting.

By 2015, Dr Zeman had conducted more research and given the condition a name, 'aphantasia', meaning 'no ability to visualise'. Some aphantasiacs report a vague ability to conjure up a **fleeting** and **fuzzy** image of a person or place they know well, but it requires a great deal of effort. The idea of adding movement, sounds and smells to those images is literally unthinkable.

As aphantasia became more prominent in the media, it was the turn of another group to be stunned. For people with hyperphantasia, or an extreme ability to visualise, there is no distinction between the real, imagined and remembered worlds – all are equally **vivid** in all the senses. They can taste a meal they ate twenty years earlier and feel its textures in their mouth. They can play back a childhood event in their mind's eye – see every tiny detail and smell every **odour** and **aroma**. In fact, they are unable to turn off their mind's eye, so that when they read a novel, for example, they experience the same **crystal-clear** sights, sounds, smells and pains as the protagonists. Like aphantasiacs, most hyperphantasiacs are unaware that they're in any way unusual.

Research into aphantasia and hyperphantasia has barely started, so we can only guess how widespread they are. But there could well be thousands more conditions like them, just waiting to be discovered, if only we would talk a bit more about what it's like to be 'me'. The idea that other people process the world in radically different ways is astonishing, but also rather reassuring. Perhaps it can help us to treat other people (and ourselves) with a bit more respect: 'Not weird, just different ... and that's fine.'

Reading

1 a Work in pairs. Take turns to close your eyes and imagine the following scenes in as much detail as possible. Tell your partner what you can see.

1 An imaginary countryside scene (e.g. a forest).
2 A room you knew well in the past.
3 A friend or family member walking or running.

b Discuss your experiences of visualisation.

1 Did you find the visualisation activities easy or difficult?
2 How clear and detailed were the images in your mind?
3 Did your mental image include smells, tastes, etc?
4 Were you surprised by anything your partner said?

2 Read the article. Which conditions do statements 1–6 below refer to – aphantasia (A), hyperphantasia (H) or both (B)?

1 Researchers don't know how common it is.
2 People with this condition can't imagine some things.
3 This condition might make reading fiction painful.
4 Most people with this condition assume they're completely normal.
5 The condition can be overcome to some extent with hard mental work.
6 It affects a range of senses (e.g. sight, hearing, smell).

3 Work in pairs. Think back to your experiences in Exercise 1a. Are you more like an aphantasiac or a hyperphantasiac – or somewhere in the middle?

Vocabulary

4 Find words and phrases in bold in the article that mean the following:

1 almost too quick to notice
2 a pleasant smell
3 an unpleasant smell
4 without clear lines/edges, like an out-of-focus photo
5 clear and (almost) alive
6 not expressed strongly; quiet, as if the sound is 'turned down'
7 strong, powerful
8 colourful, full of energy
9 in perfect focus

5 a **Work in pairs. Which senses (sight, hearing, touch, smell, taste) do the adjectives in the box refer to? Some words refer to more than one.**

blurry crisp faint fluffy hazy indistinct mellow metallic muffled musty pungent resonant savoury shrill silky succulent textured

b **Work in pairs to think of things that the adjectives might describe.**

a blurry photograph

6 **Use some of the words in Exercises 4 and 5 to describe the following:**

- the sounds you can hear now in the distance
- the taste and smell of something you ate recently
- your memories from primary school (your desk, your teacher's voice, etc.)

Go to page 169 or your app for more vocabulary and practice.

Language focus

7 a 4.6 **Listen to two people describing the same experience. How are Jenny and Marge's experiences different? Which person feels more certain about what they have experienced?**

b 4.7 **Read the language focus box, then listen to Jenny's experience again. What language does she use to make the description less definite?**

Giving impressions

To communicate that our memories or sensations are not completely clear, use phrases like these with nouns:

*I see **something resembling** a tree.*
*I come to **what could almost be a** castle.*
*It's like a doughnut, **or that kind of thing.***
*It **might possibly be** a cave.*
*I see **what can only be described as** a sausage*
*I can just **make out** the shape of the whale.*

Use *ish* or *y* with adjectives to make them less precise.

*It's a kind of **blueish greenish** colour.*

Use modifiers to make adjectives sound less definite.

*It's **somewhat** cold.*
*It's **verging on** unbearable.*

Also use the adverb *vaguely* with adjectives such as *familiar, aware, troubling* or *guilty.*

*It's **vaguely** familiar.*

With actions, use phrases like these:

***Somehow**, we cross the bridge.*
***I don't know how**, but we're suddenly on a beach.*

8 a **Work in pairs. Look at the words. How do you think they are pronounced?**

1 yellowish
2 blueish
3 lowish
4 longish
5 highish
6 greyish

b 4.8 **Listen and check. What is the sound before** ***ish*** **in each word?**

c **Listen again and repeat.**

9 **Add one word to make the sentences correct.**

1 I see resembling a house.
2 I come to could almost be a castle.
3 It's like a leopard, or that kind thing.
4 I see what can only be described a giant shoe.
5 It's sort like a postbox but not exactly.
6 I don't know, but somehow we escape.
7 In the distance, I can just make the shape of a hill.
8 We're verging exhaustion.

10 **Make the description sound less precise.**

We're walking up a mountain, and we see a sheep. We get near to it, and we see it has a yellow mark on its back, a mark from the farm it comes from. We hear a whistle, and the sheep runs off, and we follow it to an old house. There's a man there. He's a farmer.

Go to page 152 or your app for more information and practice.

Speaking

PREPARE

11 **You are going to do a guided visualisation and check whether you might be an aphantasiac or a hyperphantasiac. Work in pairs. Student A: Turn to page 180. Student B: Turn to page 182. Read the text and add two more questions of your own.**

SPEAK

12 a **Take turns to ask and answer the questions on pages 180 and 182.**

b **Do you think your partner might have aphantasia or hyperphantasia? Why/Why not?**

Master your listening page 99

4D English in action

› **Goal:** resolve conflicts in negotiations

› **Vocabulary:** negotiating

Vocabulary

1 **Work in pairs. Think of five people that you encounter fairly often (e.g. partner, parents, teacher, boss, neighbour, etc.). Then think of some situations where you have negotiated with each person. What happened?**

I often negotiate with my parents about whether I can stay out late. They usually want me to ...

2 a **Match 1–9 with a–i to complete the idioms.**

1 If both sides stay positive and open-minded, it's usually possible to **reach a**
2 All successful negotiations involve a lot of **give and**
3 OK, so we're prepared to **make a**
4 Don't give up so easily – you ought to **stick to**
5 We made a very generous offer, but they just **dug their**
6 Listen, you're offering £80, but we want £100. Shall we just **split**
7 I think they're just using the 3-year warranty as a **bargaining**
8 A good starting point in any negotiation is to **find common**
9 The negotiation was going nowhere, but then I had a brilliant idea to **break**

a **chip** – they don't really care about it, but they want something in return for giving it up.
b **the deadlock** and move things forward again.
c **your guns** and fight for what you want!
d **compromise** that keeps everyone happy.
e **ground** – things that you already agree on.
f **take** – you can't expect to get your way 100%.
g **concession on** the price, if you'll show some flexibility with the dates.
h **heels in** and refused to compromise.
i **the difference** and call it £90?

b **Which idioms from Exercise 2a have a generally positive meaning? Which are generally negative? Which can be both?**

c **Work in pairs. What sort of negotiator are you (or do you think you would be)? Try to use all the idioms in Exercise 2a in your discussion. Use examples from the situations you discussed in Exercise 1.**

3 **Read the text and think of a heading for each paragraph. Use language from Exercise 2a where possible.**

Negotiating skills: de-escalating a conflict

We might think of negotiating as a business skill, but in fact we negotiate all the time in our day-to-day lives. These simple techniques can reduce the risk of turning a difficult situation into a battle … and may help both sides find an amicable solution.

1 ______________

In a negotiation, your 'position' is what you want – a higher salary, a quicker delivery, a longer guarantee, whatever. But your 'interest' explains *why* you want those things. If you negotiate over positions, you won't get very far. But if you make the effort to understand each other's interests, you're much more likely to find a creative solution.

2 ______________

If you accuse the other person of having a flawed character and making stupid mistakes, you'll likely provoke a hostile defence, as they battle to prove you wrong. Instead, talk about how a situation makes you feel, which is an indisputable fact.

3 ______________

It may be cathartic to use emotional language to attack the other person, but it rarely, if ever, moves the negotiation forward. And if the other person uses aggressive language towards you, or misrepresents your motives and your actions, it's often better to de-escalate the situation by letting it go.

4 ______________

Sometimes the simplest way to deal with a fire is to let it burn itself out. The same goes for an angry person: allow them to let off steam. Encourage them to keep talking. After a few minutes, they'll run out of things to say and calm themselves down.

5 ______________

Try to see the situation through the other person's eyes. Why are they so angry? Would you be angry in the same situation? What would calm you down?

6 ______________

Remember almost all negotiations have two goals: resolve the current issue and develop a lasting relationship. Don't let the first goal distract you from the second.

Listening 1

4 a Work in pairs and discuss the questions.

1 Have you ever rented a flat to/from somebody? Did everything go smoothly?

2 What is involved in renting a flat? What are some possible sources of conflict between a landlord/landlady and a tenant? Make a list.

3 What can happen if the relationship between landlord/landlady and tenant turns sour? What options do they each have?

b 4.11 Listen to a conversation between a landlady and a tenant. What sources of conflict did they mention? Were any of them the same as your ideas in Exercise 4a?

5 a 4.12 Complete the Useful phrases 1 box with one word in each space. Then listen and check.

Useful phrases 1

Understanding emotional language

1 Pay the money you owe me tomorrow ______ you'll have to find somewhere else to live.

2 If you ______ stick to your side of the agreement, I'll find somebody else who will.

3 I won't ______ you spoiling my good relations with my neighbours.

4 I'll ______ you know, Toby, that this is still my flat.

5 Any more excuses ______ it's over.

Responding to emotional language

I know and I'm really sorry. I'll try to sort it out as soon as I can.

Yes. It's just that …

Was there anything else?

I'll be a model tenant from now on – believe me.

b Which three pieces of emotional language in the Useful phrases 1 box are threats? What structures did the speaker use to make them?

c Work in pairs. Think of less emotional ways of saying the things in Exercise 5a.

6 a Imagine you are Mrs Ricardo. Complete the emotional statements with your own ideas.

1 Break one more of my … and …

2 … or you're out of here.

3 I won't have you …-ing …

4 If you won't … then …

5 I'll have you know that …

b Work in pairs. How could Toby respond to the statements in Exercise 6a in order to calm the situation down? Roleplay the scenarios.

Listening 2

7 4.13 Listen to the next part of the conversation, which takes place 24 hours later. Are the statements true (T) or false (F)?

1 Toby still hasn't paid this month's rent.

2 Toby thinks Mrs Ricardo should get rid of her old furniture.

3 Mrs Ricardo was initially reluctant to rent out the flat.

4 Toby's client has refused to pay him for a lot of work.

5 Mrs Ricardo is completely confident that Toby is telling the truth.

8 a Match the phrases from the Useful phrases 2 box with the functions. Some phrases may have more than one function.

a Showing empathy (= understanding the other person's situation)

b Reassuring the other person not to worry

c Trying to find compromise

d Apologising/Admitting mistakes

e Identifying reasons

Useful phrases 2

1 It must have been quite upsetting to see everything in a mess.

2 I may have lost my temper a little yesterday.

3 How come you decided to rent out this flat, if you don't mind me asking?

4 I can see why you're so desperate for me to pay the rent on time.

5 That can't be easy for you!

6 Perhaps I was a little harsh with you yesterday.

7 Maybe we can try and work something out.

8 I suppose I might be able to wait a few more days.

9 Well, I'm sure it won't come to that.

10 It's not that I don't trust you, of course.

b 4.14 Listen to two versions of some of the extracts. Which version, a or b, sounds more empathetic? Why?

c Work in pairs. Practise the phrases to sound as empathetic as possible.

Speaking

9 a Work in pairs to roleplay two situations, using the advice and language from this lesson. Student A: Turn to page 181. Student B: Turn to page 182.

b Report back to the class. What hidden interests did you discover? What compromises did you reach? Was there anything that you were unable to resolve?

Go online for the Roadmap video.

Check and reflect: Units 3 and 4

1 Rewrite the questions using the words given.

1 What do you want to speak to me about?
What is

2 How much experience do you have?
Could you tell me

3 Do you want to speak to Clare? I'm sure you said you did.
Didn't

4 Should we ask them for more money?
You mean

5 Who came up with this idea?
Who was

6 Where did you go after the meeting?
You went

2 Choose the correct alternatives.

1 This meeting is a chance for us to *occur/bounce* ideas around for the new product launch.
2 Whose *bright/spring* idea was it not to lock the door?
3 I've had a *brainwave/dawn* – let's forget about studying and head to the beach!
4 What *gives/springs* to mind when you think of your school days?
5 Help me, I'm out of *ideas/brainwaves*.
6 You've *given/bounced* me an idea! Why don't we ask Cheryl to organise the food?

3 a Replace the words in bold in each sentence with the words or phrases in the box.

befuddled	intuitive	misinterpret	mull over	underestimate

1 I get **really confused** when I try to understand quantum physics.
2 I much prefer to **think about** a problem on my own.
3 I always **guess too little about** the amount of time it will take me to get somewhere, and arrive late.
4 I'm a rational person. I'm not **relying on feelings**.
5 I'm very honest, and sometimes people **understand incorrectly** what I say as criticism.

b Work in pairs. Discuss which sentences are true for you. Give more information.

4 a Match the sentence halves.

1 Not wanting to wake anyone up,
2 I worked hard at maths at school,
3 I left really early,
4 She was hard to work with,
5 Seeing as I didn't have any money left,
6 I was on the phone for over half an hour,

a since it was my favourite subject.
b I had to walk home.
c for fear of arriving late.
d trying to get someone to help me.
e I crept out of the house really quietly.
f in that she never really shared her ideas.

b Work in pairs. Choose two of the sentences in Exercise 4a and think of a time that they were true for you (or change them so that they were). Tell your partner about them.

5 Complete the sentences with the adverbs in the box.

completely	deeply	perfectly	quite	seriously	utterly

1 We're ______ sorry for your loss. Let us know if we can do anything.
2 You just need to be ______ open with her about how you feel.
3 I'm ______ capable of doing that myself, thank you.
4 To say that the new measures are effective is ______ ridiculous.
5 His new book was ______ good, but not as interesting as his earlier work.
6 Several people were ______ hurt in the accident.

6 Choose the correct alternatives. In one sentence, both options are possible.

1 It was nothing short of *character assassination/publicity stunt* of the old president.
2 The news story took an *impartial/bending* view of the situation.
3 We have yet to receive any reliable information on the incident. All claims to date have been *unsubstantiated/impartial*.
4 The news station prides itself on its *impartial/objective* coverage of the facts over the years.
5 The tabloid press were criticised for their simplistic *interpretations/disclose* of the facts.
6 Some viewers may find the following *publicity stunt/footage* of the accident disturbing.

7 a Complete the questions with the words in the box.

attack	buzz	churn	exhilaration	prospect	thrill

1 Why kind of thing might cause someone to have a panic ______?
2 Do you get a ______ out of being terrified?
3 Is the idea of speaking or singing in public a daunting ______ for you?
4 Does your stomach ______ when you look down from high places?
5 Do you enjoy a sense of ______ from being in dangerous situations?
6 Do you ever do something dangerous just for a ______?

b Work in pairs. Discuss three of the questions. Ask follow-up questions.

8 Complete the sentences using *will/would* and the verb in brackets.

1 There's a cat that pesters me for food every day. She ____________ until I've fed her. (not go away)
2 I hear you've got a big exam next week. You ____________ hard at the moment, I imagine. (study)
3 I was stuck in the lift for two hours. The door ____________. (open)
4 I'm not surprised you're tired. You ____________ late watching TV, won't you? (stay up)
5 You've left your phone at home, have you? In that case, you ____________ the text I sent. (not see)
6 When Jake was a child, he ____________ the most amazing pictures. (draw)

9 Complete the sentences to make strong adjective-noun collocations.

1 When it comes to family, I have a **s______g sense** of duty.
2 I help our elderly neighbour with **h______d chores**.
3 After their traumatic experience, they gained a strong sense of **m______l respect** for each other.
4 I moved out of my flat because of the **e______t rent**.
5 I catch up with my friends on a **r______r basis**.
6 Helen didn't get the job because she didn't have enough **p______r work experience**.

10 Use the phrases in bold to make real conditionals.

1 There's a chance that **I'll fail my exam**. If so, **I may have to retake it**.
2 Many people **loved her previous book**. If you're one of those people, **you'll love her new one**.
3 Apparently **your boss won't listen to your opinions**. In that case, **you should find a new job**.
4 Perhaps **you'd prefer to be alone**. If so, **I'll leave you in peace**.
5 Some of **you have never skied before**. If you're one of those people, **please raise your hand**.
6 **You can read my poems** on one condition: you promise **you won't laugh**.

11 a Put the adjectives in the box in the correct place in the sentences.

hazy fleeting mellow muffled pungent vivid

1 My most childhood memory is of my first day of school – it is still clear in my mind.
2 I can remember people's faces even if I've only had a glimpse of them.
3 I love listening to music – something relaxing to calm me down.
4 If I try to remember my childhood home, I can conjure up a image, but nothing clear.
5 I love flavours like garlic, ginger, mustard and raw onions.
6 I find it hard to sleep if I can hear a conversation in the next room.

b Work in pairs. Change the statements so that they are true for you.

12 Choose the correct alternative.

1 It's sort of *like/as* a wedding cake.
2 *Somehow/Somewhere* we manage to run away from the criminals.
3 We met a woman closely *remembering/resembling* the old Queen, Larissa.
4 There was no need for a big meeting, or *that kind of thing/somehow*.
5 I can just make *out/up* the shape of a cat on the roof of the shed.
6 She was verging *in/on* collapse from the heat.
7 I see what *can/will* only be described as a nightmare come to life.
8 We arrive at *what/which* could almost be one of those old houses from my country.

13 Match the sentence halves.

1 We can't reach a compromise
2 There are no issues we can't resolve
3 OK, we'll make a concession
4 Stick to your guns
5 We tried to convince them, but they just
6 Can we just split the difference
7 They don't really want the goods quickly, they're just using that
8 Good, I think we've found some common ground –
9 Unless there's a way to break the deadlock

a and don't let them push you around.
b and settle on five thousand for everything?
c we both need this done quickly.
d I'm afraid we're done here, Nigel.
e dug their heels in and refused to negotiate any further.
f on the delivery date if you're willing to offer us better payment options.
g with a little give and take.
h as a bargaining chip so we'll bring the price down.
i if you're not willing to offer us anything.

Reflect

How confident do you feel about the statements below? Write 1–5 (1 = not very confident, 5 = very confident).

- I can use brainstorming techniques.
- I can solve a problem.
- I can discuss how to fact-check news stories.
- I can summarise information.
- I can talk about personal experiences in detail.
- I can discuss political or social issues.
- I can answer questions about abstract topics.
- I can make proposals to resolve conflicts in negotiations.

For more practice go to your Workbook or app.

5A Unsung heroes

Goal: discuss unsung heroes

Language focus: linking devices

Vocabulary: importance and usefulness

Reading

1 **Work in pairs. Look at the definition below. Can you think of any examples of unsung heroes? Think about these fields:**

- films, TV and music
- sport
- scientific research
- business
- creating and maintaining a great city/country

un·sung adjective
not praised or famous for something you have done, although you deserve to be

2 **Read the article and answer the questions.**

1. Why are waste pickers described as 'invisible superheroes'?
2. How and why did Mundano's project start?
3. How does Mundano's project help waste pickers in São Paulo?
4. How is the project in Casablanca different from the one in Brazil?
5. What would the writer like us to do after reading the article?

3 **Work in pairs and discuss the questions.**

1. Do you agree that waste pickers are invisible superheroes? Why/Why not?
2. Why do you think the volunteers in Casablanca struggled to find people to take part?

THE INVISIBLE SUPERHEROES

Supposing you had the power of invisibility and could walk around crowded cities completely unnoticed. Amazingly, millions of people around the world have this phenomenal superpower. They spend their time picking up waste from the streets, collecting it in handcarts and selling it for recycling. The job is dirty and physically demanding, **not to mention** highly dangerous, **given** the risk of injuries when handling sharp objects without proper safety equipment. They're invisible **inasmuch as** the rest of us barely notice them. Most people are blind to the fact that, but for these waste pickers, our cities would be overflowing with trash.

In 2007, a Brazilian graffiti artist in São Paulo called Mundano decided to give *catadores* (as waste pickers are called in Brazil) the recognition they deserved, so he decorated dozens of handcarts with colourful artwork to raise the self-esteem of their owners. Thanks to social media, pictures of Mundano's work – and the stories behind them – spread around the world like wildfire. Almost by accident, Mundano had created a global movement of people who feel that these invisible superheroes, as he calls them, deserve our respect and our support. Mundano's project now provides free protective clothing and healthcare to *catadores*. The handcarts are renovated by volunteers, who also add safety features such as reflective tapes, horns and mirrors, and finally they're painted by a street artist to become part of a huge, mobile art exhibition.

Mundano's movement has now spread well beyond Brazil. One group of volunteers in Morocco attempted to replicate the project in their home city, Casablanca. At first, it was hard to persuade any waste pickers to listen to their seemingly crazy plans, **let alone** allow them to paint graffiti all over their precious handcarts. But they finally found one man, Yassine, who agreed to participate, albeit reluctantly. They offered to build him his own brand-new handcart, to replace the one he was currently renting, **provided that** he'd help them to encourage other waste pickers to join the project. **Now that** the project has taken off, the organisers are expanding it to encourage recycling all over Casablanca.

Projects like these aren't really about recycling; they're about respect and recognition for overlooked members of society, **regardless of** how dirty or unpleasant their jobs are. **Granted**, these projects can only make a limited difference to people's lives, but they're **nonetheless** an important step in the right direction. So next time you spot a waste picker, or indeed any other invisible superhero, take a moment to think of the vital service they perform – and how you can support them.

Language focus

4 a Look at the words in bold in the article. What is the function of these words in a text?

b Read the language focus box below. Then complete sentences 1–8 with your own ideas.

1 Given that nurses work so hard, ...
2 Footballers get paid far too much. Granted, ... but ...
3 Now that we're in the 21st century, ...
4 People working in low-paid jobs often have the longest hours, not to mention ...
5 People working in low paid jobs often don't have enough to live on, let alone ...
6 Supposing that we lost all our key workers overnight, ...
7 Regardless of the status of their jobs, ...
8 Street cleaners are heroes, in as much as ...

c Work in pairs. Compare your sentences with your partner. Which sentences do you agree with?

Linking devices

Linking devices are words and phrases that show the relationship between pieces of information.

- ***Given*** can be followed by a *that*-clause or a noun phrase.
  __Given__ (that) we had problems before/__Given__ our previous problems, what should we do?
- ***Granted*** usually comes at the beginning of a sentence, separated by a comma.
  I finished third in the race. __Granted__, there were only four people in the race, but ...
- ***Inasmuch as*** is followed by a subject + verb.
  The meeting was a disaster, __inasmuch as__ we couldn't make any decisions.
- ***Let alone*** can be followed by an infinitive without *to* or a noun phrase.
  He didn't even notice me, __let alone__ thank me.
- ***Nonetheless*** often comes between two clauses/sentences but sometimes comes after *but*, a subject and *be*.
  The plan met with some resistance. __Nonetheless__, they kept going.
  His stories may seem like works of fiction, but they're __nonetheless__ true.
- ***Not to mention*** is often followed by an adjective or a noun phrase.
  It's expensive and dangerous, __not to mention__ illegal.
- ***Now***, ***provided*** and ***supposing*** are followed by a *that*-clause, but you can omit *that*, especially in informal English.
  __Now__ (that) you're here, we can start, __provided__ (that) everyone else is ready.
- ***Regardless of*** can be followed by a noun phrase or an indirect question.
  Everyone is welcome __regardless of__ age/__regardless of__ how old they are.

5 a Work in pairs. Read the examples in the language focus box aloud. Do we usually stress linking devices?

b 5.1 **Listen and check.**

Go to page 154 or your app for more information and practice.

Vocabulary

6 Look at sentences 1–8. Underline the words that relate to importance or lack of importance.

1 This is a groundbreaking project. It will have far-reaching consequences.
2 It's completely futile trying to change other people's attitudes.
3 Nobody respects me or my work. I feel totally worthless and undervalued.
4 You're an indispensable member of the team. Your contributions are pivotal.
5 He made no noteworthy suggestions at all – he had a negligible impact on this project.
6 It's immaterial how badly you want this job. The only important thing is how good you are.
7 I'm not a key member of the group. In fact, I'm quite a peripheral member of the team.
8 I think his books are a little overrated. They're nowhere near as important as many people say.

7 Work in pairs. Disagree with the statements, using the words in Exercise 6.

1 This project is completely worthless.
No, it's actually a really groundbreaking project.
2 Your work is absolutely pivotal.
3 It's completely immaterial what we say.
4 His talents are overrated.
5 Those skills are indispensable these days.

Go to page 170 or your app for more vocabulary and practice.

Speaking

PREPARE

8 5.2 **You're going to make a list of unsung heroes. First, listen to two people doing the same and answer the questions.**

1 What jobs do they discuss?
2 Which job do they disagree about? Why?

9 Make a list of people you feel are 'unsung heroes'. Make notes about why you think they should receive more recognition.

SPEAK

10 a Work in pairs. Work together to make a list of the top five unsung heroes. Where your partner disagrees with you, attempt to persuade them.

b Share your ideas with the class.

Master your listening page 100

5B The power of failure

- **Goal:** tell an anecdote
- **Language focus:** unreal conditionals
- **Vocabulary:** risk, success and failure

Reading

1 Look at some proverbs. What do you think they mean? Which do you agree with?

- The great question is not whether you have failed, but whether you are content with failure. (Chinese Proverb)
- The first pancake is always a failure. (Russian Proverb)

2 Read the article quickly. How many examples does it mention of people who seem to have failed?

1 The internet is full of hilarious videos of people failing: clumsy skateboarders attempting overly complex tricks and falling over, incompetent parkour runners performing death-defying leaps and landing in a crumpled heap on the ground and overconfident gymnasts doing triple back flips and ending up flat on their backs. The stars of these videos seem too accident-prone to walk down the street, let alone attempt crazy stunts!

2 The internet is also full of breathtaking videos of extreme sportspeople performing seemingly superhuman stunts. What a difference between the losers and the pros, you might think? But what you might not realise is that they're actually the same people: the losers become the pros. Or, to put it another way, the only way to become a pro is to spend years and years experiencing soul-destroying failure … and then picking yourself up to try again.

3 According to one study of elite figure skaters, the key difference between the best and the rest is that the best skaters spend far more time falling over than their slightly less-elite counterparts. That's because they continually attempt jumps that are beyond their current abilities. Most other skaters, on the other hand, prefer to stick to their comfort zones to avoid embarrassment and injury, so of course they fall over less. By some estimates, you need to fall over more than 20,000 times on the way to becoming an Olympic figure-skating champion.

4 The same is true in many other walks of life. When you're watching a group of musicians, look out for the ones who keep making mistakes, as they're the ones who are pushing themselves beyond their limits. In business, look out for innovators who generate a thousand crazy ideas: amid 999 that sink without a trace, there might well be one that will change the world. And yes, show a bit more respect for the accident-prone losers in those online videos, because they're the ones pushing the boundaries of failure on the way to great success – albeit with a few cuts and bruises.

3 Work in pairs and discuss the questions.

1 Do you agree that failure is necessary for success?
2 Are mistakes and accidents always a sign of progress? Think of counterexamples.

Vocabulary

4 Look at the article again. Underline any words or phrases which relate to risk, success or failure.

5 a Complete the sentences with the words in the box.

drawing	fell	losing	losses	pick	safe
soul	trace	went	wind	zone	

1 Losing that job was pretty ______ **-destroying**.
2 Well, that didn't work. It's time to **go back to the** ______ **board**, I think.
3 When I didn't get the scholarship I had to ______ **myself up** and start again with applications.
4 Our plans for a fruit-flavoured coffee **sank without** ______.
5 My attempt at humour ______ **flat** – everyone assumed I was just being rude.
6 I'm afraid you're **fighting a** ______ **battle**. I suggest you **cut your** ______ and give up.
7 Sometimes you've got to get out of your **comfort** ______ and try something risky.
8 At first we decided to **play it** ______ and not take any risks, but later we **threw caution to the** ______ and ______ **for it.**

b Which phrases in Exercise 5a are connected with:

1 failing?
2 responding positively/keeping going after failure?
3 giving up?
4 taking and avoiding risks?

6 Work in pairs. Describe a time where you failed or took a risk. Use some of the phrases in Exercise 5a.

I didn't get the grades I needed for university, and that was pretty soul-destroying. I was surprised because …

Go to page 170 or your app for more vocabulary and practice.

Language focus

7 **5.6 Listen to part of a speech about success and failure. Answer the questions.**

1 What went wrong?
2 What was the cause of the problem?
3 How did Hannah benefit from the experience?

8 a **5.7 Complete these extracts from the conversation. Listen and check.**

1 If I ______ (not lose) the job all those years ago, I don't think I ______ (be) where I am now.
2 In those days, if you ______ (have) a job in a clothes shop, you ______ (be) the coolest of the cool.
3 Shop work ______ (be) so much easier if it ______ (not be) for all the customers!
4 If I ______ (not be) such a perfectionist, I ______ (not do) so well in my career over the years.
5 I ______ (be fired) on the spot if my colleagues ______ (not plead) with the manager.
6 If I ______ (not be) so terrible, I ______ (not be sacked) and I ______ (still work) there today!

b **Look at the sentences in Exercise 8a. Find a relevant section in the language focus box to explain each conditional sentence.**

Unreal conditionals

Unreal conditionals are sentences with *if* (or similar words/phrases) which refer to unreal or unlikely situations.

We use second conditionals (with *if* + past, *would*) to talk about the unreal present (*If I were fitter, I'd be able to run faster now*) and the unlikely future (*If I won a medal next week, I'd be amazed*).

Conditionals with *if* + past can also be about the real past. We can usually work out the meaning from context.

*When I was a teenager, **if** I **had** some free time, I'**d** go running.* (= whenever I had free time, I used to run.)

*I'm so busy these days! **If** I **had** some free time, I'**d** go running.* (= but I don't so I can't)

We use third conditionals (with *if* + past perfect, *would have done*) to talk about unreal past events. *If I hadn't eaten so much earlier, I'd have won last week's race.*

We can mix second and third conditionals to talk about present/timeless situations with past results (*If I were fitter, I'd have won last week's race*) and past situations with present results (*If I hadn't eaten so much earlier, I'd be able to run faster now.*).

We can change the patterns to suit our needs, e.g. use continuous verb forms, use *could*/*might* instead of *would*, etc.

*If you **were paying** attention, you **might** understand a bit more; If you'd **been paying** attention last week, you **could** have passed your exam.*

We can say *if it weren't for*/*if it hadn't been for* + somebody/something to talk about the importance of that person/thing. ***If it weren't for** your help/**If it hadn't been for** your help, I'd have failed.*

We can use *if I were* + *to*-infinitive to make it clearer that we're talking about the unlikely future, not the real past.

If I were to offer you a small gift, would it make any difference?

9 **Use the words in brackets to make conditional sentences about the situations.**

1 Hannah was fired because she was disorganised. (Hannah wouldn't …)
Hannah wouldn't have been fired if she had been better organised.
2 She didn't get sacked immediately because of her colleagues. (If it …)
3 She was focusing on the jumpers, so she neglected the rest of the department. (If she hadn't …)
4 She didn't try very hard because she didn't know she was on a trial period. (She would …)
5 She never takes any jobs for granted now because of her dread of being fired again. (She might take …)

10 a **5.8 Listen to the examples of unreal conditionals. How is *have* pronounced in very fast speech?**

1 If you hadn't been wearing a helmet, you could **have** been seriously injured.
2 You might **have** made faster progress if you'd taken a few more risks.
3 If I'd known how he felt, I'd **have** done something about it.

b **Practise saying the sentences with the same pronunciation of *have*.**

11 **Complete the sentences so that they are true for you.**

1 If I were more …, I might not have … (in the past).
2 If it weren't/hadn't been for …, I might have …
3 If I hadn't …, I'd probably be … now.

Go to page 154 or your app for more information and practice.

Speaking

PREPARE

12 **You're going to tell a true or invented anecdote about a positive or negative event in the past that has affected your life. Make brief notes on the following:**

- **Background:** Where and when did it happen?
- **Event:** What exactly happened? Why?
- **Emotion:** How did you (and other people) feel before/during/after the event? Why?
- **Results:** What happened next?
- **Impact:** How did it affect your life? How would life be different now if things had worked out differently?
- **Lessons:** What did you learn from the experience?

SPEAK

13 a **Work in groups to tell your anecdotes. Ask questions to show interest in each other's stories.**

b **Share the best anecdotes you heard with the class.**

Master your reading page 114

5C The great clean-up

A

› **Goal:** discuss problems and hypothesise solutions

› **Language focus:** hypothetical language

› **Vocabulary:** near-synonyms

Reading

1 a **Work in groups and discuss the questions.**

1 Think of five chores/tasks that are necessary but dull or unpleasant (e.g. cleaning windows, picking fruit, learning vocabulary, etc.).

2 For each chore/task, how could you turn it into a game or a fun social activity? Try to come up with a range of creative ideas.

b **Explain your best ideas to the class.**

2 **Read the article quickly. What activities do the photos show?**

A world without litter

Imagine a world where people picked up litter, not because they were being paid to do it, but because it seemed like fun. Bizarre as it may seem, such a world really exists. Welcome to the world of plogging, strawkling and trashtagging.

Plogging is the sport of picking up litter (*plocka upp* in Swedish) while jogging. The first events were organised by Erik Ahlström in Stockholm, Sweden, in 2016, and quickly became a global phenomenon. Of course, some joggers were picking up litter long before it had an official name: one plogger in England, David Sedaris, has kept his whole neighbourhood **immaculate** for years, simply by taking a bin bag on his daily jog and picking up all the **refuse** he sees. Plogging is great for your health, with all that bending and stretching. However, handling all that **muck** isn't especially **hygienic**, so you'll need to **scrub** your hands thoroughly at the end of your plog to **disinfect** them.

Strawkling involves collecting drinking straws while snorkelling. In 2017, Harriet Spark was snorkelling in Manly Cove (in Sydney, Australia) when she realised that it was full of straws and other plastic **debris**. She decided to try to restore the cove to its original **pristine** state. Over the summer of 2018, she organised hundreds of volunteers, who collected over 2,000 straws from the cove – while keeping fit and enjoying a shared social activity. She's also persuaded dozens of cafés to stop supplying plastic straws, and set up an education campaign to dissuade locals from using them. So if all goes well, strawkling won't be necessary in a few years.

Trashtagging uses social media to organise groups of people to **spruce up** a particular place on a particular day. The trashtag challenge was launched in 2015, but didn't go viral until 2019, when a man called Byron Román posted before-and-after photos of his own accomplishments, together with a challenge for 'bored teens' to emulate his work. Within a week, there were 25,000 #trashtag posts on Instagram, including jaw-dropping photos of litter-strewn parks, beaches covered in **flotsam** and forests filled with the **remains** of picnics and barbecues, followed by the same locations a few hours later, now completely **spotless**.

Each of us can make a huge difference to the scourge of litter. Instead of arguing over whose fault it is, or wishing somebody would finally do something about it, let's just go outside and pick it up!

3 **Work in pairs and discuss the questions.**

1 Which of the named people in the article made the most/least effort?

2 Which people made the most/least difference?

Vocabulary

4 a **Look at the words in bold in the article and find:**

1 five nouns for types of rubbish/waste.

2 four adjectives meaning 'completely clean'.

3 three verbs meaning 'make something clean'.

b **Answer the questions about the near-synonyms (words with almost the same meaning) in Exercise 4a. Which word ...**

1 describes only waste/rubbish on or near water?

2 is always plural?

3 refers to mud and other sticky/unpleasant substances?

4 refers to something that has never been dirty?

5 means 'clean' but in a way you might not see?

6 involves using force to remove dirt?

7 is an informal way of making something look better?

5 a **Choose the correct alternatives.**

1 I'd be very willing to pick up *litter/muck* in the park when I'm running.

2 Some of my childhood toys are still in *pristine/hygienic* condition, as I never took them out of the box.

3 I'd never work on a farm, as I don't want to get covered in *litter/muck*.

4 I'd like to *disinfect/spruce up* my flat with some new curtains and a rug.

5 I think a lot more needs to be done to make offices more *spotless/hygienic* places to prevent the spread of some diseases.

b **Work in pairs. Guess whether your partner would agree with the statements in Exercise 5a.**

Go to your app for more vocabulary and practice.

B

C

Language focus

6 5.9 **Listen to a conversation between Jack and Kira. What are they discussing?**

7 a Read the language focus box below. Then complete the extracts from the conversation with the correct forms of the verbs in brackets.

1 I wish they ______ (sort) it out.
2 Everyone would rather someone else ______ (clean) it up, but I think it's about time people ______ (start) taking responsibility.
3 Imagine if every jogger on the beach ______ (do) the same as me. All the litter ______ (disappear) within a week.
4 I wish it ______ (be) that simple.
5 I wish I ______ (think) of that before my run! And hand sanitiser ______ (be) useful too.
6 I wish we ______ (do) a bit more.
7 People would treat it as though it ______ (be) some kind of competition.

b 5.10 **Listen and check.**

Hypothetical language

We use past tenses (e.g. past simple, past perfect, past continuous) and the modal verbs *would, could, might* and *should* to tell the reader/listener to imagine unreal situations.
Imagine you had a month off work. Where would you go?

Wishes (*I wish …/If only …*)

To make wishes about:

- what we want people to do differently, use *would*.
  I wish you'd help me (and I'm annoyed that you won't).
- our own actions (which we'd like to control but can't), use *could*, not *would*.
  I wish I could help you (but I can't).
- present states, use the past simple.
  If only we had more time (but we don't).
  I wish I didn't have to go (but I've got no choice).
- the unreal past, use the past perfect.
  I wish you'd told me earlier (but you didn't).

Similar structures

- *Would rather*: *I'd rather you didn't tell anybody.* (= I'd prefer it if …)
- *It's (about) time*: *It's about time we left/we were leaving.* (= we should leave/be leaving very soon)
- *As if/as though*: *She looked at me as if I were crazy.* (= in the same way as she would look at me if I were crazy)

8 a 5.11 **Listen to two sentences and number them in the order you hear them. What's the difference in meaning between them?**

A: I wish you'd tried to help.
B: I wish you'd try to help.

b Work in pairs to practise saying the versions quickly.

9 a Rewrite the sentences using the words in brackets.

1 It's frustrating that we don't have more time. (wish)
I wish we had more time.
2 We ought to start cooking very soon. (about)
3 Why don't you clean your room more often? (wish)
4 I'm not very happy you invited so many people. (rather)
5 There's nothing we can do, unfortunately. (only)
6 You're treating me like it's my fault. (though)

b Work in pairs. Complete the sentences so they are true for you.

1 I'd rather people …
2 I wish people …
3 It's about time …
4 If only there …

Go to page 154 or your app for more information and practice.

Speaking

PREPARE

10 You're going to take part in a meeting about how to make your local park a better place to visit. First, think of five problems that a park might have.

SPEAK

11 Work in pairs. Describe the problems you came up with in Exercise 10, and how you'd like to see people's behaviour change.
I wish people wouldn't leave their rubbish on the grass.

12 a Work in pairs. Discuss what kind of activities you could put in place to improve the park.
We could ask joggers to pick up litter.

b Compare your solutions with other groups. Are they similar or completely different?

Master your writing
page 134

5D English in action

Goal: politely refuse a request

Vocabulary: excuses

A

B

Vocabulary

1 **Work in pairs and look at the pictures. What do you think the people are requesting? How do you think the other people feel about those requests?**

2 a **Look at the text. Find words and phrases in bold that mean the following:**

1 busy with more work than I can handle
snowed under
2 impossible for me to control/influence
3 busy with something else (NB rather formal)
4 a huge pile of work that has built up over a long time
5 extremely busy
6 difficult, inconvenient
7 happened, appeared
8 in a situation where I don't have enough skills
9 leave the room/building for a moment
10 causing me problems

Need to get out of helping somebody? Here's every excuse you could ever need!

Sorry, I'd love to help you but …
… I'm a bit tied up.
… I'm **otherwise engaged**.
… my back's **playing up** again.
… I'd be completely **out of my depth**.
… something else has **cropped up**.
… life's a bit **hectic** right now.
… I'm in the middle of something urgent.
… it's **out of my hands**.
… I've got a lot on my plate.
… I've just got to **pop out** for a moment.
… I've got **an almighty backlog** of emails.
… I'm totally **snowed under**.
… it's a little out of my way.
… it's an **awkward** moment.
… I can't help for, er, personal reasons.

b **Which excuse in Exercise 2a might you use in these situations?**

1 You have something else to do at that particular time.
2 You're too busy in general.
3 You don't feel competent.
4 You have health problems.
5 You don't want to travel far.
6 You can't think of a real excuse/you don't want to say.

3 **Work in pairs. Take turns to make the requests. Use the excuses in Exercise 2a to refuse your partner's requests.**

1 Could you carry my bag for me? It's too heavy for me.
2 Could you drive me to the shopping centre … and wait for me while I'm shopping?
3 Could you clean my windows?
4 Can I come to your house/flat for a meal … and bring a few of my friends?
5 Could you look after my pet snakes for a few weeks?
6 Could you go to the airport to welcome my visitors?
7 Could you …?

Listening 1

4 a 5.12 **Listen to the conversation between Suzie and Daniel. Answer the questions.**

1 What exactly does Suzie want Daniel to do?
2 Why did she choose him to ask?
3 Why can't she ask other people to help?
4 What additional request does she make?
5 What exactly does Daniel promise to do?

b **Work in pairs and discuss the questions.**

1 Do you think Suzie's requests were reasonable given her situation? Would requests like these be acceptable in your culture?
2 How does Daniel feel about Suzie's requests? Why?
3 Do you think Daniel intends to help Suzie? How can you tell?
4 How would you have reacted if you were Daniel?

C

5 🔊 5.13 **Complete the phrases in the Useful phrases 1 box with one word in each space. Then listen and check.**

> ### Useful phrases 1
> **Difficult requests**
> 1 Do you ______ if I ask you a small favour?
> 2 I don't ______ you'd be able to help me, would you?
> 3 It really would make a huge ______ if you could help out.
> 4 Is there any ______ you could help me?
> 5 I ______ it's a lot to ask.
> 6 I have another small ______ for you.
> 7 Do you think we ______ be able to use your car?
> 8 I know it's a big ______.
> 9 I don't want to put any ______ on you.
> 10 It really would ______ a lot to me.

6 **Make the requests more polite, using the words in brackets.**

1 Can you help me with my website? (suppose)
I don't suppose you could help me with my website, could you?
2 Will you give me a hand with it? (difference)
3 Can you help me? (able)
4 Can you take a look at it this evening? (chance)
5 Look after my dog for a minute. (suppose)
6 Can you spare half an hour to look at it now? (chance)

Listening 2

7 a **Work in pairs. Look at the extracts from the conversation. Discuss what Daniel really meant and what Suzie thought he meant.**

1 I'm not sure.
2 Er, possibly. I need to think about it.
3 I'll see what I can do.
4 I'll do my best.
5 I wouldn't just turn up unannounced.
6 Yeah, well, we'll see.

b 🔊 5.14 **Listen to a later conversation between Daniel and Suzie. Check your answers to Exercise 7a.**

8 a **Complete the Useful phrases 2 box with the headings in the box.**

Indirect phrases	Direct but polite refusals
Reasons for refusals	

> ### Useful phrases 2
> 1 ______
> No, I'm afraid that's not going to be possible.
> Unfortunately, it's out of the question.
> Sorry, but it's not possible today.
> I'd love to help but I can't.
> 2 ______
> I really need to unpack all those boxes when I get home tonight.
> I'm totally snowed under at work at the moment, chasing impossible deadlines.
> … for personal reasons.
> 3 ______
> Yeah, possibly.
> I'll see what I can do.
> I'm not sure.
> I'll do my best.

b **Work in groups and discuss the questions.**

1 In your culture, do people generally use direct or indirect language to refuse requests?
2 What are some examples of cultures/nationalities that prefer direct or indirect language?
3 Think of examples of possible 'culture clashes' where people from different cultures misunderstand each other. Have you ever been in such a situation? What happened?

9 a 🔊 5.15 **Listen to two versions of the same sentence. In each case, is the person agreeing or refusing to help? Practise saying the sentence in both ways.**

b 🔊 5.16 **Listen and repeat the sentences. Try to copy the intonation to show that you're happy to help or that you're going to give an excuse.**

Speaking

10 **Work in pairs to prepare what you will say in two situations. Follow the procedure in the diagram. Student A: Turn to page 183. Student B: Turn to page 184.**

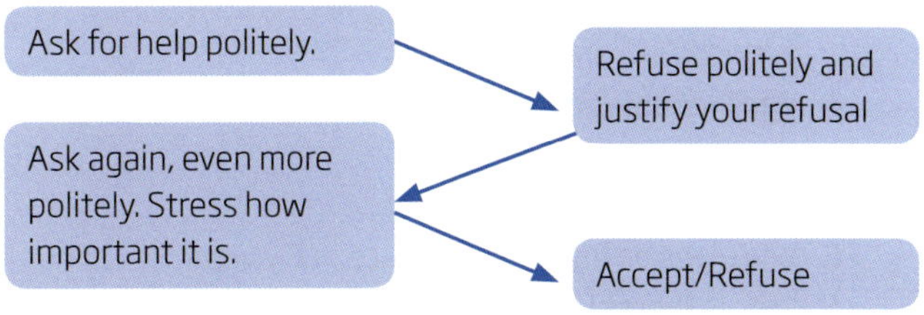

Go online for the Roadmap video.

6A Dystopias

Goal: discuss abstract topics about society
Language focus: the passive
Vocabulary: making connections

Listening

1 Work in pairs. Read the definition and discuss the questions.

> **dystopia noun [countable]**
> an imaginary place where life is extremely difficult and a lot of unfair or immoral things happen

1 What examples of dystopian books and films can you think of?
2 What are the main characteristics of dystopian books and films?
3 Do you like this type of book/film? Why/Why not?
4 Why do you think this theme is popular?

2 6.1 Listen to an interview about dystopias. Match the titles 1–5 with the type of dystopia they describe in a–e.

1 *The Machine Stops*
2 *Nosedive*
3 *We*
4 *Elysium*
5 *Player Piano*

a People live in a world made of glass.
b People live underground and communicate by video and text message.
c People live on Earth and in space.
d The world is run by machines.
e People live in a system where they earn 'points' for behaving well in society.

3 Listen again and answer the questions.

1 What two reasons does Davion give for the popularity of dystopian books and films?
2 What two examples does he give of accurate predictions?
3 Which themes does he say reflect social issues at the time?
4 Why are buildings made of glass in *We*?
5 Who lives on Earth and in space in *Elysium*?
6 Why is there class conflict in *Player Piano*?
7 What has Davion been working on for a long time?

4 Work in pairs and discuss the questions.

1 Do you agree with the reasons Davion gives for the popularity of dystopian books and films? Why/Why not?
2 Why do you think there is so much interest in dystopias?

Language focus

5 Match extracts 1–5 from the interview with points a–e in the language focus box.

1 It just couldn't have been made any quicker.
2 These themes in turn are often combined with the idea of class inequality.
3 These messages are sent to people via the machine.
4 A lot has been written about technology.
5 People have often been shocked by the remarkable accuracy of this prediction.

The passive

There are many different reasons why we use the passive in English.

a To maintain the focus on what we put at the beginning of the sentence.
Humans are no longer in control. ***They*** *have been virtually wiped out by robots.*
NOT: ~~*Robots have virtually wiped them out.*~~

b When the agent is a long phrase.
Viewers are enthralled by being able to escape to a completely different world.
NOT: ~~*Being able to escape to a completely different world enthrals viewers.*~~

c To avoid responsibility by 'depersonalising' the action or event.
The new film was criticised heavily.
NOT: ~~*We criticised the new film heavily.*~~

d When a verb has a dependent preposition, the preposition remains directly after the verb.
The story starts when the main character ***breaks into*** *the control centre.* (active)
The story starts when the main control centre is ***broken into****.* (passive)

e Some verbs have two objects (a person and a thing). The passive form depends on what we put at the front of the sentence.
If the new agent is the thing, we add *to*.
They gave the information ***to*** *the government.* (active)
They gave the government the information. (active)
The government *was given the information.* (passive)
The information *was given* ***to*** *the government.* (passive)

We don't use the passive:
- when we want to avoid the construction *be being* or *been being*.

They'll be painting the walls this evening. NOT: ~~*The walls will be being painted this evening.*~~

- with intransitive verbs.

It's set in a time when nearly all humans have died out.
NOT: ~~*It's set in a time when nearly all humans have been died out.*~~

4 Choose the correct alternatives.

1 After being found guilty, the state *froze/banned* all his bank accounts.
2 There have been a number of *restricted/unauthorised* and inaccurate copies of her work.
3 Cars have been *banned/unlicensed* from the town centre since 2015.
4 The minister has been charged with tax *evasion/self-regulation* and faces a huge *restriction/penalty*.
5 Parents should closely *comply/monitor* the content of websites their children visit.
6 The chairman's actions constitute a severe *breach/ban* of the trust of the shareholders.

5 a Complete the sentences using your own ideas.

1 The president should freeze …
2 I think the government needs to curb …
3 … should be banned.
4 … should be monitored more carefully.
5 … is a clear breach of the law.

b Work in pairs. Share your ideas with your partner.

Go to page 171 or your app for more vocabulary and practice.

Language focus

6 6.3 **Listen to an interview with a consumer expert and answer the questions.**

1 What is Melissa's problem?
2 What advice does Keira Scott give?
3 What example of a regulation does she give?

7 Read the language focus box. Choose the correct alternatives.

Making formal recommendations

After certain verbs (e.g. *insist, suggest, recommend, propose, request, order, demand*) we use the infinitive [1]*with/without* to. This is known as the present subjunctive.

*I **suggest** she **block** the websites she buys most from.*

The subjunctive is most noticeable when the verb *be* is used.

*We demand that all copies **be** removed.*

We also use it after certain [2]*nouns/adjectives* (e.g. *essential, advisable, vital, crucial, imperative, desirable, best*).

*It's **essential** she **remove** that easy initial access to them.*

We also use it after certain [3]*nouns/adjectives* (e.g. *recommendation, proposal, suggestion, advice*).

*One group has come up with a **proposal** that this minimum only **be applied** to higher-end products.*

Some fixed phrases also use the present subjunctive, such as: *Come what may*, … (= whatever happens,); *Far be it from me to* … (= introduce something that is not intended to disagree, even though it sounds like it might); *Suffice to say*, … (= to show you think something is obvious or to summarise).

***Come what may,** she will be able to save money with a bit of determination.*

***Suffice to say**, things can be done.*

8 6.4 **Listen to the strong recommendations. Which word(s) is stressed most in each one?**

1 I demand the minister explain how he got those figures.
2 It's essential these practices be regulated.
3 It's absolutely crucial you remove temptations to buy more.

9 Rewrite the sentences using the prompts.

1 The company must comply with the new regulations.
It's essential …
2 You really need to submit your application early.
I strongly recommend …
3 She should speak to her parents.
My advice is …
4 He should be cautious about what he buys online.
I suggest …
5 The content of websites children visit should be monitored by their parents.
It's important that …
6 Whatever happens, we'll be there to support you.
Come what …

10 a Use the prompts to write recommendations for the people given in brackets.

1 It is vital … (people with an addiction to shopping)
2 My suggestion … (people who want to get rich)
3 I recommend … (someone learning English)
4 I propose … (a company you know)

b Work in pairs. Share your ideas and give more information.

Go to page 156 or your app for more information and practice.

Speaking

PREPARE

11 a You're going to present some formal recommendations. First, choose two of the following situations:

- measures to protect the environment
- the media
- social media
- mobile phone use in schools

b Make notes on the following points for each practice:

- what measures can be taken
- who should be responsible for introducing each measure

SPEAK

12 a Work in small groups and present your ideas.

b Choose two measures from your group to be implemented. Share your ideas with the class.

Master your reading page 116

6C Signs of the times

› **Goal:** choose a sign or marketing slogan
› **Language focus:** comparatives
› **Vocabulary:** responding to ideas

Reading

1 **Work in pairs. Look at the signs and answer the questions.**

1 Can you explain the humour in the wording of each sign?
2 Which do you like best? Why?
3 Do you know of any signs like this in your local area?

2 **Read the blog post and match the types of word play with the signs in Exercise 1.**

The film director Alfred Hitchcock once said 'Puns are the highest form of literature'. Whether you share his view, or whether you just like a good laugh, normal, hum-drum language isn't a patch on word play, which can truly reveal the intricacies of a language. English has a long history of word play, from that used in jokes to the kind found in shop signs and slogans. Word play makes things just that little bit catchier and easier to remember (though we'd often sooner forget them!) Here are some of the main types.

One of the most common types of word play is the pun. Puns are jokes which exploit the fact that one word can have different meanings or that there are words that sound the same but have different meanings. For example: *I was wondering why the ball was getting closer, then it hit me.* A relation to the pun is the aptronym, which is often formed more accidentally. This is when someone's name is related to what they do. So *Flora Gardner*, for example, works as a florist. Then there are backronyms. These are types of acronyms in which the letters spell out something related to the topic or area e.g. *Constable On Patrol (COP)*. There are also portmanteau words where new words are formed by combining other words, such as *advertainment (advertisement + entertainment)*. Finally, there are spoonerisms, which are formed by swapping the initial letters (or groups of letters) between two words for comic effect: *I'm going to shake a tower. (= take a shower)*.

There are, of course, many more types of word play, too many to list here, and if you're anything like as boring as I am, then word play can provide endless hours of entertainment.

3 **Work in pairs and discuss the questions.**

1 Does your language use word play?
2 Can you think of any examples?

Language focus

4 **Read the language focus box. Then find an example of each type of comparatives in the blog post in Exercise 2.**

Comparatives

1 We can use adverbs and adverbials to make big or small comparisons.

His jokes are ***just that little bit*** *funnier when he's feeling confident.*

Funny slogans are ***way*** *better than standard ones.*

We can also use *anything/nothing like/nowhere near* + *as* + adjective + *as* to describe very big differences.

That joke was ***nowhere near as*** *funny* ***as*** *you thought it was.*

He's ***nothing like as*** *clever* ***as*** *his father.*

2 Some adverbs have a comparative form similar to adjectives.

She can think of puns ***faster*** *than anyone I know.*

Adverbs formed from adjectives (with a *-ly* ending) are formed with *more* or *less*.

She can think of puns ***more quickly*** *than anyone I know.*

3 Use *prefer* + *to* to talk about general preferences.

I ***prefer*** *spoonerisms* ***to*** *puns.*

Use *'d prefer/'d sooner/'d rather* + *than* to talk about a specific or hypothetical preference.

*I'****d rather*** *watch paint dry* ***than*** *listen to another of your jokes.*

4 There are a number of idiomatic expressions we use to compare things:

- *X is not a patch on Y* (*Y* is much better)
- *X can't hold a candle to Y* (*Y* is much better)
- *X is nothing compared to Y* (*Y* is much better)
- *X is not (even) in the same league as Y* (*Y* is much better)
- *X doesn't bear comparison with Y* (*Y* is much better)
- *X is beyond comparison* (*X* is the best)

5 a 6.5 **Listen to the sentences. How do the letters in bold link together?**

1 You should have been here much earlie**r o**n.
2 Your ide**a i**s one of the best I've heard for ages.
3 Your jokes are nowhere nea**r a**s awful as his, don't worry.

b Listen again and check.

6 a Complete the sentences with the correct form of the words in the box. There are four words that you do not need.

anything book easy funny easily nothing than that this to

1 I can think of puns in my language much ______ than in English.
2 *On My Granny's Farm* is one of the funniest ______ I've ever read.
3 My dad's jokes are nothing like as ______ as he thinks they are.
4 I prefer traditional jokes ______ puns.
5 In my opinion, creating puns is just ______ little bit easier than writing poems.
6 I'm not ______ like as witty as my sister.

b Work in pairs. Which of the sentences are true for you? Change the others so that they are.

7 a Use the prompts to write sentences.

1 … is not a patch on …
2 I'd rather stay at home …
3 … is one of the funniest films I've ever seen.
4 Driving a car is nowhere near as …

b Work in pairs. Share your sentences with your partner.

Go to page 156 or your app for more information and practice.

Vocabulary

8 6.6 **Listen to two people discussing names for a specialist cheese shop.**

1 Do they agree on a name?
2 Do you like any of their suggestions?

9 a Listen again. Which of the adjectives in the box do they use?

bland captivating catchy clumsy corny fitting inventive novel quirky run-of-the-mill repulsive stale surreal witty

b Work in pairs. Decide if the adjectives in the box are positive (P), negative (N) or both (B).

10 Choose the correct alternatives.

1 It's a *novel/run-of-the-mill* idea, I've never seen anything like it.
2 I always find those kinds of jokes so *witty/corny* and old-fashioned. They make me groan, not laugh.
3 That kind of art is *repulsive/bland*, it just looks ugly.
4 It's a really *captivating/corny* story, I couldn't put the book down.
5 That joke's gone a bit *stale/inventive*, I've heard it so many times it's not funny anymore.
6 That's a *clumsy/fitting* pun, it doesn't really work.
7 She's very *witty/bland*, she'll always come up with a clever response which will make you laugh.
8 That's a very strange idea, almost *surreal/witty*.

11 a Choose four of the sentences in Exercise 10 and think of a person, thing or example of word play you know that each one can describe.

b Work in pairs. Share your ideas and give more information.

Go to your app for more vocabulary and practice.

Speaking

PREPARE

12 Imagine you are part of a marketing team, and have been asked to choose a name or slogan for four things. Turn to page 185 and look at the lists of ideas. Decide what you think of each one. Use the adjectives in Exercise 9 to help you.

SPEAK

13 a Work in pairs and share your ideas. Choose the best one for each thing.

b Share your ideas with the class and vote for the best one for each place.

Master your listening page 101

6D English in action

Goal: take part in a panel discussion

Vocabulary: idioms

Vocabulary

1 Work in pairs and discuss the questions.

1 How do you feel about discussing issues where people may have strong, opposing views? Think about the topics in the box.

animal testing	banning violent video games	
banning bottled water	homework	human cloning
minimum wage	universal healthcare	

2 What might influence you most when debating an issue: the content of the argument, the way it's presented, or how engaging the speaker is?

2 Look at the idioms in bold in 1–9 used for business and debate. What is the common theme?

1 The marketing department will **get a lot of flak** for this. That controversial advert was their idea.

2 I know I'm good at maths, but I've really **set** my **sights on** studying history at university.

3 Everyone seems to have a different opinion on the issue. **It's a minefield**.

4 Too much information can be **a double-edged sword**: it's good to be informed, but too much can be overwhelming.

5 The company's **going great guns**, with three new stores opening this year.

6 I know it's **a long shot**, but do you think they'll agree to these terms?

7 Employees have been **up in arms** lately about the decision to end flexible working hours.

8 Just remember: **stick to your guns** and don't take no for an answer.

9 We're **fighting a losing battle** here. People just don't want to buy cameras any more.

3 Match the idioms in Exercise 2 with definitions 1–9.

1 unlikely to succeed, but still worth trying

2 a situation in which there are a lot of dangers and difficulties, and it is difficult to make the right decision

3 something that has advantages, but also potential disadvantages

4 very determined and ready to argue or fight

5 receive strong criticism

6 try to do something that you probably can't succeed in doing

7 doing extremely well

8 aim and want to do something very much

9 refuse to change your mind about something, even though other people are trying to persuade you that you are wrong

4 Work in pairs and discuss the questions.

1 What goals do you have your sights set on in the next year? How achievable are they?

2 Which companies are going great guns in your area at the moment? Why do you think they're successful?

3 Which celebrities have taken a lot of flak recently? What for?

4 Have you ever felt like you were fighting a losing battle at home, work or school? What happened?

Listening

5 a Read the entry in a program for a panel discussion at a business exhibition. What arguments for and against the question do you think the panel members will give?

2:15 p.m.,
Main Auditorium: Is it worth getting a degree?
This panel discussion will discuss the benefits and drawbacks of getting a traditional academic degree, and whether the costs of doing so make the potential benefits worthwhile. Host Alvin Green will be joined by three experts in the area: Gayle Torres, Dean at Newton University, Brynn Bagnold, of XCEL Business School and Carrie Verne, of the Employability Foundation.

b 6.9 **Listen to the discussion and check your ideas. Does each panel member think it's worth getting a degree or not?**

6 a Listen again. Who mentions these things? What do they say about each one? Make notes.

1 an expert
2 employability skills
3 three years
4 summer jobs
5 life skills
6 debt
7 higher earners

b Listen again and tick the Useful phrases the speakers use.

Useful phrases

Reframing and paraphrasing (the chair)

So what you're saying is ...
You mean ...
What you're trying to say is ...
What you're actually implying ...
Correct me if I'm wrong, but ...
Do you mean to say that ...
... for want of a better word ...

Referring back to what others have said (participants)

As X said/mentioned (earlier), ...
If I could build on/add to what X said about ...
Going back to what X said about ...
It's interesting that you mention X.
Speaking of X, ...

Referring back to other ideas (participants)

Along with X, this is one of the reasons why ...
This has/would have serious repercussions for ...
Going back to the idea of ...

7 Add these phrases to the correct place in the Useful phrases box.

1 X touched on an important point earlier, in that ...
2 This comes back to the idea of ...
3 Let me add to what you said about ...
4 As I said earlier, ...
5 So basically .../... in a nutshell.

8 a 6.10 **Listen to the sentences. Which sentence, a or b, shows the correct stress?**

1 a **That's** simply not **true**.
b That's simply **not** true.
2 a Is **that really** the **case**?
b Is that **really** the case?
3 a They've **spent three years** and a **lot** of **money**.
b They've spent **three years** and a **lot** of money.
4 a **Graduates finish** with a **huge debt**.
b Graduates finish with a **huge** debt.

b Listen again and repeat.

9 Work in pairs and discuss the questions.

1 Which of the speakers do you agree with most? Why?
2 What other pros and cons of getting a degree can you think of?

Speaking

PREPARE

10 a Work in groups. You're going to practise taking part in a panel discussion. First, choose one of the topics below to discuss.

- Is social media overwhelming us?
- Do sportspeople earn too much money?
- Homework should be banned in schools.
- Grammar is important when learning English.
- Should schoolchildren wear uniforms?
- Should companies be allowed to employ unpaid interns?

b Assign roles. Decide who will be the host, who will be for the question/statement and who will be against it. Make notes on the reasons for your opinion.

SPEAK

11 a Carry out your panel discussion. The host should introduce the topic and paraphrase the main points to make it easy to follow. Use the language from the lesson to help you.

b Report back to the class. What conclusions (if any) did you reach?

Go online for the Roadmap video.

Check and reflect: Units 5 and 6

1 Find and correct one mistake in each sentence.

1 All tickets cost the same, regardless whether you buy them now or later.
2 I didn't even read the poem, let alone learning it by heart.
3 Supposed you woke up with no hair. What would you do?
4 There's not much chance of success, it's nonetheless worth trying.
5 I suffered a fractured wrist and a sprained ankle, not to mention I had lots of cuts and bruises.
6 Juggling isn't a very practical skill, inasmuch it won't help you much in your everyday life.

2 a Put the underlined letters in the correct order to make adjectives.

1 What are some vloptia moments in the history of your country?
2 What kind of situations can make people feel orwhltses?
3 Have you ever tried repeatedly to do something, although you knew it was tufiel?
4 What is the most vdorretea film you've ever seen?
5 What's your most nsinsdipealeb possession that you can't imagine living without?
6 Have you ever spent a lot of money on something that made only a nilegglibe difference to your life?

b Work in pairs. Discuss three of the questions in Exercise 2a.

3 Complete the sentences.

1 I'm not a great risk-taker. I prefer to stick to my ______ zone.
2 There's no way she's going to change her mind. ______ your losses and go.
3 When life knocks you down, ______ yourself up and try again.
4 We've got nothing to lose. Let's throw caution ______ the wind!
5 Olivia wrote twenty books, all of which sank ______ a trace, before her first 'overnight success'.
6 Losing that opportunity was pretty ______ destroying.

4 a Complete the unreal conditionals with one word or a contraction in each space.

1 If I ______ failed my final exam at law school, I'd never ______ become an actor.
2 Our lives ______ be a lot more complicated if it ______ for mobile phones.
3 If I ______ a bit more assertive, I ______ have told my boss I couldn't work this weekend.
4 If somebody ______ to offer me a job on a remote island, I'd ______ very tempted to take it.
5 If it hadn't been ______ a stranger giving me a lift, I ______ have made it to the airport on time.
6 Just think – we ______ be the regional champions now if you ______ missed that goal.

b Work in pairs. Do you agree with sentences 2 and 4? Why/Why not?

5 a Choose near-synonyms from the box to replace the words in bold. Make any necessary changes to the grammar.

remains	scrub	spotless	spruce up	strewn
thoroughly	debris			

1 How can we discourage people from leaving the **rubbish from** their picnics in the forest?
2 The garden doesn't need to be **clean**, but it'd be good if you **tidied it** a bit.
3 Make sure you **wash** your hands **carefully** after touching all that rubbish.
4 Where a house had stood was just **piles of stones and bits of wood.**
5 Will we ever be free from the nuisance of plastic-**covered** beaches?

b Work in pairs. Discuss questions 1 and 5 in Exercise 5a.

6 Choose the correct alternatives.

1 Don't you think it's about time you *had been/ were/ would be* getting a job?
2 I wish *it stops/ it'd stopped/ it'd stop* raining. I'm sick of this bad weather.
3 I wish I *could be/ had been/ would be* there for you on your big day, but it's just not possible.
4 If only *I'd know/ I'd known/ I knew* you were coming! Then I could have bought some extra food.
5 I'd rather you *couldn't/ don't/ didn't* wear your shoes in the house. I've just washed the floors.
6 The other driver yelled at me as though the accident *had been/ would be/ would have been* my fault!

7 Choose the best option, a or b.

1 a It has received a lot of praise so far.
  b They have given it a lot of praise to it so far.
2 a The wall will be being built next week.
  b They're building the wall next week.
3 a The research hasn't been finalised yet.
  b The research hasn't been finalised by us yet.
4 a The fact that they could bring their own food and drink to the cinema pleased viewers.
  b Viewers were pleased by the fact that they could bring their own food and drink to the cinema.
5 a They arrived early.
  b They were arrived there early.

8 a Match 1–6 with a–f to make phrases.

1 have a	a backdrop of
2 an underlying	b concerns
3 against the	c theme
4 explore	d knock-on effect
5 tap	e an alternative reality
6 echo	f into

b Choose two of the phrases and write an example sentence for each one. Share them with a partner.

9 **Choose the option, a–c, which cannot be used to complete each sentence.**

1 The country faces tough ______ for not following the terms of the peace agreement.
  a sanctions
  b breach
  c penalties
2 The new laws are designed to ______ the power of non-elected organisations.
  a restrict
  b curb
  c comply
3 It's important we don't ______ the terms of the new regulations.
  a curb
  b violate
  c breach
4 Employees must ______ the safety guidelines.
  a not violate
  b restrict
  c comply with
5 Never give money to ______ agents when booking your trip.
  a unauthorised
  b unlicensed
  c sanction

10 **Correct the mistake in four of the sentences.**

1 Come that may, we will do everything we can to avoid this outcome.
2 Several groups have put forward the proposal that the rules only are applied in certain circumstances.
3 We demand the minister apologise for his earlier comments.
4 We suggest you are checking the facts carefully.
5 It's essential they carry out the work immediately.
6 Suffice it say, the situation needs to change.

11 **Put the words in the correct order to make sentences.**

1 is / country / Canada / as / as / near / big / My / nowhere
2 little / I'm / dad / my / that / than / just / taller / bit
3 father's / Your /a / on / mine / patch / job / is / not
4 to / I / films / books / prefer
5 as / as / My / is / language / English / difficult / like / nothing
6 weekend / the / rather / sport at / I'd / play / nothing / do / than
7 can't / Her / voice / to / mine / hold / candle / a
8 is / food / to / This / nothing / mother's / compared / my / cooking

12 **Complete the sentences with adjectives. The first letter is given.**

1 I didn't like that meal. The food was **b**______ and the atmosphere was boring.
2 The humour in the play was rather **c**______ , the audience didn't laugh much.
3 Well that film was **s**______ . I felt like I was having a weird dream!
4 We watched the film about Slovenia while we were in Slovenia, so it was quite **f**______ , really.
5 His talk was absolutely **c**______ , we all listened in complete silence.
6 That bit where the alien came out of her body was **r**______ , I thought I was going to be sick!
7 This song is so **c**______ . I just can't get it out of my head.
8 People say he's so serious and conformist, but I've noticed he has a **q**______ way of looking at things sometimes.
9 He thinks he's being **w**______ with his little comments, but I don't find them funny. I find them annoying.

13 **Complete each sentence with two of the words in the box.**

as	awkward	don't	for	moment	on
repercussions	serious	so	suppose	that	
want					

1 Polite requests: Would you be ______ kind ______ to copy me in when you email the report?
2 Polite requests: I ______ ______ you'd be able to look after my dogs, would you?
3 Polite but direct refusals: Sorry, I'd love to help you but it's a/an ______ ______ . I'm busy right now.
4 Reframing and paraphrasing: Your proposals would be a disaster, ______ ______ of a better word.
5 Referring back: Dr Lewis touched ______ an important point earlier, in ______ there are no easy solutions.
6 Referring back: We could cut costs, but this would have ______ ______ for the quality of service we could provide.

Reflect

How confident do you feel about the statements below? Write 1–5 (1 = not very confident, 5 = very confident).

- I can discuss unsung heroes.
- I can tell a detailed anecdote.
- discuss problems and hypothesise solutions..
- I can politely refuse a request.
- I can discuss abstract topics about society.
- I can present formal recommendations.
- I can choose a sign or slogan.
- I can take part in a panel discussion.

For more practice go to your Workbook or app.

7A Journeys

- **Goal:** plan an unconventional journey
- **Language focus:** determiners
- **Vocabulary:** idioms related to exploration

Reading

1 Work in groups. Choose a distant location in your country. Discuss the best way(s) to get there. Think about the following:

- time
- money
- environmental impact
- comfort and pleasure

2 Read the article quickly. What is the best way to travel a long distance, according to the writer?

It's the journey, not the destination

Flying is an incredible experience, not least because it enables you to cover **ten times the distance** in **half the time** (albeit with severe jetlag). **Your first few flights** are also awe-inspiring, as you look down at the clouds and the landscapes far below you and get a sense of the jaw-dropping beauty and vastness of our planet. Yet for many a traveller, there's something missing when you fly: the experience of passing through charming towns and villages, crossing rivers and deserts, observing gradual changes in the landscape and meeting people as you go. Above all, you miss the sense of achievement that comes from covering a great distance under your own steam and overcoming any challenges you face. In other words, you miss the journey, the adventure.

Overlanding is a new name for an old activity: travelling huge distances overland. Whereas in the past it was **rather a niche activity** for hardy adventurers with time on their hands, in the 21st century it has experienced **something of a boom**. You can stick to congested motorways and stay in hotels if that's your thing, but the real challenge, and the real pleasure, comes from going off the beaten track and roaming across wild and remote countryside. That means your car will become your life-support system for the entire journey, so you'll need to stock up with food and other supplies – or at least, plan where to replenish your stocks. You'll also need to be ready to deal with **the many problems** with your car that are bound to crop up along the way. After all, you won't be able to call a mechanic if you suffer a puncture or your engine seizes up in the middle of the desert.

So overlanding involves a good deal of planning and preparation, to ready yourself and your vehicle for the physical and psychological challenges ahead, as well as the resilience to cope when the unexpected happens – as it inevitably will. But if you think that means you'll be roughing it, with no mod cons, think again. A huge industry has built up to supply **all the equipment** you could ever want and to help you to overcome **virtually any challenge**. For an incredible 1.5 million dollars, you can pick up a top-end luxury overland vehicle, impressively equipped with gadgets galore to meet **your every need**. But on the other hand, wouldn't that undermine the whole purpose of the exercise? Maybe all you really need is a reliable old car, a tent, some tools, a first-aid kit and a sense of adventure.

3 Work in pairs and discuss the questions.

1 Why do you think there has been a boom in overlanding recently?

2 What sort of people do you think overlanding might appeal to? Why?

Language focus

4 Read the language focus box. Complete the box with the words in bold in the article in Exercise 2.

Determiners

Definite determiners (e.g. *the, this/that/these/those, my/your/his/her*, etc.) tell the reader/listener that the noun refers to something they already know. When there's no definite determiner, it's a signal for the reader/listener to expect new information.

Indefinite determiners (e.g. *a/an, another, some/any/no, much/many, all/most/each*, numbers, etc.) mainly give information about quantity.

Using two or more determiners

1 Most indefinite determiners can come before a definite determiner, usually with *of* (e.g. *some of the time*; *three of my friends*).
You don't need *of* after *all, both, half, twice* or *X times* (e.g. *both (of) those people*; ______; ______; ______).

2 Numbers, as well as *many/few/little*, can come after a definite determiner (e.g. *my* ***three*** *ideas*; *those* ***few*** *visitors*; ______).

3 You can sometimes add an ordinal number (e.g. *first, tenth*) or a similar word (e.g. *next, previous, last*) between two determiners (e.g. *the* ***next*** *three days*; ______).

Modifying determiners

4 You can modify determiners with adverbs (e.g. ***exactly*** *the problem*; ***almost*** *all the people*; ***not quite*** *half the time*; ______).

5 You can use *quite, rather, such* or *something of* before *a/an* and an adjective or noun expressing an opinion (e.g. ***quite*** *a challenge*; ***such*** *a bad experience*; ______; ______).

5 a 7.1 **Listen to two extracts from the article. Is the word *any* stressed or unstressed? Why?**

1 … covering a great distance under your own steam and overcoming any challenges you face.
2 … and to help you to overcome virtually any challenge.

b 7.2 **Decide whether to stress *any* in these examples. Listen and check.**

1 You can't simply take any car off the beaten track – it needs to be adapted for rough terrain.
2 Make sure to buy any medical supplies you'll need before you set off.
3 You don't need to stay in a hotel – any field where you can pitch your tent will do.

c Work in pairs to practise saying the sentences in Exercises 5a and 5b.

6 a Complete the sentences with the words in the box.

a almost another any few first half many quite relatively something such that your

1 I like the idea of overlanding, but I'm not sure it would be ______ a great experience in practice.
2 You don't need to plan ______ every move in advance, but you should plan your ______ few days quite thoroughly.
3 I find driving rather ______ drag, so the novelty of driving through all ______ spectacular scenery would wear off quite quickly.
4 Travelling by train has ______ all the benefits of driving with ______ few of the costs.
5 Getting visas to travel around the world is ______ a complicated business, but there's ______ a website that could help you get a visa to literally ______ country.
6 I haven't travelled abroad much, but the ______ trips I've been on have all been ______ of a disaster.
7 To save money, you can sleep on the train for much less than ______ the price of a hotel.
8 We're almost there – only ______ 800 kilometres to go!

b Work in pairs. Complete the statements with as many determiners and modifiers as possible.

1 ______ countries I've visited are in Europe.
Well over half of the approximately thirty countries I've visited in the last few years are in Europe.
2 During ______ journeys, I experienced ______ problems.
3 I've read ______ books by my favourite author.

c Plan similar sentences about your own experiences. Share your best ideas with the class.

Go to page 158 or your app for more information and practice.

Vocabulary

7 a 7.3 **Listen to two colleagues talking about three games. How does each game work?**

b Discuss in groups which (if any) of the games you would like to play. Why/Why not?

8 7.4 **Complete the extracts from the conversation with the words in the box. Listen again and check.**

away beyond clear crow herd gut nowhere outdoors scenic steps

1 … about 40 kms from here, **as the** ______ **flies**.
2 We **steer** ______ **of** anywhere we've been before.
3 It's a great way of **getting** ______ **from it all**.
4 It beats **following the** ______ to overcrowded tourist attractions.
5 The trick is to **go with your** ______ and do whatever feels right.
6 I love **the great** ______ too.
7 We always **take the** ______ **route**, even if it's twice as far as the direct route.
8 You end up **in the middle of** ______ .
9 We once got stuck in **the back of** ______ .
10 … trying to **retrace our** ______ and find our way back home again …

Go to page 172 or your app for more vocabulary and practice.

Speaking

PREPARE

9 You're going to plan a journey to a place in your region/country that you've never visited before. Work in pairs and follow the instructions.

1 Choose one of the games from the listening in Exercise 7a.
2 Discuss how to ensure that the journey is as memorable and satisfying as possible.
3 Discuss what might go wrong.

SPEAK

10 Now work with a different pair to share your ideas. Try to identify any weaknesses in the other pair's plans, then work together to rectify them.

11 Compare journeys as a class. Which group has the most interesting plan?

Master your listening
page 102

7B It's a scam!

› **Goal:** talk about financial problems
› **Language focus:** relative clauses
› **Vocabulary:** deception

Reading

1 Work in pairs. Look at the adverts and discuss the questions.

1 Do you think they might be good investments? How can you tell?
2 What techniques do both adverts use?
3 How could you find out more information without risking your money?

2 Read the article about financial scams. Is the advice mainly about offers like the one in advert A or advert B?

When it comes to financial **scams**, many of us are far too complacent. We congratulate ourselves for **seeing through** blatantly **bogus** adverts or messages. We won't be **taken in by** such an obvious **ruse**, we think. Many scams are indeed glaringly obvious, not least because they're full of typos. This may be a deliberate **ploy** by the **scammers** to filter out all but the most **gullible** potential victims, those who have fallen for their lies, hook, line and sinker. They don't want to waste time corresponding with **streetwise** people who are unlikely to hand over any money. But it is this very obviousness that lulls us into a false sense of security: we think we know what a scam looks like and how to avoid it. But not all scams target the naïve; plenty have their sights set on more **discerning** victims – people like you and me.

One common technique is the bait and switch, which involves **luring** victims with the promise of something irresistible. Once you've swallowed the bait and handed over your money, it's time for the switch, where you realise you've bought something less attractive than you expected. The scammers reassure you that you can still get those benefits … for a 'small' additional fee. And so you throw good money after bad, refusing to acknowledge that you've been **duped**.

To avoid being **ripped off**, you need to be **vigilant**: if the advert includes endorsements from well-known brands or celebrities, double-check on the endorsers' websites. If the ad **purports** to have been featured on TV, search the internet to verify that. Whatever you do, don't click on the links in the ad. At best, they'll lead to fake endorsements; at worst, you'll end up with a virus.

If you're not sure whether to trust an ad, don't simply phone or write to check. Many scammers have highly trained 'consultants' who will say whatever it takes to reassure you. Don't forget that the word '**con**' comes from 'confidence'; the key to the **con artist's** art lies in getting you to trust them. So avoid any direct communication until you're 100% sure that everything is **above board**.

Finally, remember that most scams **prey on** our greatest weakness: greed. Be wary of offers that promise a quick way of getting rich. If it looks too good to be true, it probably is. Keep your wits about you!

3 Work in pairs. Do you agree with all the advice in the article? What advice would you add?

Vocabulary

4 Find words and phrases in bold in the article that mean the following:

1 A trick that involves deception: a *scam*; a *con*
2 A person who uses such tricks to deceive people: a ______; a ______
3 A technique that involves turning a situation to your advantage: a ______; a ______
4 Correctly identifying when somebody is trying to deceive us: ______ something
5 Be deceived by something: be ______; been ______; being ______
6 Easy to deceive, naïve: ______
7 Aware of and resistant to deception: ______; ______; ______
8 Attracting somebody into a trap: ______
9 Real, true, legal, not a scam: ______
10 Focus your attack on somebody/something: ______ somebody/something
11 Not real, fake: ______
12 Claims that something is true: ______ to do/be something

5 Work in pairs and discuss the questions.

1 What are some ploys that con artists use to lull their victims into a false sense of security?
2 Are you generally gullible or streetwise when it comes to seeing through scams?

Go to page 172 or your app for more vocabulary and practice.

Language focus

6 7.9 Listen to an extract from a radio phone-in. Answer the questions.

1 Why does the man call the radio show?
2 What steps did he take to verify whether the offer was above board?
3 Why didn't he withdraw all his money earlier?
4 How does the man feel about his daughter's allegations? Why?

7 a Complete the extracts from the conversation with the phrases in the box. Listen again and check.

after which	by which time	from whom
half of which	in which case	~~which + to~~
on top of which		

1 I understand you're going to tell us about a financial scam *which* you've fallen victim *to*.

2 It's often just a ploy to charm and disarm people ______ they plan to steal.

3 I invested £10,000 in their funds, ______ I put in a low-risk, low-returns fund.

4 My low-risk investment had appreciated by an amazing 10%, ______ my high-risk investment had almost doubled.

5 I sent a request to withdraw my £5,500 from the low-risk fund, ______ my money appeared promptly back in my account.

6 It took me a few months to organise the loan, ______ my initial £10,000 had more than quadrupled in value.

7 Those amazing returns sound a bit too good to be true, ______ your investment isn't really worth a hundred thousand.

b Read the language focus box. Match points a–d with the examples in Exercise 7a.

Relative clauses

a Short prepositions (e.g. *with, about*) usually come in the middle or at the end of relative clauses, but they can also come before *which/whom*, especially in formal English.

This is the scam (that/which) I warned you ***about*** *last week.*

Formal: *This is the scam* ***about which*** *I warned you last week.*

b Longer prepositions (e.g. *according to, in spite of*) or prepositions with modifiers (e.g. *several weeks after, four metres above*) come before *which/whom*.

We spoke to a financial advisor, ***according to whom*** *it was all above board.*

Not: ~~*... who it was all above board according to.*~~

I paid a lot of money for the software, ***shortly after which*** *I realised it was only a one-month subscription.*

c We can add a number or quantifier (e.g. *three, several*) + *of* before *which/whom*.

I bought ten cameras online, ***five/half of which*** *never arrived.*

d There are a few fixed expressions with preposition + *which* + noun that can introduce a relative clause.

We arrived at ten, ***by which time*** *all the food was gone.*

I saw that my account was empty, ***at which point*** *I realised I'd been taken in.*

8 a 7.10 **Listen to two sentences. How is *to* pronounced in each one? Why?**

b Make more sentences with relative clauses which have *to* in the middle and at the end of the sentence.

c Practise saying the two versions of each sentence.

9 Combine the sentences using relative clauses.

1 I receive about 20 emails a day. Almost all those emails are scams.
I receive about 20 emails a day, almost all of which are scams.

2 My PIN number stopped working. At that point, I realised something was wrong.

3 The victims were expecting to retire on their savings. Instead of retiring on their savings, they found themselves heavily in debt.

4 I lost a lot of money in a scam. I'd been lured into the scam with promises of easy riches.

5 I received an email from an inheritance lawyer. According to the lawyer, I'm due some money from a distant relative who died without a will.

6 They bought some crypto currencies from an online retailer last month. A few days after buying them, the retailer's website disappeared.

7 The website offered instant riches. The prospect of instant riches was very appealing.

10 Work in pairs. Use the prompts to discuss your own experiences. Ask follow-up questions.

1 I was expecting (to do what?), instead of which (what happened?)

2 I receive (how many?) emails each day, most/all/some/none of which ...

3 I recently received an email from (whom?), according to which/whom ...

Go to page 158 or your app for more information and practice.

Speaking

PREPARE

11 7.11 **Listen to the end of the radio phone-in. What four things do they advise victims of scams to do?**

SPEAK

12 a Work in pairs. Student A: You've invested in one of the schemes in the adverts on this page. Tell your friend your exciting news. Student B: You're concerned that your friend has been taken in by a scam. Give them advice.

b Swap roles, and repeat the conversation.

Master your reading page 118

7C Skills for life

- **Goal:** discuss skills and abilities
- **Language focus:** reduced relative clauses and similar structures
- **Vocabulary:** skills and abilities

Reading

1 **Work in groups. What skills and abilities does a young person need before leaving home and living alone? Make a list, including practical skills and more theoretical skills.**

Changing a light bulb, managing a budget, …

2 **Read the blog post. Which skills and abilities does it mention?**

We're always pressed for time – there are [1]**people to meet**, places to go and mouths to feed. Our work consumes an ever-increasing share of our time, as does the need to be a perfect parent or [2]**a full-time friend, available 24/7** for anyone who needs [3]**a shoulder to cry on**. Whatever happened to 'me-time'?

Many of us have chosen to outsource non-essential parts of our busy schedules. [4]**No time to go shopping**? No problem. There's [5]**an app to choose your groceries for you**. Even better, tap on a different app and there'll be [6]**a hot meal delivered to your door** within the hour. Hate washing and ironing clothes? A few more clicks and somebody will pick up your dirty washing and deliver a stack of freshly laundered clothes 24 hours later. Got a puncture on your bike? Just drop it off at the repair shop and pick it up later with a new inner tube.

These are sensible ways of managing your priorities. But with all this convenience comes the realisation that we're losing vital skills along the way. For example, many young professionals can't cook even the most basic meal from fresh ingredients, and as a result they depend on [7]**instant meals from supermarkets** or takeaways. This obviously has a major impact on their finances – [8]**the money spent on a takeaway** could make enough soup to feed a family of ten for a week. But there are also health benefits to preparing your own meals: you control which ingredients you use and the size of portions, which really helps you to count calories. Home cooking also reduces your impact on the environment, as it doesn't involve a delivery driver. Finally, once you get the hang of the basics (which doesn't take long), home-cooked food tastes far better than instant meals and takeaways.

So … I hope you enjoy the blog. I'll have plenty to say on all those topics and many more, including everything from changing a light bulb to filling out your own tax return! Don't forget to add your questions and comments! Tell us about the skills you've lost – and [9]**the skills most vital for us to preserve**.

3 **Work in pairs and discuss the questions.**

1. How much 'me-time' do you get? What do you like to do with it?
2. Do you (or anybody you know) use any apps to outsource non-essential parts of your life?
3. Do you agree with the purported advantages of home cooking in the article? Can you think of any others?

Vocabulary

4 **Read the comments on the blog post below. Which of the expressions in bold in are connected with:**

1. being highly skilled in something?
2. having reasonable skills in something?
3. having a wide range of skills?
4. gaining or losing skills?
5. lacking skills?

- **Dave:** I'd be completely **out of my depth** if I had to repair my own bike – I'd be **totally incompetent!** I usually ask my mum to fix it. She's an old hand at bike maintenance – she's been doing it for years.
- **Hannah:** When I was a child, I had **an aptitude for** maths. I had an **innate ability** to do calculations in my head. But now I'm really **rusty**. Without the calculator on my phone, I'm **clueless**.
- **Ben:** I'm more of an **all-rounder** than a specialist – I'm a Jack of all trades and a master of none! But I'm pretty **versatile** around the house – I **can turn my hand to** most DIY jobs.
- **Tara:** I used to be completely **computer illiterate**, but now I'm much more tech-**savvy**. I'm even learning how to build websites. I'm still a **novice**, but hopefully it won't take me too long to **learn the basics**.
- **Omar:** When I first left home, I **could get by** in the kitchen, but cooking wasn't really my thing! Nowadays, I'm much more **proficient at** cooking, but I'm not exactly an **accomplished** chef – I've never won any awards.
- **Ada:** I used to be pretty **adept at** needlework, but I wasn't exactly **a natural** – it took a lot of effort to learn those skills. I even dabbled in designing my own clothes when I was a student, but I was totally **inept** at that so I gave up quickly.

5 **Describe your level of ability at a particular skill.**

*I'm **pretty adept** at fixing cars.*

Go to your app for more vocabulary and practice.

Language focus

6 a **Read the language focus box. Match examples 1–9 in the blog post in Exercise 2 with points a–d.**

b **Expand the nine examples from the blog post in Exercise 2 into full relative clauses.**

Reduced relative clauses and similar structures

Reduced relative clauses

a We can often shorten a relative clause by removing the relative pronoun (e.g. *who, which, that*) and the verb *be* from the beginning of the relative clause, to leave an *-ing* form (e.g. *looking*) or a past participle (e.g. *made*).

Active voice: *This blog is for anybody ~~who is~~* ***looking*** *for useful skills.*

Passive voice: *I liked the suggestions ~~that were~~* ***made*** *by the writer.*

Reduced relative clauses have the advantage of being short, but the listener has to make more effort to work out the missing information.

We can make reduced relative clauses with *-ing* forms even when a continuous verb form would be unnatural in a full relative clause.

I once bought a takeaway ***costing*** *half my weekly salary.* (= *which cost*, NOT ~~*which was costing*~~)

Similar structures

The following structures after nouns often work like relative clauses:

b *to*-infinitives, usually with a meaning of *must* or *can*:

There are a lot of ingredients ***to buy***. (= which we **must** buy).

I have no time ***to think***. (= when I **can** think)

c Prepositional phrases: *an article* ***by a famous writer*** (= an article which is/was by a famous writer)

d Adjectival phrases: *an article* ***full of ideas*** (= an article which is/was full of ideas)

7 a 7.12 **Listen to the first paragraph of the blog. Which example includes a pause after the noun? Why?**

b 7.13 **Listen to two sentences with and without commas/pauses. What difference does the pause make in each case?**

1 'I'd love to be a full-time writer (,) working from home.'
In which version is the idea of working from home a key part of the ambition?

2 'I prefer takeaway meals (,) delivered to my door.'
In which version does the speaker like all types of takeaways, but especially home deliveries?

c **Listen again and repeat the sentences.**

8 **Shorten the relative clauses in bold.**

1 I once ate a meal **which had been cooked by a top chef**.
cooked by a top chef.

2 They don't have anything **that they can do at the weekend**.

3 Anybody **who expects this to be easy** will be disappointed.

4 Do you have any tools **with which I can fix my bike**?

5 The skills **which are developed in early life** are forgotten later on.

6 I've got a book **which is full of good tips and ideas**.

7 I attended a course **which was run by a famous DIY guy.**

8 I don't understand instructions **that have been written for experts**.

Go to page 158 or your app for more information and practice.

Speaking

PREPARE

9 7.14 **You're going to take part in a discussion about skills and abilities. First, listen to some people holding a similar discussion. Who expresses each opinion, Shanika (S) or Kasem (K)?**

1 I'm clueless about cooking.
2 It's rare for people not to have cooking facilities.
3 Cooking is a vital skill in an emergency.
4 Learning new things is nice but not essential.

10 a **Work in pairs. Choose one of the skills below or your own idea. Think of a few brief arguments for and against the idea that this skill is necessary for the modern world.**

- DIY/repairing things around the house
- doing mental arithmetic
- finding our way around without GPS
- sewing/repairing clothes

b **Discuss the questions about your chosen skill, using examples from your own experience.**

1 Are we really losing this skill? Why?
2 Is this skill important in the modern world? Why?
3 Is this simply an old skill that's being replaced by new skills?
4 Overall, should we be worried about this situation?
5 What should we do to resolve this problem?

SPEAK

11 **Present your ideas to another pair. Do they agree with your conclusions?**

Master your writing
page 138

7D English in action

> **Goal:** chair and participate in a debate
> **Vocabulary:** debates

Vocabulary

1 Work in pairs and discuss the questions.

1 Think of some situations where these people might argue for things that they don't personally believe in.

a business manager	a lawyer	a parent
a politician	a salesperson	a student

A lawyer might have to defend a client in court, despite suspecting that the client is guilty.

2 Have you ever had to argue for something that you don't believe in? What happened? How easy was it?

2 a Put the stages of a typical debate in the correct order.

a Team B present their own **rebuttals and counterarguments**.

b The winning team is chosen by a **show of hands**, usually based on the speakers' **rhetorical skills** rather than the **substance** of their arguments.

c Team A argue in favour of the motion, as **eloquently and coherently** as possible.

d There may be questions **from the floor**, followed by brief summaries and closing statements from the team leaders.

e The **chair** introduces the **motion** and reminds the speakers of the **ground rules**. *1*

f Team A attempt to **refute** Team B's arguments.

g Team B try to **sway** the audience with their own arguments against the motion.

b Find words and phrases in bold in Exercise 2a that mean the following:

1 a vote to choose the winner *show of hands*
2 asked by the audience
3 idea being discussed
4 abilities to construct and deliver a persuasive argument
5 show why an argument is wrong
6 the solid facts presented in an argument
7 the formal procedure for a meeting, etc.
8 using powerfully persuasive language and building up logically to a single conclusion
9 the person who manages a debate
10 explanations of why an argument is wrong/irrelevant and positive arguments for the opposite point of view
11 persuade somebody to change their mind

3 Work in pairs. Discuss the questions using the vocabulary in Exercise 2.

1 What skills can we learn from taking part in (and watching) debates?
2 Why do you think the audience is expected to focus on the speakers' rhetorical skills rather than the substance of their arguments?

Listening

4 a You're going to listen to part of a debate. Before you listen, read the motion. Work in pairs to think of three arguments in favour of it and three against it.

ENGLISH CLUB DEBATING SOCIETY

Today's motion: Tourism is bad for our city and should be discouraged.

Proposing the motion: Matteo Colombo (first proposer) and Lorenzo Ricci (second proposer)

Opposing the motion: Angelina Esposito (first opposer) and Chiara Bruno (second opposer)

Chair: Mia Trentino

b 7.15 Listen to the beginning of the debate. What three arguments does the speaker make? Are they the same as your ideas?

5 **Which rhetorical technique(s) 1–6 does the speaker use in extracts a–i below? Some extracts include more than one technique.**

1 The speaker uses the concept of 'us' against 'them'.
2 He uses powerful negative imagery (e.g. metaphors, mental pictures).
3 He encourages the listeners to use their imaginations and remember their own experiences.
4 He uses structures like 'worse and worse' to describe seemingly endless processes.
5 He uses questions to encourage the listeners to think of their own answers.
6 He presents his ideas in sets of three – usually two short ideas and one longer idea.

a Ladies and gentlemen, over the past few years, tourists have well and truly taken over our city centre. *1*
b Our residential areas have become a wasteland for locals, with schools, corner shops and other essential services replaced by short-stay bed-and-breakfasts.
c I'm sure you've all experienced the frustration of racing to get to work or college, only to find your way blocked by a herd of slow-moving sightseers.
d For them, it's just a museum, a photo opportunity, a place to tick off their bucket list before moving on to the next place.
e So they move out too, to be replaced by yet more overpriced restaurants and tacky souvenir shops.
f As more and more long-term residents leave, and prices skyrocket, so the few remaining locals come under greater and greater pressure to follow suit.
g Think about the state of our 600-year-old wooden bridge, which I'm amazed hasn't yet given way under the strain of all those visitors.
h What about all the pollution caused by the planes and cruise ships bringing all those tourists to the city?
i And what of the vandalism, littering and other mindless damage caused when the city is filled with people with no respect for its rich heritage – or for its long-suffering residents?

6 **Look at the Useful phrases. Who would say them, the chair of a debate (C) or a debater (D)?**

Useful phrases

Thank you all for coming.
Tonight, we are debating the motion that …
Finally, I'd like to point out that …
That's why I firmly believe that …
I'd like to present my case by drawing your attention to …
Without further ado, let me introduce the first speaker.
To sum up, …
Secondly, there's the fact that …
I'm sure you've all experienced …
I'd like to remind the audience that …
Your allotted two minutes start now.

7 **Work in pairs and discuss the questions.**

1 Do you agree with the speaker's three arguments?
2 Were you in any way influenced by his techniques?
3 Do you think he really believes them, or is he just trying to win the debate?

8 a 7.16 **Read the extracts from the debate. Where do you think the speaker added a long pause (or 'power pause')? Listen and check.**

1 Our city's priceless architectural treasures are crumbling under the strain of too many feet, too much pollution and too little respect from our unwelcome visitors.
2 That's why I firmly believe that tourism should be discouraged, if not banned altogether.
3 I'd like to present my case by drawing your attention to three irrefutable facts.
4 They seem to have no conception that this is a living city.

b **Work in pairs. Why did the speaker pause at those moments?**

9 a **Work in pairs to write three points against the motion (i.e. reasons why tourism shouldn't be discouraged). Plan where to add a power pause to each point.**

b **Practise presenting your points to another pair.**

Speaking

10 a **Work in groups of three or five. Choose one of the motions below to debate.**

- Cars should be banned from city centres.
- Joggers in cities should be restricted to designated 'jogging zones' (e.g. parks).
- Tourists should pay large fees to visit certain places.
- E-scooters should be subsidised by city governments.

b **Allocate the following roles on a random basis:**

Student A: You are the chair. Turn to page 184.
Student/Team B: You are in favour of the motion.
Student/Team C: You are against the motion.

c **Students/Teams B and C plan your three arguments, introduction and conclusion. Decide where to add power pauses. Use the Useful phrases to help you.**

11 **Student A will conduct the debate.**

Go online for the Roadmap video.

8A We all do it

> **Goal:** carry out a survey
> **Language focus:** describing habits and compulsions
> **Vocabulary:** idioms related to feelings

Listening

1 **Work in pairs. Read the article and discuss the questions.**

1 Do you do any of these things?
2 What other 'strange' things do you do (that everyone else probably does too)?

2 a 8.1 **Listen to eight people describing their habits. What things do they do? Make notes.**

b **Listen again. Which speaker:**

1 keeps changing their mind about something?
2 fantasises while they're doing it?
3 says they're usually comfortable around strangers?
4 feels guilty when it happens, even though they've done nothing wrong?
5 doesn't react so extremely these days?
6 is affected by heights in some way?
7 describes being caught doing this in public?
8 gives an example of when this happened to them recently?

3 **Work in pairs and discuss the questions.**

1 Which of the things the people described do you think is the funniest? Why?
2 Which of the things do you do?

Language focus

4 **Work in pairs. Look at extracts a–h and discuss questions 1 and 2 below.**

a I'm always doing that in the lift at work.
b I'll look at the other people in the lift out of the corner of my eye.
c Yet I keep doing it whenever it happens.
d I find myself speaking out loud, without thinking.
e I tend to do this outside in the street.
f I usually catch myself glaring at the ground in time to stop.
g I can't stop myself from turning it down.
h I have this overwhelming urge to drop my phone.

1 Are the people describing single events or habits?
2 Are the actions intentions or things the people do without thinking?

THINGS WE THINK ARE WEIRD, BUT WE ALL DO

From wearing the same socks two days in a row, to having a sneaky look at ourselves in the reflection of a shop window, there are some things we all do (but are maybe too afraid to admit). Here are some of our readers interesting habits.

Pro tip: when cooking something, always throw the packaging away immediately, so that when you come to cook it you forget how long it needs and have to fish the packaging out of the rubbish again to check. **Tina**

It's amazing how dextrous I become when I'm too lazy to bend down and pick something up. Toes are amazing grabbing tools. **Lemmy**

Never walk into a dark room without first reaching your hand inside and feeling for the light switch, people. There are definitely monsters in there! **Charlotte**

I swear my printer has a personal vendetta against me. I often ask it why it hates me. **Barry**

If I shout loudly enough at the people on the TV, they'll hear me, right? **Keith**

Does anyone else turn down the music when driving, believing it will help them find the way? **Oscar**

Stopping the microwave at two seconds left to avoid the 'ping!' sound makes me feel like a cool bomb diffuser in a movie. **Leo**

5 **Read the language focus box. Then match the extracts in Exercise 4 with examples 1–4 in the box.**

Describing habits and compulsions

1 Use *will* + infinitive without *to* to describe typical behaviour in the present.
I'll open *the fridge to find a snack when I'm bored, even if I'm not hungry.*

2 After *I have this tendency/(overwhelming) urge/I tend*, use the infinitive with *to*.
I have this overwhelming urge ***to dance*** *when I hear this song.*

3 After *I have this habit of/I find/catch myself/I can't stop myself (from)/I keep*, use verb + *-ing*.
I sometimes catch myself ***doing*** *a little dance to the music when I'm driving.*
I can't stop myself from ***touching*** *a plate if some says, 'Careful, it's hot'.*

4 You can also use *always/forever* + present continuous to describe habits.
I'm forever walking *into a room and forgetting why I went in there.*

6 a **Look at the sentences. Decide which of the words carries the most stress.**

1 I'm always doing that kind of stuff.
2 I just can't stop myself doing those things sometimes.
3 I'll find myself getting annoyed when things like that happen.

b 8.2 **Listen and check.**

c **The last few words at the end of sentences 1–3 in Exercise 6a don't carry much stress. Look at the words and decide why.**

7 **Use the prompts to write sentences.**

1 I / forever / pretend / yawn / so / check / breath
2 I / habit / talk / myself
3 I / tend / say 'uh-uh' / not hear / what someone said
4 I'll / yell 'Ouch!' / even / not hurt
5 I / urge / laugh / quiet places
6 I / catch / talk animals / as if / babies.

8 a **Use the prompts to write sentences which are true for you.**

1 I'm always talking to …
2 I sometimes find myself … when I'm home alone.
3 I have this tendency to … while I'm driving
4 My friend will …
5 I keep …

b **Work in pairs and compare your sentences. Do you have anything in common?**

Go to page 160 or your app for more information and practice.

Vocabulary

9 a **Work in pairs. Read the sentences and discuss the meaning of the idioms in bold.**

1 When I saw my top was on backwards I was so embarrassed **I wanted the ground to swallow me up** right there!
2 That comedy we watched last night **had me in stitches** the whole way through.
3 When I first met my boyfriend's parents **I had butterflies in my stomach**, but they were really nice and soon made me feel comfortable.
4 I nearly fell off my bike on the way here. I'm OK but feel a bit **shaken up**.
5 When the waiter took ages to serve them, Jake **saw red** and demanded to see the manager.
6 I **felt on top of the world** when I finally passed my driving test.
7 I always **feel out of it** when I first arrive in a foreign country.
8 You're going to her party? Just don't **make a fool of yourself** again, OK?
9 Customers were **up in arms** when the supermarket ran out of milk.
10 We were **over the moon** when we found out that we're going to have a baby.

b **Look at the idioms in Exercise 9a again. Decide which ones have similar meanings to uncomfortable (U), nervous (N), scared (S), embarrassed (E), happy (H) and angry (A).**

10 a **Choose four of the idioms in Exercise 9 and think of a situation when you feel like this.**

b **Work in pairs. Take turns to give your descriptions of the situations and guess the idioms.**
I feel like this when my team wins.

Go to page 173 or your app for more vocabulary and practice.

Speaking

PREPARE

11 **You're going to carry out a survey to find out how many people do the quirky things that you do. Work in groups of three. Student A: Turn to page 185. Student B: Turn to page 186. Student C: Turn to page 188.**

SPEAK

12 a **Walk around and ask other students questions to find out if they do the same things. Keep a record of their answers. Respond, asking the person to explain the details of their habits.**

b **Work in the same groups. Compare your answers. Which was the thing most people do?**

Master your reading page 120

8B Pivotal moments

› **Goal:** describe a pivotal moment in your life
› **Language focus:** the future in the past
› **Vocabulary:** decision making and reflection

Reading

1 a **Work in pairs. Read the list of events and decide whether you think they really happened.**

1 The first English colonists in America died of starvation.
2 Sir Isaac Newton wrote one of the most important books in modern science.
3 Britain put the first man in space.
4 The corporation, Intel, invented the microprocessor.

b **Read the article and check your answers.**

2 **Work in groups and discuss the questions.**

1 Which of the events in the article were most surprising?
2 Do you know of any other events like this in history that nearly had huge consequences?

Language focus

3 **Work in pairs. Look at phrases 1–7 in the article and discuss the questions.**

1 What time are they all set in?
2 What time do they refer to?
3 Which describe changes that were imminent or about to happen?

Moments in History that Nearly Changed Everything

It's funny how some of the most important historical events are often shaped by seemingly inconsequential things, which in hindsight have proved to be almost as historic as the events they inspired. Here we look at four of those.

America as we know it almost didn't happen

Hungry, tired and increasingly alone, the first English colonisers were having a tough old time of it. After a hurricane destroyed supply ships to the fledgling Jamestown Colony (the first permanent English settlement in the Americas) in 1609, the few remaining survivors [1]**were on the verge of** giving up and going back home. At the last minute, however, another fleet of ships arrived with a year's supply of food, and they were rescued.

Britain nearly won the space race

At the end of World War II, Britain was testing old German rockets (by basically just blasting them into space). While doing so, Ralph Smith of the British Interplanetary Society came up with a design for a space rocket which could carry a person, called *Megaroc*. The design was well received and it [5]**was envisaged that** Britain could be regularly sending people into space by 1951. Britain [6]**was on the threshold of** a new era of space exploration, when in 1946 the government rejected the project due to lack of funds – Britain was broke after the war.

A picture of a fish nearly stopped science

Sir Isaac Netwon's *Principia* was published in 1687 and is considered to be one of the most important works in the development of modern science. But it very nearly didn't happen. Because of a fish. Well at least, a picture of one. The year before, the Royal Society published *De Historia Piscium* (The History of Fish), which included very ornate pictures of fish. These were very expensive to produce, the most complex (and most expensive) being that of a flying fish. It [2]**was expected to** sell well and the Royal Society [3]**were due to** recoup their costs. However, it didn't pan out that way and the book sold poorly, depleting their publishing budget. They [4]**were on the point of** cancelling Newton's book (and in turn cancelling science), when at the last minute Newton's friend Edmund Halley came up with the money, and science was subsequently changed forever.

Some people decided to invent computers, then didn't, then did

In 1957, the Shockley Semiconductor Laboratory [7]**was on course to** complete research into silicon-based semiconductors (an early version of the modern microchip), when the head of the company decided not to continue the research. As a result, eight of his top researchers walked out and went on to invent the microprocessor as originally planned, forming companies such as Intel.

4 **Read the language focus box and check your answers in Exercise 3.**

The future in the past

There are several ways to describe the future from a past perspective.

We use *was/were due to* describe scheduled/formally planned events.

The new measures ***were due to*** *come into effect last year.*

We use *was/were (all) set to* and *was/were on course to* to describe something that was almost certain because of conditions/plans at the time.

The company ***was all set to*** *launch its new product line when they found serious faults.*

The new technology ***was on course to*** *revolutionise the industry, but it was rejected.*

We use *was/were about to* to describe things which were imminent or almost happening.

They ***were about to*** *pack up and go home when we saw them.*

We use *was/were on the point/verge of* to describe changes that had already begun.

We ***were on the verge of*** *entering the new market, when we were forced to retreat.*

We use *was/were on the threshold of* to describe a wider change or situation that was already beginning.

They were ***on the threshold of*** *a new world order.*

Certain verbs (e.g. *expect, plan, envisage*) also have a future meaning.

We ***expected*** *the book to be hugely successful, but sales were poor.*

It was ***envisaged*** *that it would change the world.*

5 a 8.3 **Listen to the sentences. What happens to the two sounds at the underlined word boundaries?**

1 I didn't expect to see this happen.
2 The company were set to unveil its new plans at the conference.
3 We were about to launch the new product.

b **Listen again and repeat.**

6 **Rewrite the sentences using the words in brackets.**

1 Scientists were very close to a breakthrough. (verge)
Scientists were on the verge of a breakthrough.
2 The government planned to bring in the new regulations last year. (due)
The new regulations ______.
3 We were going to become the market leader before the crisis. (course)
We ______.
4 People thought the product would sell well. (envisage)
It ______.
5 I was very nearly going to leave the party when an old friend arrived. (about)
I ______.
6 We nearly left, but then I remembered I didn't have the tickets. (set)
We ______.

7 a **Think of an example for each of the following and make notes.**

- a time you changed your plans at the last minute
- a decision which you regret
- a technology or other invention in the past which turned out not to be popular

b **Work in pairs and compare your experiences.**

Go to page 160 or your app for more information and practice.

Vocabulary

8 a **Match 1–8 with a–h to complete the phrases in bold.**

1 **With the benefit**
2 I thought we were going to get on well, but it didn't **pan**
3 They were ready to abandon the project, but they **stopped**
4 I **agonised**
5 She was **torn**
6 It was a difficult choice, so we decided to **weigh**
7 We were really **in a quandary**
8 **On reflection**, I think I made

a **out** that way.
b **short of** giving up completely.
c **of hindsight**, it's easy to see now that it was the wrong decision.
d **over** the various options for hours before finally making a decision.
e **up the options**, and the first one came out better.
f the right decision.
g **over** what to do at the time.
h **between** carrying on and looking for another job.

b **Use the idioms in bold in Exercise 8a to write true sentences about your own life.**

I agonised over whether to wear a thick jumper or not today.

Go to page 173 or your app for more vocabulary and practice.

Speaking

PREPARE

9 **You're going to describe a pivotal moment in your life or in the history of your country. Make notes on what happened. Use the questions to help you.**

- What were you doing when it happened?
- What happened?
- What did you think would happen with each option?
- How do you feel about it now?

SPEAK

10 **Work in groups. Present your story to your group.**

Master your listening page 103

8C Urban survival

> **Goal:** create a list of survival tips
> **Language focus:** emphasising advice
> **Vocabulary:** idioms related to risk

Reading

1 a **Think of the top three advantages and disadvantages of living in a big city. Make notes.**

b **Work in pairs and compare your ideas. Are there any positive aspects to the disadvantages?**

A: It gets really crowded.
B: Yes, but it never gets lonely.

2 Read the article. What is its purpose?

1 to offer serious advice for urban living
2 to offer humorous advice for urban living
3 to discourage people from urban living

3 Work in pairs and discuss the questions.

1 Which of the advice in the article do you agree/disagree with? Why?
2 Have you ever had issues related to any of these situations? What did you do?
3 What other advice would you give for living in a big city?

Life in a big city can be hazardous, with daily trials and tribulations draining your energy and testing your patience to the limit. But don't worry, you can easily get by with our handy survival guide. No matter what you do, don't panic!

1 Crossing a busy street

This can be quite unnerving, as you know that as soon as the lights change at a pedestrian crossing, two walls of steely-faced people will clash in the middle of the road, both sides determined to reach the other side before the lights change. Whatever you do, don't make eye contact with anyone. This will help you avoid any unnecessary 'dancing', darting from side to side against someone coming the other way.

2 Deciding where to sit on public transport

Whenever you see two seats free on the bus, always take the window seat. It's just polite. Under no circumstances whatsoever should you be tempted to sit in the aisle seat or block the window seat in any way. Yes, you might be more physically comfortable, but you'll feel much more awkward when the old lady comes on and has nowhere to sit because you're selfishly taking up two seats. While we're on the topic of transport – whichever seat you take, don't eat your breakfast on the bus – it won't make you any friends!

3 Navigating the pavement with friends

Don't be a pavement hog. There's nothing more annoying than when you're trying to get somewhere quickly and a group of people are slowly walking side-by-side, blocking the pavement in front of you. Whoever you're with, whether they're your best friends you haven't seen for a while, or new friends you've just met, the best way forward is to regroup into pairs and allow space for people to walk past. After all, everyone has a right to walk along the pavement unhindered.

4 Dealing with people on the hard sell

'Excuse me, could you spare me a minute of your time?' the young man approaching you says. However rude it feels not to stop and respond, don't be tempted to succumb. The best tactic here is to pull out your phone, say something like, 'Ah, Mike, finally!' or something similar, and once again avoid eye contact at all costs. Another good tactic here is to always walk along with earphones in, even if you're not listening to music. You can easily feign ignorance then and pretend you haven't heard them.

5 Check your surroundings

Wherever you are in the city, always check your surroundings before taking a deep breath, even if you've been stuck inside for hours. The city is awash with weird and wonderful smells, especially if it's the day the rubbish is collected.

Language focus

4 Read the language focus box. Match examples 1–5 from the article with points a–e.

1 Whichever seat you take, don't eat your breakfast on the bus.
2 Under no circumstances whatsoever should you be tempted to sit in the aisle seat or block the window seat.
3 Whatever you do, don't make eye-contact with anyone.
4 However rude it feels not to stop and respond, don't be tempted to succumb.
5 No matter what you do, don't panic.

Emphasising advice

We can emphasise advice by using:

a *Whatever/However/Whichever/Whenever/Wherever* + subject + verb, + imperative/*should*
***Wherever you** are in the city, always **check** your surroundings.*

b *However/No matter how* + adjective, + imperative/*should*
***No matter how difficult** it is, you **should** try not to talk to anyone.*

c *Whatever/Whichever* + noun + subject + verb, imperative/*should*
***Whatever route you take**, you **shouldn't** walk too slowly.*

d *No matter* + *what/which/who/where/when/how* + subject + verb, imperative/*should*
***No matter where you are, don't take** a deep breath.*

e *Under no circumstances/On no account* + *whatsoever* + inversion (for very strong emphasis)
***On no account whatsoever should you** make eye contact.*

5 a 8.6 **Listen to the sentences. Which two words carry the main stress?**

1 Whenever you're lost, don't panic.
2 Whoever you meet, be polite.
3 Whatever the weather, take an umbrella.
4 However you feel, try to stay calm.

b Listen again and repeat.

6 Rewrite the advice using the words in brackets.

1 It doesn't matter where you are, you should always be careful. (wherever)
2 You should count to ten slowly if you feel angry. (whenever)
3 Don't be rude when you speak to anyone. (whoever)
4 It's absolutely vital that you don't just push through. (under)
5 Tell people if you're going to be late for something important. It doesn't matter what time it is. (whatever)
6 Never stop to answer, even if you feel bad. (however)
7 Pull out your phone and pretend to take an important call in any place. (matter)
8 It doesn't matter which form of public transport you choose, but you should definitely use it. (whichever)

7 Think of a situation in which you might give each piece of advice in Exercise 6.

Go to page 160 or your app for more information and practice.

Vocabulary

8 a Complete the sentences with the correct form of the idioms in the box.

keep your head down	out of the woods	
play it safe	play with fire	run the risk
take a calculated risk	the coast is clear	
watch your step		

1 You're ______ if you don't follow the proper safety rules.
2 You'd better ______ when you talk to him – he's the boss after all.
3 I did what I was told and ______ because I didn't want to cause any trouble.
4 You can come out now, ______, she's gone.
5 The country's economy is not ______ yet, they still need to reduce unemployment.
6 Let's ______ and give that chicken another ten minutes, we want to make sure it's properly cooked.
7 We'd better leave really soon or we ______ of missing our flight.
8 They ______ in investing in the company, only after carefully reviewing all the data available.

b Do the phrases in Exercise 8a describe taking a risk (R) or being safe (S)?

9 a Choose four of the phrases in Exercise 8a and think of a situation when you do this action. Make notes.

b Work in pairs. Describe the situations to your partner.

Go to your app for more vocabulary and practice.

Speaking

PREPARE

10 a Work in pairs. You're going to create a list of tips on how to survive in a situation. First, choose one of the situations below (or your own idea).

- a boring meeting
- a family get-together
- living in the countryside
- meeting your partner's parents for the first time
- a traffic jam

b Work individually and make a list of advice.

11 Work with the same partner. Choose the five best pieces of advice about how to survive your chosen situation.

SPEAK

12 a Work with another pair. Share your tips. Can they add any more?

b Work with another pair and share your tips again.

Master your writing page 140

8D English in action

Goal: deal with problems on a call

Vocabulary: making a call

Vocabulary

1 Work in pairs and discuss the questions.

1 What communication problems can there be when you make a call?
2 What additional problems might there be when making calls in English?
3 How do you usually call people? Do you usually use your phone or a computer?

2 Complete the sentences with the correct form of the words and phrases in the box.

audio call   landline   mute   on hold
reception/signal   speakerphone   text (message)
video call   voicemail   audio call

1 Hang on, I've got another call coming in. Can I put you ______ for a few seconds?
2 Can you hear me? Oh sorry! I ______ my microphone by mistake.
3 Do you mind if I put you on ______? Carl's here and he wants to say hello.
4 We won't have any mobile ______ at the country house, but you can call us on the ______.
5 If you don't get through, then leave a message on my ______.
6 Great, can you send me a ______ with your postcode?
7 I don't want to do a ______, I'm still in my pyjamas! Can we do an ______?

3 8.7 Listen to five extracts from calls and match problems a–e with each one.

a The line is **crackly** and keeps cutting out.
b There's an **echo**.
c The person's voice is **muffled**.
d The person is **cutting out/breaking up**.
e It's a **automated message**.

4 Work in pairs and discuss the questions.

1 Do you prefer to communicate by text or call? Why?
2 What do you do to try and improve the signal when it's poor?
3 Do you still use a landline? If so, what for?
4 How do you feel when you leave messages on voicemail?
5 Do you prefer video calls or audio calls? Why?

Listening 1

5 a 8.8 Listen to a conversation between Ricardo and Gary. Why do they have trouble communicating?

b Which of the following statements are true?

1 Gary's indoors when he picks up the phone.
2 Ricardo is coming to visit soon.
3 Ricardo has booked a place to stay in an area that Gary doesn't recommend.
4 The Queen's Park area is a cheap place to stay.
5 Gary won't be able to meet up when Ricardo is there.
6 They're going to meet at a restaurant called Molly's.

6 a **Read the Useful phrases 1 box. Tick the phrases Gary and Ricardo used.**

b **Listen again and check.**

> ## Useful phrases 1
> **Dealing with call problems**
> It's a really crackly line and you're cutting out.
> Can you hold the phone away from your face?
> **Asking for clarification**
> A/Two ... what?
> Sorry, I don't (quite) get you/what you mean.
> You mean it's ...?
> It's (a)/They're what?
> You lost me at ...
> Fifty or fifteen?
> How do you spell that?
> **Clarifying what you mean**
> I mean it's/I (just) meant ...
> Sorry, my fault. Let me say that again/explain what I mean.
> M for 'mike', A for 'alpha', ...
> In other words, ...
> Let me put it another way/try that again.

c **Add the phrases to the correct section of the Useful phrases 1 box.**

1 I didn't quite catch that.
2 Sorry, it's/that is ...
3 I can't hear you. Is your mic muted?
4 That's to say ...
5 Sorry, I'm probably being stupid, but ...
6 The signal's terrible. Can I call you back on the landline?
7 Can I just (double) check what you mean by ...?
8 What I meant to say was ...

7 **Work in pairs. Discuss what you would say in situations 1–4.**

1 You don't understand what someone says.
2 You need to check a number or spelling.
3 You need to spell out the name *Hanoko*.
4 You need to rephrase something.

Listening 2

8 a 8.9 **Listen to two telephone conversations and answer the questions. In which conversation:**

1 does the person stall for time?
2 are the speakers friends/partners?
3 are the speakers at work?

b **Complete the extracts from the conversations. Then listen again and check.**

Conversation 1

1 **A:** Where did you put it? I need the code from it.
B: Ah, [1]______. Let me think ...
A: Dan, I don't have much time. My train leaves in ten minutes.

2 **A:** Don't you remember where you put it?
B: Um, yes, of course. [2]______, OK?
A: I only have a few ...

3 **A:** OK, [3]______. Don't panic. I'm just firing up the computer...
B: Grr!

4 **A:** Wait, wait ... here it is ... Right. What's your password?
B: Danbo89.
A: Yep, right ... [4]______ ... Bingo! Here it is. The code's XY76 ...

Conversation 2

5 **A:** And the children? Is school OK?
B: Yes, absolutely fine, thanks. Rafael, [5]______ to talk to me about?

6 **A:** Well, apparently she's up for promotion.
B: Right. Well anyway Rafael, [6]______.

7 **A:** Yes, and people aren't very happy about it, because –
B: Look, Rafael. I'm really sorry but I've got to go. I'm really [7]______ it here. Can I call you back soon?

9 **Complete the Useful phrases 2 box with the phrases in Exercise 8b.**

> ## Useful phrases 2
> **Stalling for time**
> (That's a) **1** ______.
> **2** ______.
> Let me think.
> **3** ______.
> **4** ______.
> One moment, I won't keep you.
> Almost there ...
> **Getting the other speaker to the point**
> Was there something I can help you with?
> **5** ______?
> Anyway, I expect you're calling about ...
> Right. So you were calling about ...
> **Getting the other speaker to finish**
> Well, I mustn't keep you.
> **6** ______.
> It's been great talking to you.
> Sorry I've got to go.
> Look, I'm sorry but I'm really busy at the moment.
> **7** ______.

10 a **Work in pairs and discuss the questions.**

1 Does our intonation go up or down if we have more to say?
2 Does our intonation go up or down when we finish our turn?

b 8.10 **Listen to six phrases. For each one, decide if the person is stalling for time (S) or wants to finish the conversation (F).**

c **Listen again and repeat.**

Speaking

11 **Work in pairs. Student A: Turn to page 186. Student B: Turn to page 188. Read the instructions and think about what language to use.**

12 **Have your conversations. Swap roles and try the conversations again.**

Go online for the Roadmap video.

Check and reflect: Units 7 and 8

1 Find and correct the mistakes with determiners. Two sentences are correct.

1 It was something of shock when almost all my students passed.
2 Fewer than half the people we invited turned up, but those who came had a great time.
3 Each of our employees will be delighted to take care of every your need.
4 It was quite an ending to the match – both teams scored goals in the last thirty seconds.
5 I've spent many a night in cheap hotels, but I've never had a such bad experience as this.

2 a Choose the correct alternatives.

1 Have you ever got so lost that you had to *backtrack/ retrace/ undo* your steps?
2 What are the pros and cons of living in the middle of *beyond/ faraway/ nowhere*?
3 Are you more of a city type, or do you prefer the *free/ great/ wild* outdoors?
4 How far is it from here to the sea, as the *bee/ crow/ eagle* flies?
5 Do you ever take the *scenic/ nowhere/ crow* route to work rather than the fastest one?
6 Are there any parts of your country that tourists *remain/ steer/ step* clear of?

b Work in pairs. Choose three questions in Exercise 2a to discuss.

3 Complete the sentences with one word. The first letter is given.

1 I receive a lot of email scams, but it's usually fairly easy to see **t**_______ them.
2 Are you sure this investment is above **b**_______ ? It looks like a scam to me.
3 He said he was ill, but it was all a **r**_______ to get Monday off work.
4 You're so **g**_______ – you believe whatever he tells you.
5 When I read all those positive reviews, it lulled me into a false sense of **s**_______ .
6 We were totally **r**_______ off at the restaurant – they charged us £25 for coffee!

4 Complete the relative clauses with one word.

1 You should check the contract, according to _______ you're obliged to give me two weeks' notice.
2 The floods affected thousands of people, many of _______ were forced to flee their homes.
3 We had a bad beginning, in spite of _______ we became great friends.
4 We organised a demonstration, the purpose _______ which was to demand better conditions.
5 I threatened to report them to the police, shortly _______ which they agreed to give me a refund.
6 I waited a week before applying for the job, by which _______ it was too late.

5 a Complete the sentences with the words in the box.

all-rounder aptitude get innate novice proficient ropes rusty turn

1 I discovered I had a/an _______ for that kind of thing at an early age, so it didn't take too long to learn the _______ .
2 I haven't been doing it long, so I'm still a bit of a/an _______ , but I can _______ by reasonably well.
3 I'm something of a/an _______ . I can _______ my hand to most things.
4 Ever since I was young, I've had this _______ ability to do maths in my head really quickly.
5 I used to be pretty _______ at it, but after a long break, I'm really _______ now, unfortunately.

b Work in pairs. Discuss which sentences apply to you and your skills.

6 Put the words in the correct order to make sentences.

1 When / be / my phone, / I / person / for / they'll / responsible / find the / breaking / in big trouble!
2 I / suit / the / bought / wear to / a new / job / to / interview.
3 The / being / crime scene / the / sought by / near / was / seen / man / the police.
4 The / its / in front / suddenly slammed / of / car / on / us / brakes.
5 We accidentally / our / in / belonging / the hotel / packed / towels / to / some / suitcase.
6 Can / bag / my / to / borrow / wet / I / a / clothes / put / in?

7 a Choose the correct alternatives.

1 I have this habit of *pretend/ pretending* I'm hosting a cookery show every time I cook a meal.
2 I'm forever *having/ have* conversations with inanimate objects.
3 I'll *cook/ to cook* a big meal so that I can save some for lunch the next day, then eat it all.
4 I tend *smile/ to smile* when I have no idea what's going on.
5 I often catch myself *laugh/ laughing* out loud when I think of something funny.
6 I keep *losing/ to lose* my mobile phone in my bed.
7 Whenever I see pigeons, I have this urge *to frighten/ frightening* them.
8 I sometimes find *myself/ me* quoting Shakespeare at my cat.

b Which sentences in Exercise 7a are true for you?

8 a Complete the sentences with one word.

1 I always feel a bit out of ______ first thing on a Monday. I usually wake in a bad mood.
2 I see ______ when I find a ticket on my car. It's impossible to park near here!
3 I was over the ______ when I passed my driving test first time.
4 I once performed on stage and was so nervous I wanted the ground to ______ me up right there.
5 I saw a comedy recently which had me in ______ .
6 I never promise more than I know I can deliver, because I don't want to end up making a ______ of myself.

b Work in pairs. Discuss which of the sentences in Exercise 8a are true for you. Give more information.

9 Make sentences using the prompts.

1 *We / point / leave /* when we realised we'd forgotten our tickets.
2 *Management / due / review /* the case last month, but they didn't.
3 *I / about / leave /* when you arrived.
4 The high-speed rail link / *course / open /* this year, but there have been several delays.
5 At the turn of the century, *we / threshold / new era.*
6 *We / expect / the new product / be /* hugely successful, so sales figures were disappointing.

10 a Complete the sentences with the words in the box and a preposition.

benefit	pan	agonised	reflection	short	weigh

1 The course didn't ______ the way I expected, and I left before finishing it.
2 ______ , I could have studied more for my last test.
3 I never make decisions on impulse, I always prefer to ______ the options carefully first.
4 I often stop ______ telling people when I disagree with them.
5 I ______ whether to ask him or not but I'm glad I did.
6 With the ______ hindsight, I can see that I made some bad decisions when I was younger.

b Work in pairs. Discuss which of the sentences in Exercise 10a are true for you. Give more information.

11 Put the words in bold in the correct order to complete the sentences.

1 **matter / to / speak / you / no / who**, always be polite.
2 **do / whatever / you / always** carry ID with you.
3 **think / however / is / you / difficult / it**, remember that you can do it.
4 **you / on / whatsoever / should / no / account** make any noise after 10 p.m.
5 **action / whichever / of / you / course / on / decide**, make sure you weigh up the options carefully first.
6 **feel / whenever / alone / you**, remember that I'm thinking of you.

12 Match the sentence halves.

1 Because of his unpopularity with the voters, the minister decided to keep
2 I'm not going to the party because I don't want to run the
3 We're not out of
4 You can come out now, the coast
5 Don't play
6 You need to watch your

a risk of seeing Adam again.
b with fire, just do what she says for now.
c is clear.
d step around the new boss, at least until you get to know her better.
e his head down until after the elections.
f the woods yet, but if we watch what we spend we should be OK.

13 Choose the correct alternatives.

1 I'd like to present my case by *drawing/pulling* your attention to three irrefutable facts.
2 That's why I *hardly/firmly* believe that this is the best way forward.
3 Well, I've got *new/news* for you.
4 To some *extent/extend*, your points are valid.
5 Sorry, I don't quite *get/have* you.
6 Let me *put/give* it another way.
7 One moment, I won't *keep/catch* you.
8 *Look/See*, I'm sorry but I'm busy *on/at* the moment.
9 Was there something I can help you *with/for*?
10 Anyway, I *expect/aspire* you're calling about …
11 It's been great talking *to/with* you.
12 Sorry, I've got to *go/hang* up.
13 Sorry, it's a really *crackly/automated* line.
14 Let me *try/speak* that again.

Reflect

How confident do you feel about the statements below? Write 1–5 (1 = not very confident, 5 = very confident).

- I can plan a journey.
- I can talk about financial problems.
- I can discuss skills.
- I can chair and participate in a debate.
- I can carry out a survey.
- I can describe a pivotal moment in my life.
- I can create a list of tips.
- I can deal with problems on a call.

For more practice go to your Workbook or app.

9A Oral storytelling

› **Goal:** relate a non-chronological narrative

› **Language focus:** narrative tenses

› **Vocabulary:** verb-adverb collocations

Listening

1 Work in pairs and discuss the questions.

1 Do you like telling stories? Do you like listening to them? Why/Why not?

2 What are some reasons that people tell stories?

3 How is oral storytelling different from written fiction?

2 a 9.1 Listen to an extract from a podcast. In what order does the speaker mention experiencing these emotions?

embarrassment	hopelessness	nervousness *1*	
overconfidence	pride	relief	surprise

b Does the speaker tell the story in the order the events occurred?

Language focus

3 Read the language focus box. Match points a–i with the words and phrases in bold in extracts 1–9.

1 … and now **I was wrapping up** the first part of my talk.

2 I was hoping they hadn't noticed that **I'd been shaking** uncontrollably throughout.

3 As I looked out at the auditorium, I just **wanted** to crawl into a hole in the stage and disappear.

4 **I'd never spoken** in front of a large audience before.

5 It **was going to be** a long semester.

6 One of the students near the back of the auditorium **stands** up and **says**, 'We already know lots of theory.'

7 They **listened** attentively. They **asked** questions. They **kept** coming back, week after week.

8 Of course, **I'm not claiming** it was all down to me.

9 But from that day on, **I've never again underestimated** the power of a good story.

Narrative tenses

Narrative tenses are **past** verb forms we use to tell a story about the past.

a Past simple (actions): The main events in the story, in the order that they happened.

*I **took** a deep breath, **turned** off the slide projector, **put** down my notes and **looked** out at the audience.*

b Past simple (states): Feelings, possession, etc., around the time of the main events.

*They **didn't care** who I was or what I had to say.*

c Past continuous: Events in progress around the time of the main events.

*The lecture **was going** badly.*

d Past perfect simple: Completed events before the main events.

*I**'d presented** my carefully rehearsed introductory slideshow.*

e Past perfect continuous: Incomplete processes before the main events.

*I don't know what I**'d been expecting**, but it certainly wasn't that.*

f Future in the past: Expectations and plans at the time of the main events.

*And at the end of the semester, when my course **was due to finish**, …*

Present verb forms aren't normally used in narratives. However, we sometimes use the following:

g Present perfect: At the end of a story, to show how it's still relevant today.

*Several of them **have become** extremely successful managers in their own right.*

h Present simple or continuous: To add comments for the listener.

*And **do you know** what? They loved it too.*

i The historic present: Storytellers sometimes switch to present (and future) verb forms to add a sense of drama, as if the events are happening right now.

***I'm just about to give up** and go back to my computer. **I'm thinking** to myself, 'This is the worst experience of my career.'*

4 **Choose the most suitable narrative tense to complete the extract from another story.**

I [1]*took* (take) a sip from my coffee and [2]_______ (look out) at the terrifying audience of high-powered business leaders and politicians – over 200 of them. So far, my presentation [3]_______ (go) swimmingly – or at least, the audience [4]_______ (listen) attentively and taking notes assiduously. Nothing [5]_______ (can) possibly go wrong – or so I thought. As I [6]_______ (place) my coffee cup back on the lectern, my hand [7]_______ (slip) and I watched helplessly as the cupful of hot brown liquid [8]_______ (wash) all over my beloved laptop, which [9]_______ (start) hissing and fizzing. I knew instantly that my beautiful presentation slides, which I [10]_______ (spend) weeks working on tirelessly, were lost forever, together with countless other invaluable files. My computer [11]_______ (die).

As I stood there, I could only think of one thing: how [12]_______ (I/survive) the next 40 minutes of my presentation without my computer? But then I [13]_______ (notice) something unexpected: the people in the audience [14]_______ (smile) encouragingly at me and even giving me the thumbs up, as if to reassure me that everything [15]_______ (be) fine after all. And do you know what? It was fine … up to a point.

5 a 9.2 **Listen to the second paragraph of the story in Exercise 4 and answer the questions.**

1 Which parts does the speaker say at normal speed?
2 Which does he say more quickly and loudly?
3 Which does he say more slowly, with long pauses?

b **Work in pairs. Why did the speaker use these techniques?**

c **Work in pairs to practise saying the paragraph using the same techniques.**

Go to page 162 or your app for more information and practice.

Vocabulary

6 a **Complete the sentences with the adverbs in the box. Underline the verb that each adverb collocates with.**

badly clearly ~~closely~~ competently continually dramatically politely uncontrollably unenthusiastically

1 They'll <u>listen</u> more *closely* and understand your message more _______.
2 Even emails can be improved _______ by turning them into compelling stories.
3 Above all, you can _______ adjust your delivery.
4 The lecture was going _______.
5 I'd presented my slideshow reasonably _______, to which they'd listened _______ if _______.
6 I was hoping they hadn't noticed that I'd been shaking _______ throughout.

b **Find more verb-adverb collocations in the story in Exercise 4.**

Go to page 174 or your app for more vocabulary and practice.

Speaking

PREPARE

7 9.3 **Listen to some friends telling stories. Put the events from the story into chronological order. How is this different from the order Celine mentioned them in the recording?**

a She lost a doll.
b She found her doll.
c She left home.
d She pushed the gate open.
e She went into the summerhouse.
f The garden became overgrown.

8 **Work in pairs to plan your own story. Use the past simple to plan the events in chronological order. Use a true story (or an exaggerated version of a true story) or one of the ideas on page 186.**

SPEAK

9 **Choose a more powerful 'focus time' to start telling your story. Retell your story from this point, using a range of narrative tenses and descriptive adverbs to make it more interesting.**

10 **Tell your story to another pair. What did you like about each other's stories? What might you improve?**

Master your writing page 142

9B Gossip

Goal: take part in a work-based discussion

Language focus: reported speech

Vocabulary: gossip and rumours

Vocabulary

1 Work in groups and discuss the questions.

1. Why is gossip often considered to be a bad habit? What problems can it cause?
2. Can you think of any benefits of gossiping?

2 Read sentences 1–10 and match the phrases in bold with definitions a–k below.

1. **Rumour has it** that they're going to get married.
2. They didn't say it explicitly, but **reading between the lines**, I think they're having a few problems.
3. I can't remember who told me, I **heard it through the grapevine**.
4. I hear you've had a bit of an argument, or have I **got hold of the wrong end of the stick**?
5. I didn't tell them your secret, but I may have **dropped a few hints** and they must have just **put two and two together** and worked it out for themselves.
6. He seems nice when you meet him, but he's really cruel behind your back. He's so **two-faced**!
7. So? Have you got any **juicy gossip** for me today?
8. I can't say who, but **a little bird told me** that you're looking for a new job. Is that right?
9. If you hear any gossip about me, I'd **take it with a pinch of salt**.
10. News of their lottery win **spread like wildfire**, so everybody knew within a few hours.

a thought about it logically
b someone, who I can't name, told me
c interesting (especially relating to scandal)
d went around quickly
e regard something as exaggerated
f misunderstood
g insincere
h was told it by someone
i there's a rumour
j thinking about the true meaning of what I was told
k given some clues

3 Work in pairs to roleplay some short conversations using the phrases in Exercise 2.

A: So? What's the latest juicy gossip?
B: Well, rumour has it that ...

Go to your app for more vocabulary and practice.

Listening

4 a 9.4 Listen to part of a business meeting (Part 1) and a later conversation (Part 2). Match the people with the descriptions.

Lena Marcel Niko Vicky Wanda

1. ______ is a senior manager who leads the meeting.
2. ______ attends the meeting and enjoys gossiping.
3. ______ is reluctant to gossip and thinks there might be alternative explanations.
4. ______ misses the meeting and is often late for things.
5. ______ didn't attend the meeting and enjoys gossiping.

b 9.5 Listen to the final conversation (Part 3). Answer the questions.

1. How does Lena feel about the rumours?
2. What is her explanation for her constant lateness?
3. Is she worried about losing her job? Why/Why not?

Language focus

5 9.6 Complete the sentences in the same way they were reported in Exercise 4. Then listen again and check.

1. 'Wanda's been in contact with some specialists in downsizing operations.'
   A little bird told me Wanda *had been* in contact with some specialists in downsizing operations.
2. 'I'm afraid I can't make it to today's meeting, Wanda.'
   Lena sent a message to say ______ it today.
3. 'Let me tell you who'll be getting the chop."
   So did Wanda say who ______ the chop?
4. 'I'm afraid there are going to be some redundancies.'
   It was mentioned at today's management meeting that ______ some redundancies.
5. 'Apparently Lena's name cropped up at the meeting.'
   Your name is rumoured to ______ at the meeting, Lena.
6. 'Lena's always late for everything.'
   It was said that you ______ always late for everything.
7. 'As I've told you many times, Lena, I'm delighted with your work.'
   Wanda has told me repeatedly that ______ delighted with my work.

6 **Read the language focus box and answer the questions.**

1. Which three examples in Exercise 5 use backshifting?
2. Why didn't the speakers use backshifting in the other examples?
3. Which three examples use passive reporting verbs?

Reported speech

When we explain what someone said, wrote or thought, we can use **direct speech** (= their actual words) or **reported speech**.

Backshifting

Backshifting involves changing from present-tense verb forms to the equivalent past-tense forms. Past-tense forms become past perfect.

*'I**'ve** already apologised so I**'m** not going to do it again.'* → *He said he **had** already apologised so he **was**n't going to do it again.*

*'I **heard** the news while I **was** driving.'* → *He said he **had heard** the news while he **had been** driving.*

We don't use backshifting:

- when the verb form is already past perfect or a past modal (e.g. *would, might, should, could*).

*He said, 'I**'d** be happy to tell you if I **hadn't promised** to keep it a secret.'* → *He said he **would** be happy … if he **hadn't promised** …*

- when the reporting verb is in a present tense, including present perfect.

He's told me many times that he's not a gossip.

- when you want to emphasise that you agree with the speaker's words.

*He told me he'**s** not a gossip, and I believe him.*

Passive reporting verbs

When we put the reporting verb into the passive voice, we usually need to start with *It*.

Somebody mentioned that you're leaving the company. → ***It** was mentioned that …*

We can sometimes raise the subject of the *that*-clause to become the subject of the main clause. The *that*-clause becomes a *to*-infinitive.

*It's said that gossiping **is** good for you.* → *Gossiping is said **to be** good for you.*

*It's believed that they **were trying** to keep it secret.* → *They are believed **to have been trying** …*

7 a 9.7 **Listen to the pairs of sentences. Which words are stressed in each one? Why?**

1. **a** Sasha mentioned that you're leaving.
   b It was mentioned that you're leaving.
2. **a** Bruce argued that it was unfair.
   b It was argued that it was unfair.

b **Listen again and repeat the sentences with the correct stress.**

8 **Change the reported statements so they start with the words or phrases in bold.**

1. It is widely believed that **malicious gossip** serves no useful purpose.
   Malicious gossip is widely believed to serve no useful purpose.
2. It is thought that **the rumour** was started as a joke.
3. It's alleged that **he** was stealing from the company.
4. The managers expected that **more people** would come to the meeting.
5. Scientists consider that **sharing gossip** is a great way to reduce your stress levels.
6. There are rumours that **Daniel** is thinking of applying for the job.

Go to page 162 or your app for more information and practice.

Speaking

PREPARE

9 **Work in pairs. You're going to roleplay three conversations involving gossip. Student A: Turn to page 187. Student B: Turn to page 189.**

SPEAK

10 a **Have the conversations with your partner.**

b **Which person from each pair is a better gossip?**

Master your listening page 104

9c Rewilding

A

- **Goal:** discuss a course of action
- **Language focus:** participle clauses and verbless clauses
- **Vocabulary:** improvement and deterioration

Reading

1 Work in pairs and discuss the questions.

1 Describe the photos. What kind of places do you think these are? Where might they be?

2 Read the introduction to an article about rewilding. How do you think the photos are connected to this topic?

2 Read the rest of the article to check your predictions in Exercise 1.

REWILDING AROUND THE WORLD

Rewilding is an approach to conservation that involves applying a limited amount of human intervention to restore indigenous wildlife to tracts of land, and then, wherever possible, taking a step back to allow nature to do all the hard work. We look at three very different projects.

Wild flowers in Rotherham Not long ago, Britain's roadside verges were all-but devoid of wildlife, having been mown intensely for years in an overzealous effort to remove so-called 'weeds'. But in 2013, one English town, Rotherham, tried a radical experiment on an eight-mile stretch of road: the council simply planted wildflower seeds and waited for nature to work its magic. Within a few months, this stunning 'river of flowers' had become a haven for butterflies, bees and birds, allowing the council to save £23,000 a year in maintenance costs, while boosting wildlife and even reducing the stress-levels of frustrated commuters. Now, councils around the country are saving the environment (and plenty of money) by following Rotherham's example. The trend is spreading to other habitats too, with parks, farms and gardens increasingly being transformed into picturesque meadows.

Patagonian ranchland Straddling the vast southern expanses of Chile and Argentina, Patagonia is home to what may well be the world's biggest rewilding project. In 2004, after making their fortune with clothing brands such as Esprit and The North Face, Kris and Doug Tompkins bought a 222,000-acre expanse of over-grazed ranchland in Chile and Argentina. They set about rewilding it by removing fences and reintroducing extinct or endangered animals, from mountain lions to giant anteaters. While controversial to some (not least the former sheep ranchers deprived of their traditional way of life), the rewilding project has been a remarkable success.

A Siberian nature reserve First proposed by Russian scientist Sergey Zimov, Pleistocene Park aims to transform one desolate corner of the Siberian wilderness into a thriving grassland ecosystem by reintroducing large grazing mammals. Its ultimate goal is to test Sergey's theory that grazing animals will slow the thawing of the permafrost, reducing emissions of greenhouse gases. If successful, scientists envisage a wide belt of grassland spreading right across Siberia and into Alaska, making a major contribution to the fight against global warming. So far, yaks, bison and wild horses have all been reintroduced, all of which used to thrive in this region in prehistoric times, before being overhunted by early humans. All being well, the next stage will be the introduction of predators such the Siberian tiger. There is even talk of recreating extinct woolly mammoths in the laboratory and releasing them into the park.

3 Work in pairs and discuss the questions.

1 What are some possible risks and problems with the three projects?

2 Which places in your country could/should be rewilded?

Language focus

4 Read the language focus box, then find more examples of participle clauses and verbless clauses in the text.

Participle clauses and verbless clauses

Participle clauses

We can often shorten clauses so that they start with a present participle (e.g. *doing*) or a past participle (e.g. *done*). This only works when we're sure the reader/listener can work out missing information (i.e. the subject, the tense), so it's especially common in careful or formal writing.

***Not wanting to appear rude**, I accepted their offer.*
(Because I didn't want ...)

***Reintroduced a few years ago**, the yak population is booming.*
(The yak population, which was reintroduced ...)

***Having spent the afternoon weeding**, I was exhausted.*
(Because/After I had spent ...)

In informal/spontaneous English, participle clauses are less common, apart from some common fixed expressions (e.g. *All being well; Having said that; Bearing in mind that ...; All things considered; That said*)

*Rewilding is a brilliant idea. **Having said that,/That said**, some projects are controversial.*

Participle clauses after linking devices

Participle clauses are extremely common after prepositions and conjunctions (e.g. *instead of, about, unless, if*).

***Instead of complaining**, you should be celebrating.*

***While driving**, you should never use a phone.*
(= While you're driving, ...)

***Unless instructed to stand up**, please remain seated.*
(= Unless you're instructed to stand up, ...)

It's sometimes possible to add a subject before a present participle.

*I'm not happy about **you rewilding our garden**.*
(... about the fact that you're going to ...)

Verbless clauses

Verbless clauses are like normal clauses with the subject and 'be' removed.

***If necessary**, you can start again. (= If **it's** necessary, ...)*

***While on holiday**, we saw a yak. (= While **we were** on holiday, ...)*

5 a 9.10 **Listen to three sentences. Write the word which contains the rise-fall intonation.**

b Listen again and repeat. Try to use the same intonation as the speakers.

6 Rewrite the sentences using participle clauses or verbless clauses. Start with the words in brackets.

1 The visitors parked their cars all over the meadow because they didn't realise it had been rewilded. (Not …)
Not realising that the meadow had been rewilded, the visitors parked their cars all over it.
2 These wildflowers, which were planted last year, have transformed this patch of wasteland. (Planted …)
3 Call me if you're in any doubt. (If …)
4 I wasn't sure what to do next because I'd never done anything like this before. (Never …)
5 These butterflies aren't exactly on the verge of extinction, although they are rather rare. (Although …)
6 I bought some flowers from a shop because I didn't want to pick them from the meadow. (Not …)

7 a Use the ideas in 1–3 to make notes about how you feel about rewilding.

1 Being …
Being a nature lover, I'm quite keen on the idea of rewilding.
2 I (never) used to think …, but now, having read/thought about it, …
3 Never/Not having …, it's hard for me to …

b Work in pairs and discuss your ideas from Exercise 7a.

Go to page 162 or your app for more information and practice.

Vocabulary

8 9.11 **Listen to an extract from a local council meeting. Answer the questions.**

1 What objections do Angus and Louisa raise?
2 What evidence does Sonia use to dispel those concerns?

9 a Complete these extracts from the meeting with the words in the box. Then listen again and check.

aggravating	alleviating	beautify	compounded
deteriorate	enhanced	exacerbate	facilitates
hampered	hinder	impair	rectify	undermines

1 We've spent years and years … trying to ______ our verges, so I don't want to do anything that ______ all that good work.
2 Without regular cutting, the quality of our verges will ______ really quickly.
3 Wherever it's been tried before, … it's actually ______ the appearance of the verges.
4 We've got enough financial problems already, which we're working hard to ______ .
5 I don't want to ______ those problems by trying expensive experiments.
6 On blind corners, tall grass and thick clumps of weeds can really ______ people's ability to see clearly.
7 So your rewilding project could really ______ our efforts to make our roads safer.
8 Keeping the grass short really ______ the process of collecting litter.
9 … that problem would be ______ by long grass.
10 The litter-collecting process can be ______ by long grass.
11 We'll need to convince the committee that we're ______ problems, not ______ them.

b Work in pairs. Look at the answers in Exercise 9a. Think of words that could be synonyms. Use the context to help you.

Go to page 174 or your app for more vocabulary and practice.

Speaking

PREPARE

10 Work in groups. You're going to roleplay a meeting to discuss a possible rewilding project. Turn to page 187 and follow the instructions.

SPEAK

11 Roleplay your meeting in Exercise 10. Try to find a compromise and reach a decision.

Master your reading
page 122

9D English in action

› **Goal:** answer questions in a job interview in detail
› **Vocabulary:** employability and competencies

Vocabulary

1 a Work in pairs. Discuss whether you agree with quotes 1–3, using your experiences of job interviews or similar situations.

1 The whole point of a job interview is to make the candidate hate the company, the interviewers and herself.
2 Job interviews are great for testing whether potential employees are good at job interviews, but not much else.
3 The only way to prepare for a job interview is to fail dozens of other interviews and spend six months agonising over what you did wrong.

b What advice would you give to interviewees, based on your discussions in Exercise 1a? Think about what to do before, during and after an interview.

2 Read the definitions. What's the difference between competencies and qualifications?

competency (n): **any skill, ability, knowledge, experience or personality trait** that enables a person to perform effectively in a job. Also called a competence.

employability (n): the combined competencies that enable a person to **gain and maintain fulfilling work**

3 a Match the examples of employability competencies in the box with explanations 1–10.

adaptability autonomy business acumen
critical thinking entrepreneurial skills
growth mindset perseverance
professional confidence ~~resilience~~
tolerance of ambiguity

1 You can cope with setbacks and criticism. *resilience*
2 You question assumptions and don't simply believe everything you hear or read.
3 You keep going when most people would give up.
4 You can change quickly to fit in with new situations.
5 You want to learn new things and improve all the time.
6 You can work alone and make decisions without constantly asking for advice.
7 You are creative, innovative, take risks that others would avoid and likely to start your own business.
8 You can make good judgements and quick decisions based on your professional knowledge.
9 You can cope in situations where the 'rules' aren't clear or change frequently.
10 You respect yourself as a person who is good at your job.

b Work in pairs and discuss the questions.

Which competencies:
1 are the most/least important?
2 can/can't be learnt?
3 have become more/less important in the twenty-first century?
4 do you need in your own career?

Listening 1

4 a Read about the STAR technique for competency-based job interview questions. Complete the explanation with questions a–h below.

Job interviewers are increasingly using competency-based questions to ask interviewees for concrete evidence of their skills, abilities and other attributes. They typically take the form, 'Tell us about a time when you demonstrated …'. These competencies are usually listed in the job advert, so it's often possible to predict and prepare for competency-based questions in advance. A good way of organising your answers is called the 'STAR technique':

1 SITUATION: *b* , *e*
2 TARGET: ______ , ______
3 ACTION: ______ , ______
4 RESULT: ______ , ______

a Why did you want/need to solve it?
b Why were you there?
c Did your plan work?
d What specific steps did you take?
e Where and when did the story take place?
f What were the longer-term consequences?
g What problem were you trying to solve?
h How did you overcome any resistance you faced?

b Work in pairs and discuss the questions.

1 Have you ever taken part in a competency-based job interview? If so, what happened? If not, how would you feel about it?
2 Why do you think competency-based questions have become so popular?

5 a 9.12 Listen to an extract from a competency-based job interview. Answer the questions in Exercise 4a.

b Work in pairs and discuss the questions.

1 What competencies in Exercise 3 (apart from entrepreneurial skills) did Laura demonstrate?
2 Why is it useful to demonstrate several competencies in each answer?

6 Complete the Useful phrases 1 box with the words in the box.

anyway eventually example experience experiment hunch offered

Useful phrases 1

Well, perhaps a good [1]______ comes from …
It was a great [2]______ for me because …
[3]______, after a few weeks, I noticed that …
So I wanted to find out whether …
So what I did was I [4]______ to …
[5]______, and very reluctantly, he/she agreed, and I started my experiment.
It turned out that my [6]______ had been correct.
My little [7]______ revealed that … was actually …

7 Write *S, T, A* or *R* from the technique in Exercise 4a next to each statement.

1 I took a deep breath and explained, as calmly as I could, that things needed to change. *A*
2 And, well, we went on to …, which was wonderful.
3 Overall, it was a dramatic change for the better.
4 I decided that instead of running away from the problem, I should confront it head on in order to find a solution.
5 And it worked. The penny seemed to drop and he …
6 So one day, I approached him/her to discuss …
7 Maybe I can give an example from my experiences as a …
8 From that day on, he/she stopped (doing X) and started (doing Y).

Listening 2

8 a 9.13 Listen to another interview extract. Complete the summary with one word in each space.

Laura used to play [1]*volleyball*, but her [2]______ kept singling her out for criticism, which was having a negative impact on her [3]______. Instead of giving up, she decided to [4]______ the problem head on in order to find a [5]______. She discussed her future with the team and threatened to [6]______. After some resistance, he [7]______ and agreed to change his [8]______, which he did (despite a few lapses). They won the [9]______ and Laura ended up as team [10]______.

b Work in pairs and discuss the questions.

1 Do you think this is a good example of resilience? Why/Why not?
2 How else did Laura demonstrate resilience during the interview?

9 a 9.14 Listen to two versions of one of the interviewee's answers. Which is more effective? Why?

b Work in pairs. Discuss ways that you can avoid too many 'um's and 'ah's during an interview.

Speaking

PREPARE

10 a Choose three of the competencies in Exercise 3. Spend a few minutes thinking of a time when you demonstrated each competency.

b Work in pairs to plan and practise your stories, using the STAR technique. Suggest ways of improving each other's stories.

SPEAK

11 Work with a new partner to roleplay job interviews. Swap roles after each question.

Interviewee: Tell your partner which competencies you have chosen. Then answer their questions.

Interviewer: Ask your partner about situations where they demonstrated each competency.

Go online for the Roadmap video.

10A The next big thing

› **Goal:** present an idea
› **Language focus:** emphasis and persuasion
› **Vocabulary:** collocations: innovation

Vocabulary

1 Work in pairs and discuss the questions.

1 What inventions would you like to see that would make your life easier?
2 Have you ever had an idea for an invention? What was it?

2 Complete the sentences with the words in the box that have a similar meaning to the words and phrases in bold.

boundaries	era	flourish	harness	herald
leading	revolutionary	state-of-the-art		

1 Recent discoveries in biology have enabled us to push back the **frontiers/limits**/ ______ of our knowledge of the natural world.
2 Hackers have been able to **exploit/utilise**/ ______ new video-editing technology in order to create fake videos of politicians and other famous people.
3 Not only does the new smartphone have a range of security features, its **cutting-edge**/ ______ design has wowed customers all over the world.
4 The new carbon-capture technology is a **pioneering/groundbreaking/trailblazing**/ ______ concept that tackles climate change head on.
5 It's an interesting idea, but I don't think it's likely to **catch on/thrive**/ ______ .
6 3D printing is likely to **pave the way for**/ ______ significant changes in how we make things.
7 With these new measures, the government is **spearheading/spurring**/______ the effort to eradicate poverty.
8 The release of the new software represents a new **dawn**/ ______ in digital literacy.

3 Work in groups and discuss the questions.

1 What can schools do to encourage an entrepreneurial spirit among students?
2 Which technology company do you think has the most cutting-edge designs?
3 What groundbreaking concepts have you seen or heard of in medicine?
4 What fashions have caught on recently? What do you think of them?
5 What weaknesses do hackers exploit?

Go to page 175 or your app for more vocabulary and practice.

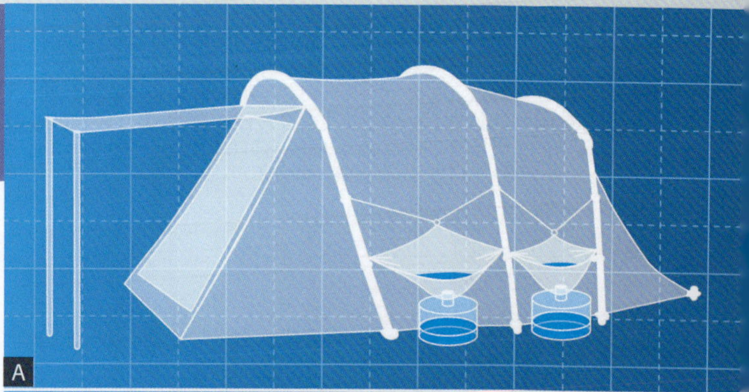

A

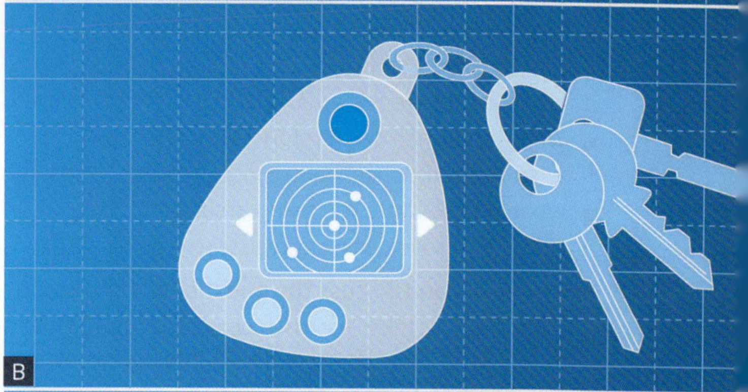

B

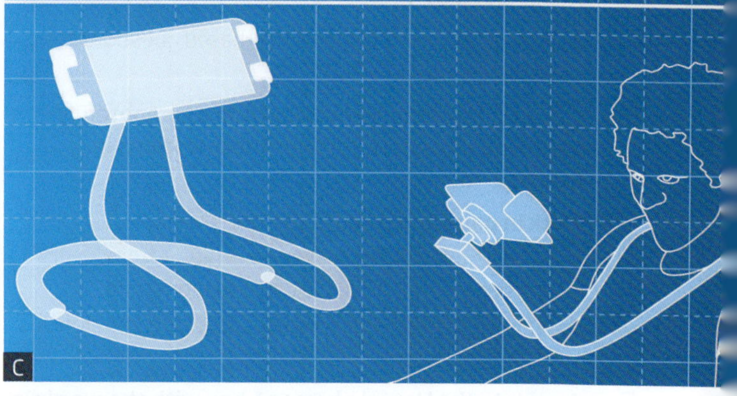

C

Listening

4 a Work in pairs. Look at the designs for three inventions and answer the questions.

1 What do you think each invention does?
2 What might be the benefits of each one?
3 What might be the drawbacks of each one?

b 10.1 **Listen to three people presenting their ideas on a TV show and check your ideas in Exercise 4a. Match each presentation with pictures A–C.**

c Work in pairs. What problem was each invention designed to address?

5 Work in pairs and discuss the questions.

1 Which of the three inventions did you like best? Why?
2 Which of the inventions do you think is the:
- most convenient?
- most useful?
- cheapest to make?
- most pointless/unnecessary?

Language focus

6 **Read the language focus box. Match extracts 1–8 from the presentations in Exercise 4 with the techniques in the box.**

1 Nobody wants to waste water ... nobody. *2d*
2 It's really, really simple to use.
3 It's simple, effective, lightweight, easy-to-use, environmentally friendly, convenient and portable.
4 But the *Ringleader* does tell you as soon as you put it down.
5 Wouldn't it be much easier if you could speak hands free? You bet it would.
6 What's more, it produces more and more water.
7 The beauty of this is that it's simple, useful and portable.
8 It's effective ... it's effective because you won't lose them in the first place.

Emphasis and persuasion

There are a number of techniques we can use in a presentation to make it more persuasive:

1 Using auxiliaries to add emphasis.
This does make things much easier.

2 Using repetition. We can do this in a number of ways:
a) repeating intensifying adverbs.
It's dead, dead useful.
b) using comparative + comparative.
It just gets better and better.
c) using statement + repetition + explanation.
It's convenient ... it's convenient because you don't need to look for a charger.
d) repeating a key word you want to emphasise.
Everybody likes chocolate ... everybody.

3 Rhetorical questions (and possibly answering them, too).
Who doesn't want a cheaper alternative?

4 Tripling: making points in 'threes' so that they're more memorable.
This app is convenient, safe and free.

5 Machine-gunning: listing lots of points quickly.
We think you'll love it, because it's interesting, innovative, well-designed, cheap, sleek, portable and beautiful. What's not to love?

7 a 10.2 **Listen to the sentences. Which of them have similar intonation patterns? Why?**

1 It's light, compact and portable.
2 It comes in small, medium or large.
3 It's cool, it's interesting, it's you.
4 Available morning, noon and night.

b **Listen again and repeat.**

8 a **Put the words in the correct order to make statements or questions. Add punctuation where necessary.**

1 convenient / travel / cheap and / rail / safe / is
2 really / software / the / really / good / is
3 nobody / nobody / caught / to / wants / get / out
4 cheaper / computers / likely / are / to / cheaper / get / and
5 life / it / does / make / really / easier
6 family-friendly, convenient / are / Sunvale holidays / fun / cheap / enjoyable and easy to book
7 just / do / ever / could / you / wish / escape / you
8 amazing / free / it's / it's / because / amazing / it's

b **Match each statement or question in Exercise 8a with the techniques in the language focus box.**

9 a **Choose four of the things below. Write a statement or question for each one, using a different technique from the language focus box each time. Write your answers in random order.**

1 Something you're in the process of doing nowadays.
2 Your favourite phone app.
3 A TV show you really like.
4 Your favourite gadget.
5 A type of clothing you often wear.
6 Someone you know and admire.

b **Work in pairs. Read out your statements/questions for your partner to guess what you're describing.**

Go to page 164 or your app for more information and practice.

Speaking

PREPARE

10 a **Work in pairs. Read about the inventions on page 190 and choose one to present (or think of your own).**

b **Work in pairs. Think about how you would use it. Make notes on the following:**

- name of the invention
- what it's made of
- how big it is
- how it works

11 **Prepare to present your idea to the class. Decide who will say what and how you'll say it. Use the persuasive presentation techniques from the lesson to help you.**

SPEAK

12 **Present your ideas to the class. As you watch other presentations, make notes of questions to ask when they have finished.**

13 **Hold a class vote for the best idea.**

Master your writing page 144

10B It's your turn

A

- Goal: explain the rules of a game
- Language focus: heads and tails
- Vocabulary: board games

B

Reading

1 Work in pairs and discuss the questions.

1. Do you ever play the type of games in the photos?
2. What's attractive about playing games like this?
3. What skills do you think you need to be good at these types of games?

2 Work in pairs. Look at the game titles in the article. What do you think each one involves? Read the article quickly and check your ideas.

As winter draws near and you're looking for something to fill those cold, dark evenings, we review what we think are the four best board games to immerse yourself in with family and friends.

1 The chameleon

This is our go-to game of the year. Players pit their wits against each other in a tense face-off, in which one player is secretly 'the chameleon' (chosen by cards given out in the **initial phase** of the game) and has to remain undiscovered. Other players have a secret code word (chosen when they **roll the dice** and look it up in a chart) and say words related to this (e.g. *tennis: ball, serve, grass, strawberries* etc.). At the end of the game, players all point to who they think the 'chameleon' is.

2 Snatch-it

Fast-paced and requiring quick wits, this is a word-building game using counters with letters on. The letters are all placed face-down in the middle, and players **take turns** to turn them over one at a time, leaving them **face up**. As soon as a player sees a word of three letters or more, they 'snatch' it and **score points** for the letters used in the word. The **ultimate goal** is to be the player with the most points at the end.

3 Carcassonne

This is a great tile-laying game for a get-together with friends or family. The game uses 'tiles' (cards with features of a city or countryside on them) and 'followers' (counters which allow you to keep the tiles you place them on). First, players **shuffle** the tiles, and place them **face down** in piles around the table and **deal** eight followers to each player. Players then take turns to **place** tiles and followers around the starting tile, building up cities as they go. Players get points for placing their followers on different city features (e.g. roads, churches, cityscapes, etc.) to **take** them. Once all the tiles have been placed, the player with the most points wins.

4 Happy Salmon

Simple but hilarious from the outset, this is a variation of the classic Snap! card game. Players have a set of cards with various actions on them. Each turn, everyone **turns over** a card and reads out the action on it. When two players have the same action, they must perform it together, then discard that card. The only drawback to this game is it's noisy, so best to wait until the neighbours go out!

3 Read the article again and answer the questions.

Which game:

1. involves trying to blend in with others?
2. is likely to be loud?
3. involves physical activity?
4. is a language-based game?
5. involves 'stealing' things from other players?
6. involves building something together?

Vocabulary

4 Complete the sentences with the correct form of the words and phrases in bold in the article.

1. Always place your cards ______ so nobody can see what they are.
2. In the ______ of the game, players set up their teams.
3. The ______ of the game is to lose all your cards.
4. First, ______ the cards, then ______ five cards to each player.
5. In this game, players can ______ their counters on yellow squares only.
6. ______ and try to get higher than four.
7. If you have more counters on a square than another player, you can ______ that square.
8. You ______ for correct answers to each question.
9. Players ______ to move their counters around the board.
10. These cards need to be placed ______ in the middle, so everyone can see them.
11. On your go, ______ a card and read out the question.

5 Work in pairs and discuss the questions.

1. Which of the games in Exercise 2 would you most like to play? Why?
2. Are there any you wouldn't like to play? Why/Why not?
3. In what situations and with whom do you think each game would be most suitable? Why?

Go to page 175 or your app for more vocabulary and practice.

C

D

Language focus

6 a 10.3 **Listen to some people explaining the rules to one of the games in the article in Exercise 2. Which game are they playing?**

b Complete the extracts with the missing words (contractions count as one word). Then listen again and check.

1 This game, ______ a card game, right?
2 The tiles, ______ the city features.
3 And ______ the followers, the little men?
4 ______ a clever boy, this Matt.
5 It's a bit like a jigsaw, ______ game.
6 The road, ______ where I'll put it.
7 ______ is great, this game.

7 Read the language focus box and decide if extracts 1–7 in Exercise 6b are *heads* or *tails*.

Heads and tails

Heads and tails are common in informal, spoken English. Heads allow us to focus attention on something specific, while tails allow us to clarify something.

Heads can be noun phrases or whole clauses which we want to focus attention on by bringing them to the beginning of the sentence. They're followed by a pronoun which then refers back to the header.

***The pink counter**, that goes first.*
***The player with the red card**, they're the banker.*

Tails work the opposite way round. They come at the end of the sentence, almost as an afterthought to qualify what we're talking about. They're noun phrases and refer back to a pronoun at the beginning of the sentence.

*It's a difficult game to play, **chess**.*
*It's an easy game to play, **this one**.*

8 a 10.4 **Listen to six heads and tails. Mark if the intonation goes up (↑) or down (↓) on the words in bold.**

1 I don't really play it any **more**, that game I got for my birthday.
2 The **dice**, I can't find them anywhere.
3 The game Fiona bought **you**, have you played it yet?
4 I've never played it **before**, poker.
5 I really enjoyed **it**, that meal we had last week.
6 These **cards**, are they yours?

b Listen again and repeat.

9 Rewrite the sentences with a head (H) or tail (T), as indicated in brackets, focusing on the noun phrase in bold.

1 Alice works in **information technology**. (T)
She works in information technology, Alice.
2 **Those keys** belong to Jamie. (H)
Those keys, they belong to Jamie.
3 **Adam and Kate** are moving to New York. (H)
4 **Brand-new laptops** aren't cheap to buy. (T)
5 Is **that** the **house** where the famous singer lives? (H)
6 I think **people from Liverpool** have a great accent. (T)
7 **Mark**'s really good at this game. (T)
8 I really like **going to football matches** on a Saturday. (H)

10 a Work in pairs. Make guesses about your classmates for these topics.

- something they've achieved in the last year
- the place where they were born
- what they'd buy or do if they won the lottery
- something they always do at the weekend
- what they want for their next birthday

b Check your guesses with your classmates, then report back to your partner.

Madrid, that's where Mari Carmen was born.

Go to page 164 or your app for more information and practice.

Speaking

PREPARE

11 You're going to explain how to play a game that you could play in your classroom. Think of the rules of a game you know and what you need to play it.

SPEAK

12 Work in pairs. Take turns to explain how to play the game. Listen to your partner's explanation and ask any questions you have.

13 Play one or both of the games with your partner.

Master your listening
page 105

10C Is this the future?

- **Goal:** discuss approaches to language learning
- **Language focus:** concession clauses
- **vocabulary:** evaluating

Vocabulary

1 Work in pairs and discuss the questions.

1. How did you learn to read in your first language? Was this different to how you learnt to read in English?
2. Has your approach to learning English changed as you've progressed in your studies? In what way(s)?

2 a Decide if the words and phrases in bold have positive (+) or negative (–) meanings.

1. There's a **compelling** argument for greater use of technology such as Virtual Reality (VR) in schools.
2. For an essay to be **sound**, it needs to be both well-researched and **convincing**.
3. You say it's the future, I say it's just a **cheap gimmick**.
4. Traditional approaches to learning history were fundamentally **flawed** – they just involved memorising dates.
5. New approaches to learning often look **superficially/ outwardly attractive**, but on closer examination they're found to be **lacking**.
6. Despite its criticisms, using translation when learning a foreign language remains a **valid** approach.
7. The reasons for children wearing school uniforms seem **badly thought through** to me.

b Work in pairs. Discuss whether you agree or disagree with the statements in Exercise 2a. Give reasons.

Go to your app for more vocabulary and practice.

Reading

3 a Work in pairs. What do you know about these developments in education?

1. The Initial Teaching Alphabet (ITA)
2. Learning styles
3. The Maker Movement

b Read the article and check your ideas.

Education has long been shaped by change and innovation. From the bygone days of rote-learning where children sat in rows, strictly disciplined, to the more outlandish experiments of the 1960s and 70s, new ideas have sought to improve the way students learn, often with mixed results.

Take, for example, the Initial Teaching Alphabet (ITA). Developed by James Pitman in the early 1960s as a way of simplifying learning how to read, it assigned a different symbol for each of the 44 sounds of English. For example, *one* was spelt *wun*. Odd as it may seem, it made learning to read a lot easier. The problem came when children had to make the transition to the established way of spelling words in English. Teachers were poorly trained in how to do this, and children soon became overwhelmed. Another compelling argument against its use was that the sound system didn't take account of regional accents, placing an additional burden on both teachers and children.

A recent area to come under scrutiny is the theory of Learning Styles. In its most basic form, the theory suggests that we all perceive the world in different ways, and should learn in a style that suits accordingly. For example, a visual learner learns best when they see things, an auditory learner needs to hear things, and so on. This theory gathered such widespread support that literally hundreds of learning styles have been identified, leading to such titles as 'right v left-brain learners' and 'accommodating v diverging'. However interesting this theory sounds, there is very little evidence to support it and it has been accused of being a cheap gimmick in some quarters. No studies (or even meta-studies into these studies) have ever proved conclusive.

One of the biggest trends in education of late is that of the Maker Movement. It provides 'makerspaces' for students, in which they're given a problem and supplied with the resources and tools they need to solve it. This type of hands-on learning is essentially collaborative and open-ended, and allows space for students to develop their creative skills. Despite being seen as effective in developing skills students need for the modern workplace, resources and tools can be expensive, and it requires teachers to learn new skillsets in order to be able to make the most of the spaces.

To sum up, while innovation is surely a good thing, it's important to treat each new development and its accompanying hype with a pinch of salt, subjecting it to the scrutiny it deserves before allowing it to become commonplace. Even if something sounds convincing at first, it might not prove fruitful in practice.

4 **Work in pairs and discuss the questions.**

1 Which of the writer's opinions do you agree/disagree with? Why?

2 Should education stick to 'tried-and-tested' methods or be experimental? Why?

3 Which of the ideas in the article would you like to try?

Language focus

5 **Read the language focus box and find more examples of concession clauses in the article in Exercise 3.**

Concession clauses

Concession clauses allow us to contrast two main ideas. They reduce the strength of the original idea. They take various forms:

Although/Even though + clause.

***Although** innovation is exciting, we need to take a cautious approach.*

***Even though** it was popular, there was little evidence to support it.*

Even if + clause. This means 'whether or not'.

***Even if** we give a good presentation, there's no way they'll adopt the proposal.*

While/ Whereas + clause

***While** there have been many innovations, many teachers prefer the 'tried-and-tested approach.'*

Adjective + *as/though* + clause.

***Difficult as** it may sound, the new approach is certainly effective.*

However + adjective + clause.

***However simple** it appears at first, it's not without its complications.*

Nevertheless,/Nonetheless,/All the same, + clause to refer to a previous sentence.

*The evidence is lacking. **Nevertheless**, it's widely believed to be true.*

In spite of/Despite/ + noun/noun phrase/gerund.

***Despite** the recent changes, the system is still lagging behind that of other countries.*

***In spite of** implementing the changes, the system still lags behind.*

6 a **Look at sentences 1–5. Which one will have a different intonation pattern?**

1 Even if it becomes a reality, it's unlikely to become commonplace.

2 In spite of the recent downturn in the economy, many businesses are thriving.

3 Exciting as it may sound, it doesn't come without costs.

4 However expensive it may be, people will still buy it.

5 Profits are up. Nevertheless, the company is still having difficulty.

b 10.7 **Listen and check, then repeat.**

7 **Combine the sentences using the words in brackets.**

1 It's effective. It's yet to catch on. (despite)
Despite being effective, it's yet to catch on.

2 Demand has fallen recently. It remains a popular product. (although)

3 It might be appealing. It's still dangerous. (however)

4 It's an interesting idea. There's no proof it actually works. (all the same)

5 The cost is high. I'd like to try it. (in spite of)

6 It's unattractive to most people. It's my favourite. (while)

7 There are no safety issues with it. I wouldn't want to try it. (even if)

8 It's not easy. It's still an important part of my daily routine. (difficult)

8 a **Choose four of the sentences in Exercise 7 and think of something each one could describe in your life.**

b **Work in pairs. Read out the things you came up with in Exercise 8a for your partner to guess which of the sentences in Exercise 7 they relate to.**

A: *Skydiving.*
B: *Sentence 5?*
A: *That's right!*

Go to page 164 or your app for more information and practice.

Speaking

PREPARE

9 **You're going to evaluate some possible new approaches to language learning for your school. Work in pairs. Student A: Turn to page 188. Student B: Turn to page 190. Make notes on the advantages and disadvantages of each approach.**

SPEAK

10 **Describe each approach you read about to your partner. Discuss the advantages and disadvantages of each one. Choose what you think is the most beneficial for language learning.**

11 **Share your conclusions with the class, giving reasons.**

Master your reading
page 124

10D English in action

Goal: deliver a progress report

Vocabulary: success and failure

Vocabulary

1 Work in pairs and discuss the questions.

1 Do you like getting feedback on your learning or work?
2 How often do you usually get it?
3 What things have you learnt in English lately? What do you feel you need to work on still?

2 a Complete the sentences with the words in the box.

back	downhill	it	off (x 3)	out	short	up (x 2)

1 Despite not preparing for the presentation, Caity managed to **pull it** _______ and the board was impressed.
2 Although they had a successful year, the sales team **fell** just _______ of achieving their targets.
3 The team had a bad start, then just **went** _______ from there until they crashed out of the competition.
4 The going was tough, but we **made** _______ in the end.
5 After a disastrous year last year, the team have managed to **bounce** _______ this season and are now top of the league.
6 You need to talk to Kevin, his comments have **messed** things _______ for all of us.
7 We've taken some huge risks, which, fortunately, have **paid** _______.
8 After the financial crash, we watched as all our dreams **went** _______ **in smoke**.
9 You don't want to **lose** _______ on this opportunity, so invest now.
10 After a shaky start, Trisha's business **took** _______. She's now making a regular profit.

b Work in pairs. Decide if each of the phrases in bold in Exercise 2a describe success (S) or failure (F).

3 Work in pairs and discuss the questions.

1 When was the last time you tried something difficult and managed to pull it off?
2 What local businesses in your area have taken off recently?
3 What celebrities do you know who have bounced back?
4 Have you ever fallen just short of succeeding in something? What happened?
5 Have you ever had any plans go up in smoke?
6 When was the last time your hard work paid off?

Listening 1

4 a 10.8 Listen to Sofia discussing her progress in English lessons with her teacher. What has she achieved and what does she still need to work on?

b Complete the Useful phrases 1 box with the missing words. Then listen again and check.

Useful phrases 1

Summarising progress

(You've) ¹ _______ headway with …
(You've) come on in leaps and bounds.
(You've) ² _______ significant/solid progress in …
(You've) made a breakthrough in …
(You've) achieved proficiency in …
(You're) now ³ _______ to … adeptly.
(You have) a good track record in …

Describing what still needs work

(You've) yet to …
(We've) still ⁴ _______ a bit of work to do in …
(You're) continuing to grow/develop in …
(You're) improving, but … still needs some work.
(You've) still ⁵ _______ some way to go in …

5 Work in pairs. Use the Useful phrases and the vocabulary in Exercise 2 to describe your progress and what you still want/need to do in the each of these areas:

- sport/fitness
- your career
- a book you're reading
- a hobby/interest

Listening 2

6 10.9 **Listen to Sofia reporting back on her progress in learning English to her boss. Which of these goals does she set for the future?**

1 get a new job
2 give an important presentation in English
3 get a pay rise
4 take more trips abroad for work
5 get a promotion

7 **Read the Useful phrases 2 box. Can you remember which ones Sofia used? Listen again and check.**

Useful phrases 2

Setting goals

I intend to ...
Ideally, I'd like to put this to good use by ...
I think this goal should be easily attainable.
The aim is to ...
I'd like to seek ways to put into practice ...
I'm hoping this will boost my ...
It would be great if I could ...
My ultimate goal is to ...

Referring to the future

... by (the end of the year).
In the short/mid/long(er) term, ...
(Three) weeks/months/years from now, ...
... in (three) weeks'/months'/years' time, ...
In the near/foreseeable/(not-too-)distant future, ...

8 a 10.10 **Listen to the sentences. How do the sounds in bold change? Why do they do this?**

1 This goal shoul**d** be easily attainable.
2 It woul**d** be great if I could boost my CV.
3 In four year**s** she'll be eligible for promotion.
4 You've made soli**d** progress in your goals.

b **Listen again and repeat.**

Speaking

PREPARE

9 **Think about your progress in English over the course. Look back over the book and complete the chart with what you've achieved/haven't yet achieved in the following areas. Add two more areas to the chart.**

Area	What I've achieved	What I'd like to achieve
Language focus		
Vocabulary		
Listening		
Reading		
Speaking		
Writing		
Practical English for my work/studies		

10 **Set yourself goals for each of the areas you made notes on in Exercise 9. Think about the timeframe in which you hope to achieve them.**

SPEAK

11 **Work in pairs. Present your progress and goals to your partner. Listen to each other's presentations and make notes on any useful advice you can give.**

12 **Give your partner feedback on their progress report and share any useful advice you have.**

Go online for the Roadmap video.

Check and reflect: Units 9 and 10

1 Complete the text with the most suitable form of the verbs in the box.

arrive be click leap pass shake stare tell type wait

As I turned on my laptop, my fingers ¹_______ so much that I ²_______ my password incorrectly twice. When I finally got my password right at the third attempt, and opened up my email account, my heart ³_______. The email ⁴_______. The email that I ⁵_______ for impatiently for six agonising weeks. The email that ⁶_______ me whether I had passed or failed my university entrance exam. I ⁷_______ at the unopened email for a few seconds. Finally, I took a deep breath and ⁸_______ 'open'. I gasped. I ⁹_______ with flying colours. Everything ¹⁰_______ OK. Or was it?

2 a Choose the correct alternative.

1 What work tasks do you do *competently/dramatically*, but without enjoying them too much?
2 When was the last time you agreed to do something politely but *continually/unenthusiastically*?
3 Do you know anyone who always listens to you *closely/clearly* when you speak?
4 What possession of yours breaks down *continually/uncontrollably*?
5 Has a film ever made you shake *closely/uncontrollably*?
6 Do you have a friend who never speaks *closely/clearly*?

b Work in pairs. Choose three questions in Exercise 2a to ask and answer. Ask follow-up questions.

3 Find and correct one word in each sentence.

1 Thanks to social media, rumours can burn like wildfire, so everybody knows within minutes.
2 There are lots of rumours flying around, but I'd take them with a pinch of pepper if I were you.
3 You should be able to work out what present I want – I've dropped enough clues!
4 I thought they were joking, but it turned out I'd got hold of the wrong end of the bat.
5 It's mean to gossip about people behind their faces.
6 They didn't say why I didn't get the job, but reading between the words, they probably think I'm too old.

4 Choose the correct alternatives.

1 Her dad said he wouldn't buy her a new phone because *she'd/she/she's* only had the old one for two years.
2 The manager is rumoured *that she was looking/to be looking/to look* for a new goalkeeper.
3 The thief claimed that he *had been watching/has been watching/watched* a film in the cinema at the time.
4 The fire is believed *that it was/to be being/to have been* started deliberately.
5 They've told me that they *paid/'re going to pay/were going to pay* me back but I don't believe they ever will.
6 It was rumoured that their essays *had been/have been/to be* copied from the internet.

5 Put the words in the correct order to make sentences.

1 sporting event / Held / is / the African Cup of Nations / year, / biggest / the continent's / every other
2 I / hours, / slept / for / was / having / Not / 24 / exhausted / absolutely
3 absolutely / Please / don't / this / me / unless / phone / evening / necessary
4 gets / before / arrive / well, / All / should / being / it / we / dark
5 ever / to / largest / is / the blue whale / have / the / creature / almost 30 metres, / lived / Measuring
6 lives / been / upside / lottery, / Since / turned / our / have / winning / the / down

6 a Complete the sentences with the correct form of the words in the box.

alleviate deteriorate enhance impair rectify undermine

1 I worry that my English is _______ – or maybe I'm just more aware of my weaknesses.
2 If I've upset somebody, I sometimes try to _______ the situation by buying them a present.
3 You can work hard 99% of the time, but if you're lazy once, it can _______ all your earlier efforts.
4 It's not enough to be popular – you need to work hard constantly to _______ your reputation.
5 When I'm feeling tired, it can _______ my ability to make rational decisions.
6 I find physical exercise is a great way of _______ stress.

b Work in pairs. Which statements are true for you? Change the others so that they are true for you.

7 a Replace the words in bold in the sentences with the words in the box with a similar meaning.

cutting-edge dawn harness pioneering spearheading thrive

1 The best way to reduce pollution is to **utilise** new forms of renewable energy.
2 I love gadgets, so I'm always interested in the latest **state-of-the-art** technology that comes out.
3 I don't think electric scooters will ever really **catch on** as a form of transport.
4 This government is **leading** the effort to reduce carbon emissions in public transport.
5 We are entering a new **era** in terms of the way we work.
6 Online, instant translation is a **groundbreaking** concept which will change the way we learn languages.

b Which of the statements in Exercise 7a do you agree with?

8 **Match 1–6 with a–f.**

1 Nobody wants to feel like that,
2 *Nutraline* will help you feel happier, healthier
3 It's really,
4 How can we solve it?
5 We really do
6 It's innovative,

a really fresh.
b it's innovative because nobody's ever done this before.
c nobody.
d and full of life.
e I'll tell you how.
f want to make a difference.

9 **Complete the sentences with a word from box A and a word from box B.**

A

face initial roll score take ultimate

B

dice down goal phase points turns

1 In the _______ _______ of the game, people choose which character they're going to be.
2 Place the cards _______ _______ in a pile , so nobody can see them.
3 In each round, players _______ _______ to move their counters.
4 At the start of the game, players _______ the _______ . The highest number goes first.
5 You _______ _______ for correct answers.
6 The _______ _______ is to be the first player to reach the 'Finish' square.

10 **Choose the correct alternatives.**

1 *My hat, I can't/I can't, my hat* find it anywhere.
2 It's difficult *to use, this software/this software, to use.*
3 She's *Judie, a professional singer/a professional singer, Judie.*
4 That *man, was it him over there/man over there, was it him?*
5 This *is it, laptop/laptop, is it* Claire's?
6 *She knows her stuff, Angela/Angela, she knows her stuff.*

11 a **Choose the option, a–c, which does not complete the sentences.**

1 There are _______ arguments for banning homework.
   a compelling
   b gimmick
   c convincing
2 While the reasons for banning plastic bags look _______ attractive, it's not practical in reality.
   a lacking
   b outwardly
   c superficially
3 Universal, free education is a _______ idea.
   a superficially
   b sound
   c valid
4 The idea of free healthcare for all is _______ .
   a flawed
   b badly thought through
   c outwardly
5 While social media is a(n) _______ attractive idea, it has a lot of problems.
   a superficially
   b badly
   c outwardly

b **Which statements in Exercise 11a do you agree with?**

12 **Choose the correct alternatives.**

1 It's very expensive. *Despite/Nevertheless*, it remains popular.
2 *In spite of/Although* its recent success, the company was still in trouble.
3 Even *if/though* you get the job, you'll still have a lot to learn.
4 *Whereas/Easy as* it may sound, a lot of people have trouble with it.
5 It's very challenging. *All the same/Although*, a lot of people achieve it every year.
6 *Despite/While* the fact that he won, he wasn't happy.

13 **Complete the sentences with the correct form of the words in the box.**

attainable better bound dramatic foreseeable get hunch leap turn

1 Talking about results: It _______ out that my _______ had been correct.
2 Talking about results: Overall, it was a _______ change for the _______ .
3 Dealing with interjections: Yes, well, I'm just _______ to that.
4 Summarising progress: You've come on in _______ and _______ .
5 Setting goals: I think this goal should be easily _______ .
6 Referring to the future: I think that's a great plan for the _______ future.

Reflect

How confident do you feel about the statements below? Write 1–5 (1 = not very confident, 5 = very confident).

- I can relate a non-chronological narrative.
- I can take part in a work-based discussion.
- I can discuss a course of action.
- I can answer questions in a job interview in detail.
- I can present an idea.
- I can explain rules.
- I can discuss approaches to language learning.
- I can deliver a progress report.

For more practice go to your Workbook or app.

1C Master your listening

Goal: understand a persuasive speech
Focus: recognising persuasive language

1 **Work in pairs. Think of the last time you tried to persuade someone to agree with you or do something. How did you do it? Were you successful?**

2 a **In a speech designed to influence people, how important do you think these things are? Rate each one 1–5 (1 = not important, 5 = very important).**

- Identify your goal.
- Make your credentials clear.
- Give lots of facts and figures.
- Know your audience.
- Focus on content that will persuade your audience.
- Choose the language you use carefully.

b **Work in pairs and compare your ideas. Try to reach an agreement about the three most important items.**

3 1.8 **Listen to an online lecture about how to give a persuasive speech. Which four strategies in Exercise 2a does the presenter suggest? Why?**

4 a **Which of the linguistic techniques in the box did the presenter mention? Read the Focus box and check your ideas.**

long sentences	listing points in pairs
repeating sounds	asking questions

b **What are the examples in the Focus box trying to persuade listeners to do?**

Recognising persuasive language

Understanding persuasive techniques can help us to recognise when someone is actively trying to persuade us to agree or do something, and to avoid being manipulated.

1 Using short sentences and easy to follow language
Volunteering is rewarding. Everyone should do it.

2 Using 'the power of three' i.e. points listed in groups of three to be memorable
*Volunteering can **give you a sense of purpose**, **boost your confidence** and **increase happiness**.*

3 Repetition of key words and phrases to be memorable
*Volunteering **connects** you **with people**. When you **connect with people,** you feel good.*

4 Repetition of consonant sounds (alliteration) and vowel sounds (assonance) to be memorable
Volunteer work is meaningful and motivating.

5 Using descriptive language e.g. adjectives, metaphors, imagery to help listeners see ideas more vividly
Imagine being in a situation where you need help and no-one comes.

6 Using rhetorical questions with an obvious answer to make a point
Don't we all want to be happy?

7 Using pronouns to connect with the audience
We can all spare at least one hour a month, can't we?

5 a 1.9 **Listen to Speaker A and Speaker B both giving information about six different things. Who is more persuasive in each case?**

b 1.10 **Listen to the more persuasive speaker again. What techniques do they use? Use the Focus box to help you. Give examples.**

6 a 1.11 **Listen to three people being persuasive in three different situations. What are their goals?**

b **Choose the word(s) you think the speakers used. Then listen again and check.**

1 I've project managed several successful projects; built successful relationships with existing clients and *effectively/successfully* attracted several substantial new clients to the firm.
2 In terms of *effectiveness/performance* and efficiency, I do believe that I'm as valuable as the other members of our team.
3 It's sleek. It's sporty. It's *superfast on the road/speedy*.
4 Inside *you/we*'ll find it's stylish but comfortable.
5 This car is for a smart driver who wants a *perfect/smooth* ride around town, who wants to show people that they're stylish but not flash; sophisticated and sensible; and aware of their impact on the planet.
6 *Let's stop/No more* acceptance. No more apathy. No more inaction.
7 We don't want to live in a country that damages children's futures and *crushes/destroys* their dreams, do we?
8 We want to feed them, *educate/nurture* them and watch them grow.

c **What persuasive technique(s) can you identify in each extract in Exercise 6b?**

7 **Work in pairs and discuss the questions.**

1 In what situations do people try to persuade you in some way?
2 What techniques do they usually use?
3 Do their techniques usually work?

2B Master your listening

> **Goal:** understand an informal explanation
> **Focus:** recognising understatement

1 **Work in pairs and look at the photo. If you could ask him one question about his job, what would it be?**

2 a 2.5 **Listen to three people answering a question about their jobs.**

1 Which profession does each speaker have?
2 What question has each speaker been asked?

b 2.6 **Listen and check your answers to Exercise 2a.**

c **Listen again and answer the questions.**

Speaker 1

1 According to the man, why shouldn't you complain about getting knocked out?
2 At what point does it hurt?

Speaker 2

3 Why did the passenger get upset?
4 What does the speaker think is the real reason the passenger got upset?

Speaker 3

5 Why did his supervisor ask him to check the platform?
6 What was the truth of the situation?

3 a **Choose the correct meaning for the extracts from Speaker 1.**

1 ... it can sting a bit!
  a It's not painful at all.
  b It's only a little bit painful.
  c It's very painful.
2 It wasn't the smartest question.
  a It was one of the smartest questions but not the smartest.
  b It was a stupid question.
  c It was a normal question, not smart and not stupid.

b **Read the Focus box and check your answers.**

Recognising understatement

Understatement is when someone describes something as less than it really is. For example, 'we've got a bit of a problem' for many speakers actually means 'we've got a big problem'.

We sometimes use understatement to make a problem sound smaller than it is, to avoid offending someone or to be funny. Often, however, we use understatement to emphasise the opposite of the literal meaning.

First you don't feel a thing [but] then, then it can sting a bit! (it hurt a lot)
It wasn't the smartest question (it was a dumb question to ask)
Don't say that. It's not so nice. (it's quite nasty)
That won't help much. (it won't help at all)
She's no fool. (she's smart)
It wasn't much fun. (it was unpleasant)
That's not going to be cheap to repair. (it's going to be expensive)
I wouldn't say no. (yes)

4 a **Look at extracts from the other speakers. Which three are examples of understatement?**

1 So, of course, you try to keep your cool and say you understand ...
2 ... when someone goes berserk because you haven't got the right kind of snacks well, then I think they're taking it just a bit too far.
3 ... she just wanted to take it out on someone and I was in the firing line.
4 I walked to the end of the platform – not a soul around ...
5 I didn't hang around! Didn't bother waiting for the lift!
6 They thought it was the funniest thing ever but I wasn't laughing ...

b **What does the speaker really mean in each of the understatements?**

c **Rewrite the statements using understatement.**

1 When I gave her the news, she broke down crying.
2 She bought a new electric bike. I think it was very expensive.
3 He's actually really clever even though everyone thinks he's not.
4 I don't like that kind of behaviour at all.

5 a 2.7 **Listen to two more professionals answering a question about their jobs. Identify examples of understatement from each speaker.**

b **Work in pairs and compare your answers. Then listen again and check.**

6 **Work in pairs. What understatements could you make about your own job or studies?**

3C Master your listening

Goal: understand a formal talk and informal conversation on the same topic

Focus: recognising differences in formality

1 **Work in pairs and look at the photo. How serious a problem do you think fake news is?**

2 a 3.7 **Listen to Sanjay telling an anecdote twice. When is he giving a talk? When is he chatting to a friend? How do you know?**

b **Read the Focus box and check your answers.**

Recognising differences in formality

We change the level of formality in our spoken language according to the context and the people we're speaking to. Formality influences a speaker's choice of these things:

1 Vocabulary

Formal: longer words of Latin/Greek origin, less common vocabulary, more formal collocations

*... each demanding the other move to **avoid a collision**.*

Informal: shorter words, colloquial language (e.g. phrasal verbs/slang), conversational discourse markers

*...but, **you know**, each one refusing to **budge**.*

2 Grammar

Formal: standard grammar, full sentences

However, something about this exchange seemed illogical to me.

Informal: some non-standard grammar, ellipsis (i.e. omissions)

Thing was, it was obviously fake. (Full phrase = *The thing was*)

3 Pronunciation

Formal: contractions are used but words are pronounced clearly.

*... the lighthouse keeper **would have** stated who he was.*

Informal: omission of some sounds, speech more connected and less clearly pronounced

*... the lighthouse keeper **woulda** said who he was ...*

In neutral situations, speech may include some features of formal or less formal language.

3 **Which extract, a or b, is informal?**

1 a Someone I know posted this audio recording the other day.
  b A contact of mine shared some audio via social media.

2 a ... describes the extensive military power at his disposal.
  b ... showed off about how much military power he had behind him.

3 a Anyway, I did a bit of digging and found it was fake.
  b I fact-checked it and discovered that it was fake.

4 a I knew it wouldn't make me popular but I couldn't let it go, you know?
  b I felt unable to allow him and others to continue to believe it was true.

5 a Classic example of fake news in action.
  b This is a classic example of how fake news works in practice.

4 a 3.8 **Listen to eight more extracts. Do they belong to the informal chat (I) or the formal talk (F)?**

b **Listen again and complete the sentences with one or two words. How does the language in each sentence help you identify the level of formality?**

1 The first explanation is our __________ to believe the people we trust.
2 Confirmation bias describes the way people __________ information ...
3 Exactly that __________ thing, yeah.
4 I mean, some of the news stories that __________ social media ...
5 Once it's __________, getting a fake story out of our brains is tricky.
6 It's less harmful to our self-belief to __________ our existing views ...
7 ... someone we immediately believe has different __________ to us ...
8 I guess it's just the age we're __________ in.

5 a 3.9 **Listen to the complete talk and conversation. Does Sanjay talk about these topics formally (F), informally (I) or both (B)?**

1 Why fake news succeeds
2 Why fake news sticks in our minds
3 Our changing attitudes to news

b **Listen again and answer the questions.**

1 According to Sanjay, who do we tend to trust as information sources?
2 How does Sanjay say echo chambers play a part in the spreading of fake news?
3 What two reasons does Sanjay give for being unable to convince someone that news is fake?
4 Why does Sanjay say we're becoming more sceptical?

6 **Work in pairs. Do you think you do enough to avoid the impact of fake news? Do you think you contribute to the problem of fake news? Why/Why not?**

4c Master your listening

Goal: understand a group discussion

Focus: recognising references to common expressions

1 Work in pairs and answer the questions.

1 What do you think is happening in the photo? Why?
2 Have you ever been in total darkness? If so, give details about where you were and how it felt. If not, imagine how it might feel.
3 How long do you think you could spend in total darkness and isolation without suffering ill effects?

2 4.9 **Listen to a discussion about a woman who spent a long time in total darkness as a challenge. Complete the sentences.**

1 The woman spent the entire time in a ...
2 In terms of the outside world, she was not allowed ...
3 In total, she was in there for ...

3 a Listen again and answer the questions.

1 What did the problem with the power help the female speaker to understand?
2 Why do they suspect the woman took on the challenge to live in darkness?
3 Why were meals delivered at odd times?
4 How did she stay calm and happy?
5 What two tricks did her mind play on her?
6 Why did the woman not stay in for the whole month?

b Work in pairs and compare your answers.

4 Work in pairs. Read extracts 1–6 and guess the meaning of the phrases in bold.

1 a **pitch black** bathroom
2 ... they created this set of rules that she had to **abide by** ...
3 ... she wasn't allowed any contact from outside **whatsoever**.
4 He admitted defeat and said that she **may as well** come out.
5 Did she **stick it out** for a month?
6 I'm **not remotely** surprised.

5 a Look at the extract below. What do you think Speaker B means?

A: *... I was about to say that!*
B: *Great minds!*

b Read the Focus box and check your answers.

Recognising references to common expressions

The better speakers know each other, the more likely they are to reference a common expression to summarise a situation. The expression is often shortened.

A: *... I was about to say that!*
B: Great minds!

Here the *Great minds* refers to the expression *Great minds think alike*. The speaker is humorously suggesting that they both have great minds because they both had the same thought.

Referencing common expressions can be confusing to a listener who doesn't know the expressions, but knowing the expressions and recognising references to them can help to understand all kinds of discussions.

Common expressions that are often shortened

A fool and his money ... (A fool and his money are soon parted.)
It's easy to con a fool out of his money.

If the cap fits ... (If the cap fits, wear it.)
If a particular description fits you, accept it.

Accidents will happen (in the best regulated families.)
Not every accident can be prevented.

The more things change ... (The more things change, the more they stay the same.)
It looks like things are changing but actually nothing has changed.

When in Rome ... (When in Rome, do as the Romans do.)
When you are in a new place, behave in the same way as the people who live there.

6 a 4.10 **Listen to four extracts. Note four common shortened versions of expressions.**

b Work in pairs and answer the questions. Listen again if necessary.

1 What is the meaning of each expression?
2 Why does the speaker use the expression in this situation?

7 Work in pairs. Which of these things do you think you could do? Which would be hardest?

- Stay in bed for a week.
- Eat pizza every day for a year.
- Stay silent for a full day.
- Stay offline for a week.

5A Master your listening

Goal: understand a narrative

Focus: understanding colloquial language

1 **Work in pairs and discuss the questions.**

1 How would you define an 'idol'? Why?

2 What kind of people are usually considered to be idols these days? Make a list.

3 Rank the people on your list from most heroic to least heroic. Justify your ideas.

2 5.3 **Listen to a podcast about meeting your idol. Which speaker, 1, 2 or 3:**

a felt disillusioned by the meeting?

b met someone who was generous with their time?

c had a sudden realisation?

3 **Read the Focus box. Then look at the extract below and use the information in the box to help you:**

1 understand the gist, ignoring the word in bold.

2 work out the meaning of the word in bold.

And there, in the shop was none other than actress Cara Ronson. … I've been a **humongous** fan since I saw her in *The Big Deep* a few years ago …

Understanding colloquial language

Colloquial is a word used to describe informal language used in casual conversations. If we hear a word or phrase we don't recognise in informal contexts, it may well be colloquial.

Oh, it was a sporting hero of mine; a footballer who'd helped our local team to win the league. He's not world famous or anything but in our local area, he's a ***big deal****.*

In this situation, we can:

1 ignore the word or phrase and continue listening. This is the best strategy if we don't need the word or phrase to understand the gist of what's being said, or if we need to keep listening. (gist = he's not famous, he's local).

2 infer the meaning.
If the word or phrase is important to meaning or if it's repeated, we can try to guess the approximate meaning. Consider these things:

- the meaning of parts of the word or phrase (*big* = important)
- the connotation i.e. positive or negative (*not … but* suggests it's positive)
- what the word represents e.g. a person, object, place, action or description of (describes a person)
- the meaning of the whole sentence (suggests he's not very famous but important locally)
- our understanding of what is said before and after (he's a sporting hero locally)
- our knowledge of the topic (*sporting hero* = someone important)

We can conclude that *a big deal* refers to someone or something that is important.

4 a 5.4 **Listen to six extracts from the podcast in Exercise 2 and match them with a–f (the gist of what is said). Ignore any unknown words or phrases.**

a The celebrity was less clever and imaginative than they'd anticipated. *6*

b The speaker was extremely enthusiastic about the celebrity.

c The speaker was ignored in favour of other people.

d The celebrity received what looked like bad news.

e The speaker thought it was the best time of their life.

f The speaker realised the famous person was just like everyone else.

b **Listen again. Choose the correct meaning of the word or phrase in bold. Check in a dictionary. Does understanding the gist help you?**

1 **gutted:** *really disappointed/really irritated*

2 **dawned on me:** *I misunderstood/I realised*

3 **fangirled:** *be calm/be overexcited*

4 **epic:** *amazing/surprising*

5 **blanked:** *ignored/stared at*

5 a 5.5 **Listen to the next part of the podcast. Are the statements true (T) or false (F)?**

1 The guests agree on the type of people that should be celebrated.

2 The female speaker thinks the celebrity lifestyle is attractive.

3 The male speakers have the same idea about why we're obsessed with celebrities.

b **Listen again. What do you think these words and phrases mean?**

1 muck around

2 get hung up on

3 drives me up the wall

4 rub off on

5 have ups and downs

6 buddies

6 **Work in pairs. Who is your idol? Would you ever want to meet a famous hero of yours? If yes, what would you say or do? If not, why not?**

6C Master your listening

Goal: understand a complex podcast

Focus: recognising doubts about word choice

1 Work in pairs and discuss the questions.

1 What is your favourite kind of comedy to listen to or watch (e.g. romantic comedy films, stand-up comedians, funny podcasts, etc.)?

2 What do you understand by the term 'improvisation comedy' (also called *improv*)? Have you ever seen any?

2 a Work in pairs. You are going to listen to a podcast about improv. Why might someone choose to do a course in improv?

b 6.7 **Listen to Part 1 of the podcast. Did it mention your ideas?**

3 Listen again and complete each sentence with two words.

1 According to Helena, improv is a kind of theatre or comedy where nothing is ____________ .

2 The course is aimed at ____________ who might be introverted.

3 Justin decided to take part because he wanted to break out of his ____________ .

4 He had been feeling stuck in a rut and had lost ____________ in his life.

5 Tony decided to do the course because he wanted to be ____________ .

6 Doing the course has had a ____________ on him.

4 a Look at this sentence from the podcast. What is the purpose of the phrase in bold?

I wanted to challenge myself, you know, find a way to be more playful, **if you like**.

b Read the Focus box and check your answer.

Recognising doubts about word choice

Sometimes when we speak it's hard to find exactly the right words to express what we think, so we have to use words or phrases that are imprecise or not exactly what we mean. To show that we recognise this, we often use certain expressions either before or after the imprecise word or phrase.

This is an improv workshop for ordinary people, for introverts ***so to speak****.*

I wanted to, sort of, break out of my comfort zone, ***if you like****.*

I just felt that I'd kind of lost the spark in my life, ***if you see what I mean****.*

Often these phrases indicate that the speaker finds it difficult to come up with the right word or expression.

I was feeling kind of like … ***how can I put it****, unable to really feel good about myself.*

Recognising these expressions and their purpose can help to understand a speaker's intention and predict what is coming next.

5 Choose the correct option, a or b, to match the speaker's meaning.

1 'I felt as though I was falling into a deep hole, if I can put it that way.'

a The speaker didn't know if he was really falling into a deep hole.

b The speaker didn't know if *falling into a deep hole* accurately describes the feeling.

2 'She came across as quite, how can I put it … reserved.'

a The speaker doesn't know if she was really reserved.

b The speaker doesn't know if *reserved* is exactly the right expression.

6 6.8 **Listen to Part 2 of the podcast and answer the questions.**

1 What are you trying to do in improv?

2 How do you do that?

3 Why should you actively listen to your fellow improvisers?

4 What are we normally doing when we are listening?

7 a Listen again and complete the sentences.

1 Well we break it down into the principles of improvisation, ____________ .

2 You don't have to use those exact words but the, ____________ … the spirit of those words is what you're looking for.

3 I think it's really important that you don't have a preconceived plan, ____________ .

4 So normally we listen to each other with minimal attention, ____________ .

5 You have to actively listen and engage and then usually you just, ____________ , spontaneously find you have something to add.

b Which phrase is the speaker not sure about in each extract in Exercise 7a?

8 Work in pairs and discuss the questions.

1 Would you like to do this course? Why/Why not?

2 If you did the course, what might you gain from it?

7A Master your listening

› **Goal:** understand a debate

› **Focus:** recognising digression

1 **Work in pairs. What are some arguments against travelling abroad for a holiday? Make a list.**

2 a 7.5 **Listen to the introduction to a radio debate. What topic will the guests discuss? Why is it being discussed now?**

b **Work in pairs. Do you agree or disagree with the opinions below?**

1. Travel is a way of showing off.
2. Travel allows us to break down barriers.
3. We no longer have to travel to meet different people these days.

c 7.6 **Listen to the first part of the debate. Who holds the opinions in Exercise 2b: Ellis (E), Imogen (I) or both (B)?**

3 a 7.7 **Read the Focus box. Then listen to three extracts from the radio debate. Who digresses in each one: Ellis (E) or Imogen (I)?**

Recognising digression

In discussions and debates, speakers may digress because they forget their main point, remember a different point they want to make or perhaps choose to make a joke. Digression can also be used as an argumentative tactic, to divert attention away from the weakness of the speaker's argument or to divert attention away from the strength of the other speaker's argument.

P: Imogen, let's bring you in here – does Ellis make a valid point?

I: Yes, although he makes it somewhat hypocritically given that he's been a travel writer for years! ***Anyhow****, yes, he does make a valid point …*

Other phrases a speaker might use to digress include *by the way* and *incidentally*.

To bring a conversation back to the original argument, a speaker may use phrases such as *Getting back to my original point; Going back to what I was saying earlier; Anyway, Anyhow.*

But ***getting back to my original point*** *– travel doesn't really cause you to find yourself.*

b **Listen again. How does the topic of conversation change when the speakers use the phrases below?**

1. Topic before: How people use social media to show off.
   'anyhow'
   Topic after: ________________
2. Topic before: His job has been to travel the world.
   'anyhow'
   Topic after: ________________
3. Topic before: Stereotypes can be harmful.
   'going back to what I was saying before'
   Topic after: ________________

4 a 7.8 **Predict whether the statements are true (T) or false (F). Then listen to the second part of the debate and check your answers.**

1. Ellis says that we should consider both the pros and cons before traveling.
2. Imogen says that young people should not be allowed to have the same experiences Ellis did.
3. Ellis thinks that some people should break their travel routines.
4. The presenter thinks that travel is hard work.
5. Ellis thinks that travelling is relaxing for most people.
6. Imogen says that travelling is good if done correctly.

b **Listen again and answer the questions. What are the reasons for the digressions?**

1. How does Ellis digress when Imogen says young people should not have their freedom to travel removed?
2. How does Imogen digress when Ellis says that people who don't get excited about travelling shouldn't do it?
3. How does Imogen digress when Ellis describes negative aspects of travelling?

5 **Work in groups. Do you think that travel is overrated? Should we agree to travel less? Justify your arguments.**

8B Master your listening

› **Goal:** understand a phone call

› **Focus:** recognising the context words are generally used in

1 **Who is the first person you call or speak to when something goes wrong in your life? Why do you call that person?**

2 a 8.4 **Listen to three phone conversations about something that has gone wrong. For each conversation, answer the questions.**

1 Where is the caller?
2 What has happened?

b **Work in pairs and compare your answers.**

3 **Listen again and say why the statements are not correct.**

Conversation 1

1 This is the second time the car has broken down this month.
2 He knew he was going to run out of petrol.
3 The problem is not big so the garage will repair it.

Conversation 2

4 Serena was confident she would get the role.
5 She was one of a few other people at the audition.
6 There was a mini-riot backstage.

Conversation 3

7 Rafa's boss cancelled Rafa's appraisal because of an important meeting.
8 Rafa has quit his job.
9 Rafa's friend thinks Rafa should find a better job.

4 a **Look at the sentences below. Which one is from Conversation 1? Why is it more natural than the other option?**

1 This car causes me a lot of grief.
2 This car provides me with a lot of grief.

b **Read the Focus box and check your ideas in Exercise 4a.**

Recognising the context words are generally used in

Sometimes the connotation of a word is obvious (for example, *picky* versus *selective*) and sometimes it is hidden. We only discover the hidden connotation of a word by analysing the words that it frequently collocates with. An example is the verb *cause*, which is almost always used in a negative context. This becomes obvious when you look at the words that *cause* most frequently collocates with: *problems, harm, trouble, damage, pain,* etc.

I don't want to ***cause*** *any* ***trouble****.*
Your boss is ***causing*** *the company* ***real harm.***
The riot ***caused*** *a lot of* ***damage*** *to property.*

The word *provide*, on the other hand, is commonly used in a positive context. It commonly collocates with words like *information, support, opportunities, leadership, protection*, etc.

Their job is to ***provide information****.*
We're all hoping that she'll ***provide*** *some* ***leadership****.*
I'm happy to ***provide support*** *if you need it.*

Recognising the context a word is most often used in can help to decode speech and understand someone's underlying meaning.

5 a **Look at the extracts. Do you think the words in bold are usually used in a positive or negative context?**

Conversation 1

1 This town is **rife with** cowboy businesses.
2 Well, my brother **had some dealings** with them before and it didn't … it's a long story …

Conversation 2

3 A mini-riot nearly **broke out** backstage when everyone found out how long they'd have to wait.
4 Do you have to **sit through** all the other auditions?

Conversation 3

5 It's just a **build up** of irritating things.
6 You're **building up** a lot of experience there.

b **Can you think of any other words that frequently collocate with the words in bold?**

6 a 8.5 **Listen to four extracts from phone conversations. Do you think the speakers are talking about something positive or negative? Which word or phrase suggests this?**

b **Work in pairs and compare your answers. Then listen again to check.**

7 a **Work in pairs. Listen to the conversations again and decide on a context for each conversation.**

b **Choose one of the conversations and continue it.**

9B Master your listening

Goal: follow a group discussion

Focus: understanding overlapping

1 Work in pairs. Discuss which of the statements below you agree with. Give reasons where possible.

1 Musicians shouldn't be motivated by money.
2 Famous musicians don't realise how lucky they are.
3 Talented musicians deserve what they earn.
4 Life was better for musicians before the rise of music streaming sites.
5 If musicians have to tour more to earn money, that's a good thing.

2 a 9.8 **Listen to three friends discussing the music industry. Decide which of the speakers, Leo (L), Aisha (A) or Jamie (J) expresses the ideas in Exercise 1.**

b Based on their interactions in the conversation, decide which of the friends get on the best, and which have the most difficult relationship.

1 Aisha and Jamie 2 Aisha and Leo 3 Jamie and Leo

c Read the Focus box. Then decide which forms of overlapping Aisha, Jamie and Leo are likely to have used with each other.

3 a Look at dialogues 1–5 below. Decide which might be examples of competitive overlapping (A) and which might be cooperative overlapping (B).

1 **A:** Ronaldo was so nice about the situation …
B: He always is, really nice guy.
2 **A:** I think it's east, east on …
B: … on the A52 from here.
3 **A:** I think most people would agree with me about …
B: I'm not remotely interested in what other people think.
4 **A:** And it's not exactly boiling hot, it's just, like …
B: … it's pleasantly warm.
5 **A:** If we'd left earlier, then we …
B: Your friend Diane was really nice, by the way.

b 9.9 **Listen and decide if you'd like to change any of your answers from Exercise 3a. Why do you think speaker B overlaps with speaker A in each case?**

4 a Look at extracts 1–5 from the conversation between Jamie, Leo and Aisha in Exercise 2a. Predict which ones will be examples of competitive (A) or cooperative (B) overlapping.

1 **Jamie:** Oh because of the whole streaming thing? Artists not getting paid much by music streaming services, etc?
2 **Aisha:** I don't know, I like his music, I think he should get paid for it.
3 **Leo:** There are people in the world without enough to eat.
4 **Aisha:** It's not how they work. Yeah, and also, Papa G makes a lot of people happy, that's a good thing, isn't it?
5 **Aisha:** Leo, how's your little band doing these days?

b 9.8 **Listen to the three friends again and check. Why do they overlap with each other in each case?**

5 Work in pairs and discuss the questions.

1 How does your culture compare with others in terms of the way you use overlapping in conversation?
2 Do you ever overlap competitively? If so, why?

Understanding overlapping

Overlapping, where two people speak at the same time, is common in English, and occurs most often when speakers 'hand over' at the end of their speaking turn in a conversation. It can be broken into two broad categories:

Cooperative

This form of overlapping is done to keep the flow of the conversation going and offer support to the person currently speaking. It may include:

- supporting the idea of the previous speaker

A: *And it's getting so hard, so tough …*
B: *… difficult for them to earn money, yes.*

- clarifying/helping the previous speaker with the expression of an idea

A: *And he's so, not exactly lying, he's …*
B: *… insincere, isn't he.*

- jumping in towards the conclusion of an idea

A: *And that's why they have to go on tour …*
B: *… tour, I see, right.*

Usually this type of overlapping would not be seen as disrespectful.

Competitive

This form of overlapping breaks the flow of a conversation, and is done due to the speaker's own desires rather than to facilitate others. It may include:

- raising a different viewpoint or disagreement

A: *Some of those guys are great, really talented…*
B: *They're so not great, I can't believe you think that.*

- abruptly changing topic

A: *Jane's coming today and she's …*
B: *I saw Silas this morning, did I tell you?*

- jumping in mid idea

A: *What they find difficult is …*
B: *It's always about them isn't it?*

There is a greater chance with competitive overlapping that offence may be caused to other speakers.

10B Master your listening

> **Goal:** understand a presentation
> **Focus:** taking effective notes

1 **Work in groups and discuss the questions.**

1 How do you feel about video games?
2 Do you know anyone who's addicted to video games?

2 a 10.5 **Listen to the beginning of a talk on video game addiction. What will the content of the talk be?**

b **Work in pairs and compare your answers. Listen again and check.**

3 a **Work in pairs. Discuss how you make notes when listening to a lecture. Do you have any tricks or tips?**

b **Read the Focus box and prepare a piece of paper to make notes for the lecture on video game addiction.**

Taking effective notes

There are many different ways to take notes when listening to a lecture. One way is to divide the page into three sections as shown below.

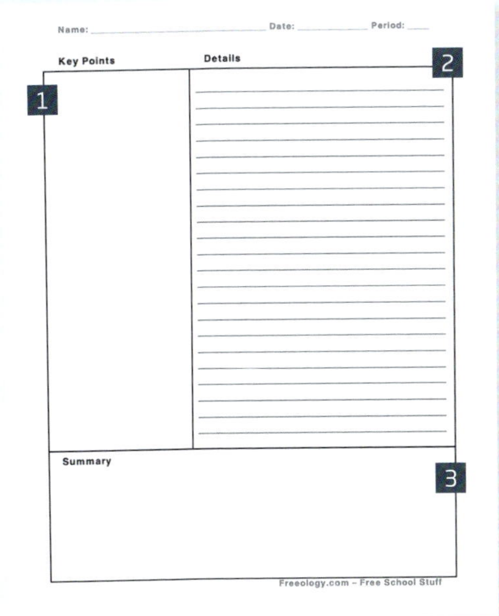

- Write the subject and date at the top of the page.
- While listening to the lecture, make notes in Section 2. Note down only the important information in short phrases. Use headings, abbreviations, symbols, bullet points and indentations and leave space to show a change of topic or new section.
- During or as soon as possible after the lecture, write key words in Section 1. The purpose of the key words is to prompt you to remember the information when you look at them.
- Then write a summary of the lecture at the bottom of the page in Section 3. Use your own words.
- When you come to revise your notes, cover Section 2 and use Section 1 to help you recall as much information as possible. Then check your complete notes to see if you have remembered everything.

4 a 10.6 **Organise your note paper in a similar way to the model in the Focus box. Listen to the lecture on video game addiction and take notes on your paper in Section 2. Then complete Section 1.**

b **Work in pairs and use your notes to answer the questions.**

1 Why does the speaker say that 'gaming is gender neutral'?
2 Who defines video game addiction and what is their definition?
3 Why does the speaker say that 'although gaming is gender-neutral, game addiction is not'?
4 In what ways does gaming negatively affect the imaginary Johan's life?
5 What law has China introduced to tackle video game addiction?
6 What law was nearly introduced in the UK?
7 What is the relationship between loneliness and video game addiction?
8 How might a video game addiction treatment programme try to help addicts?

5 **Listen to the lecture again and check your notes. Is there anything you would add or cut?**

6 a **Complete the summary section of the note-taking template.**

b **Compare your summaries to those created by other students. What makes a good summary?**

c **Work in pairs. Cover Section 2 of your notes and use Section 1 to recall as much information from the lecture as possible.**

7 **Work in groups and imagine you have a friend who is a video game addict. What rules would you create for him to cure his addiction?**

1B Master your reading

Goal: understand short anecdotes in an article

Focus: recognising cohesive devices in a text

1 **Think about the way you speak to the people in the box below. Do you speak to them all in the same way or in different ways?**

friends family employer classmates
strangers people on the phone

2 **Read the article about code switching and answer the questions.**

1 What is it?
2 What reasons are given for code switching?

3 a **Look at the words in bold in the article. What function do they have?**

b **Read the Focus box and check your ideas. Match words a–e in the article with categories 1–5 in the box.**

Recognising cohesive devices in a text

Cohesive texts are created through grammatical and lexical linking. They all help to build meaning.

1 Pronoun referencing (referring backwards, forwards or outside the text)

... my mother picks up the phone and puts on the most sophisticated accent she can manage. (*she* refers back to *my mother*)

It's not just about switching a language though. Code switching also covers changes in dialect and style. (*It* refers forward to *code switching*)

2 Substitution

... sometimes doing so within the same sentence. (*doing so* refers back to *switching from one language to another*)

3 Ellipsis

... it was not uncommon for us to switch from one language to another (*language* is omitted)

4 Linkers

It's not just about switching a language ***though****.*

5 Lexical cohesion

lexical groups: *language - bilingual, language, conversation, speaker, dialect, style, accent*

4 **Underline examples of cohesive devices in the introduction to the article. Identify their meaning.**

... by drawing on her experiences and ***those*** *of other code switchers.*

those = the experiences

Linguistic Chameleons

As the people we interact with become more diverse, code switching becomes more prevalent in everyday conversation. Elena Williams explores the reasons why people code switch by drawing on her experiences and those of other code switchers.

1 Growing up in a bilingual family, code switching was a fact of life. With a Spanish-speaking mother and an English-speaking father, it was not uncommon for us to switch from one language to another in a conversation, sometimes doing so within the same sentence. It's not just about switching a language though. Code switching also covers changes in dialect and style. I'm constantly bemused by the way my mother picks up the phone and puts on the most sophisticated accent she can manage.

2 Code switching is something we all do, whether it's intentional or subconscious. According to researchers, there are several reasons for [a]**this**. In my case, there are times when English lacks the words I need to describe a particular concept so I switch to Spanish, or vice versa. Emotions play a prominent role, too. When I get angry, I tend to shout in English, probably because I grew up watching my hot-headed father do the same, while fear and excitement usually reveal themselves in Spanish.

3 Another reason for code switching is to fit in. When Ellis moved to the US from Wales aged 12, he was desperate not to be conspicuous. 'With my Welsh accent I stuck out like a sore thumb, [b]**so** I quickly started to mimic the local accent. I have a good ear, which meant within a few weeks I sounded as American as my classmates. My parents and siblings didn't, so weirdly, when I'm at home with them, I speak in my Welsh accent. If we've got American visitors, I'll flip between the two. It gets a few perplexed looks at first, but they soon get used to it.'

4 Whether we're children or adults, we often strive to fit in, which is why we may code switch with different social groups. Lara recalls her teenage years in the UK. 'Making up our own language was a natural way for us to show we fit in, to differentiate ourselves from adults and to increase our autonomy. We'd learn to use words like 'rents' for parents or 'on fleek' to mean stylish. These phrases come in and out of fashion pretty quickly though, so I'd sound ancient if I tried to use them now!' Lara thought it was horrifying when her parents attempted to speak teen language. [c]**So did** her brother Cameron: 'My dad had obviously been seeking out teen words online as he suddenly started to sprinkle them into conversations. At first, I just rolled my eyes but after he did it in front of my friends and they all cringed, I had to plead with him to stop.'

5 Another reason for code switching is social class. David has experience of this. 'I grew up in a socially deprived area where the local dialect is one that people might look down on. So, when I went to university, I soon realised I needed to adopt one that would better help me to get on in life. Code switching gave me a kind of social power that perhaps I hadn't had before.'

6 One final reason for code switching is the desire to be persuasive. When Anabel started in sales, she discovered that people were more amenable if she spoke in a southern US accent rather than her normal east coast [d]**one**. 'There's a growing perception that a southern accent is friendlier. People seemed to warm to me a lot faster if I put on a southern drawl and, more significantly, it led to more sales. I did feel like a fraud at times, but I didn't think I was doing any harm.' Of course, code switching can get you into hot water, as Anabel remembers. 'I was wandering around a shopping mall when someone rushed over to speak to me. I couldn't place [e]**him** at all and spoke in my normal accent. It transpired that he was a customer who was really put out when he realised I wasn't quite what I seemed.'

5 **Are the statements true (T) or false (F)? Which cohesive device(s) in the text helped decide on the answer?**

1 Elena says that code switching in her family generally means having one conversation in English and another in Spanish.
F - it means switching languages in one conversation and sometimes in one sentence: '... it was not uncommon for us to switch from one language to another in a conversation, sometimes ***doing so*** *within the same sentence'. (cohesive device = 'doing so')*
2 Elena suggests that learnt behaviour has caused her habit of changing languages according to mood.
3 Ellis speaks in a particular accent with his family.
4 Lara says that one reason teenagers create language is to assert their independence.
5 Lara believes that teen language swiftly changes.
6 Cameron urged his father to stop using certain phrases as soon as he started using them.
7 David used code switching in order to move up the social ladder.
8 Anabel felt that changing her accent was an acceptable way to make money.

6 **Put the sentences in a reader's response to the article in the correct order. Use your understanding of text cohesion to help you.**

Another example is foreign politics. ______
Having grown up in that context, we're completely bilingual. ______
As these were conducted in English, I guess it makes sense we use it to discuss them. ______
My twin sister and I were brought up in Spain by British parents. __*1*__
One is memories of family holidays. ______
We employ the two languages in different ways though. We speak in English with our parents but almost always in Spanish with each other. ______
This must be down to the fact that we read about it in English-speaking media. ______
However, there are certain topics where we naturally switch to English. ______

7 **Work in pairs and discuss the questions.**

1 Is code switching common in your culture? Why/Why not?
2 When do you think code switching happens most commonly in your society?
3 Do you think that code switching is positive, negative, both or neither? Why?

2A Master your reading

Goal: understand a newspaper article

Focus: recognising scepticism

1 **Work in pairs and look at these workplace trends. Do you know anyone affected by any of these? Which do you think have the most far-reaching implications? Why?**

1 Hot-desking: No one has their own desk but workers sit at whatever desk is available.

2 Flexible working: You don't have to be at work from 9 to 5 but can choose when you work your hours.

3 Remote working: You can work from home sometimes or always.

4 Overworked or underworked: Some workers have too much work while others have too little. Those with too much can end up working very long hours.

5 Gig work: Workers no longer have a job with set hours but sign in to work through an app and work the hours they want, like taxi drivers.

2 **Read the article about Danielle Steel, a famous author of romantic fiction. Answer the questions.**

1 What is extraordinary about her output as a writer?

2 How was her claim about her working day greeted by the media?

3 Why, according to the writer of the article, is sufficient sleep important?

3 **Read the article again. Are the statements true (T), false (F) or not mentioned (NM)? Correct the false statements.**

1 Steel's desk is built from a pile of her own books.

2 The main focus of *Glamour* magazine's article was Steel's work schedule.

3 There was a positive reaction online to details of her work routine.

4 Website *Quartz* suggested that sleeping less can help us achieve our goals.

5 The National Sleep Foundation helps people with sleeping problems.

6 The writer of the article argues that it is not productive to work 24 hours a day.

7 People no longer believe that working incredibly long hours contributes to success.

8 Some people sleep only three or four hours a night and never feel tired.

IS IT POSSIBLE TO WORK 22-HOUR DAYS?

DANIELLE STEEL SAYS IT IS THE SECRET OF HER SUCCESS

The prolific romance novelist has described her 'brutal, exhausting' process. Can she really work such long hours – and does it make her a role model?

It says something about the author Danielle Steel's work ethic that her desk, built to resemble a stack of her own books, is less remarkable than the hours she puts in at it. The 71-year-old romance novelist is notoriously prolific, having published 179 books at a rate of up to seven a year. But a passing reference in a recent profile by *Glamour* magazine to her 20 to 22-hour workdays – not to mention the 24-hour session 'a few times a month, when she feels the crunch' – prompted an outpouring of awestruck admiration online.

'If she gets four hours, she considers it a restful night,' marvelled *Business Insider*. Elsewhere, the question 'why Danielle Steel is more successful than the rest of us' was answered: 'Steel does not understand this modern-day mentality of work-life balance'.

4 **Work in pairs. Choose the correct meaning of the phrases in bold.**

1 The 71-year-old romance novelist is **notoriously prolific**.

a famous in a negative way for the low quality of her work

b famous in a negative way for the high quantity of her work

2 when she **feels the crunch**

a feels the stress of a deadline approaching

b feels the stress of having missed a deadline

3 She goes from bed, to desk, to bath, to bed, **eschewing** all contact.

a rejecting

b getting angry at

4 findings that show the **cumulative effects** of sleep loss

a the effects over a single time period

b increasing because each new effect is added to the previous one

Steel has given that 20–22 hour figure when describing her 'exhausting' process in the past: 'I start the book and don't leave my desk until the first draft is finished.' She goes from bed, to desk, to bath, to bed, eschewing all contact aside from phone calls with her nine children; 'I do not comb my hair for weeks,' she says. Meals are brought to her desk, where she types until her fingers swell, her nails often bleed and 'every muscle is shrieking'.

The business news website *Quartz* held Steel up as an inspiration, writing that if only we all followed her 'actually extremely liberating' example of industrious sleeplessness, we would be quick to see results. Well, indeed. The National Sleep Foundation's guidelines recommend that, at 71, Steel should be sleeping for seven to eight hours every night; the recommended duration for those aged 18 to 65 is seven to nine.

Taken in tandem with findings that show the cumulative effects of sleep loss, and its impact on judgement and productivity, doubt has been voiced as to the accuracy of Steel's self-assessment.

While you could work that long, especially as a one-off, the impact on productivity would make it hardly worthwhile. 'The idea that someone could sustain that pattern effectively – work, write, commit things to memory, use their full brain capacity – is just unbelievable to me,' agrees Katie Fischer, a sleep consultant. If Steel was routinely sleeping for up to four hours a night, she would likely be drastically underestimating the negative impact of it, says Alison Gardiner, the founder of the sleep improvement programme Sleepstation.

Margaret Thatcher was also said to get by on four hours a night, while the 130-hour work weeks endured by the former Yahoo! chief executive Marissa Mayer and other tech heads has been held up as key to their success.

That is starting to change with increased awareness of the importance of sleep for mental health. 'People are starting to realise that sleep should not be something that you fit in between everything else,' says Emma Taylor, an expert on workplace wellbeing.

But it is possible – if statistically extremely unlikely – that Steel could be a 'short sleeper', born with a mutation in the gene regulating circadian rhythms. People with the mutation wake up after three to four hours' sleep without an alarm, feeling fully alert without the need for caffeine or naps, says Dr Sophie Bostock of the sleep improvement programme Sleepio – but it is extremely rare. 'It is probably present in fewer than 1% of the population.'

Even if Steel does happen to be among that tiny minority, says Bostock, it is 'pretty irresponsible' to suggest that 22-hour days are simply a question of discipline for the rest of us. 'It really does sound as though she's got quite an unusual body clock.'

5 a What does the writer of the article think about Danielle Steel's claim to regularly work up to 24 hours a day? How do we know?

b Read the Focus box and check your answers.

Recognising scepticism

When we are sceptical, we express doubt that something is true or really happened. The writer of the article is sceptical about Danielle Steel's claims to work such long hours. She shows that she is sceptical in several ways.

1 Emphasising the extreme parts of the claims

By choosing to quote the most extreme parts, the writer makes the information seem open to doubt: *her nails often bleed; every muscle is shrieking*

2 Suggesting that supporters are being too positive

By using a strongly positive verb such as 'marvelled' instead of a neutral verb, the writer implies that *Business Insider* is going too far in its analysis.

'If she gets four hours, she considers it a restful night,' ***marvelled*** *Business Insider.*

3 Expressing doubts in a neutral way

Using the passive form makes the writer sound balanced and fair when expressing doubt: *doubt has been voiced as to the accuracy of Steel's self-assessment*

4 Offering an alternative explanation

Steel could be a 'short sleeper', born with a mutation in the gene regulating circadian rhythms

6 Which technique from the Focus box does each extract use?

1 While you could work that long ... the impact on productivity would make it hardly worthwhile.
2 'I do not comb my hair for weeks,' she says.
3 [Steel's work schedule] prompted an outpouring of awestruck admiration online.
4 'I start the book and don't leave my desk until the first draft is finished.'
5 It really does sound as though she's got an unusual body clock.

7 Read the text. Identify the ways in which the writer shows that he or she is sceptical.

Professor Cornelissen believes that an unhappiness-free future is just around the corner. 'Unhappiness as we know it,' he declares, 'will completely disappear' thanks to 'one little pill' that we will all swallow every morning. It promises 'the greatest ever revolution in what it means to be human' gushes *Future Psychology* magazine. If your beloved pet dies, you'll simply smile and shrug your shoulders. If you lose your job, you'll still find it easy to 'effortlessly focus on the positives in your life'. Some people have suggested that unhappiness can actually serve a purpose in life. It can encourage us to change and try something new. Professor Cornelissen finds this 'old-fashioned thinking'.

8 Work in pairs and discuss the questions.

1 What is your reaction to Danielle Steel's claims?
2 Do you think people often exaggerate how much they work? If so, why?
3 How does lack of sleep affect you? Do you often suffer from lack of sleep?

3A Master your reading

Goal: understand business articles

Focus: evaluating the effectiveness of an argument

1 a Work in pairs. Which item you would choose and why.

- Coffee or tea?
- Chocolate, banana, strawberry or lemon cake?
- Pasta, curry, salad, soup, kebab, paella or fish?
- Vanilla, strawberry, chocolate, cherry, cookies and cream, peanut butter, coffee, chocolate brownie, mint chocolate chip or peach ice cream?

b Discuss the questions.

1 Was it easy or difficult to make your decisions? Why?

2 Do you think choice is a good thing? Why/Why not?

2 a Read the article below and answer the questions.

1 What is 'choice overload'?

2 What is its effect and how can it be prevented?

b Read the article again. In which paragraphs, A–D, do arguments 1–4 appear?

1 Concern for what is lost by making a choice can reduce satisfaction with the choice made.

2 The idea of consumer choice is not as positive in reality as it is in theory.

3 Consumers maintain their purchasing habits when choice becomes overwhelming.

4 A range of products on display will tempt consumers into looking but not selecting one of them.

3 a What evidence does the writer give to support arguments 1–4 in Exercise 2b? Think about the following:

- examples
- statistics
- research
- quoting experts

b Work in pairs. What do you think it means to be 'a critical reader'? Why might this be important?

Consumer choice and potential overload

By Marta Iglesias, editor of *The Buzz*, an independent business magazine

A In theory, consumer choice promises autonomy and freedom. It gives people the opportunity to make decisions for themselves and stops them being tied to particular brands. However, in practice, some of the effects of so much choice on consumers can be less than desirable.

B One effect is behavioural paralysis. When faced with too many choices, consumers feel debilitated and often make no choice at all. In a well-known study by psychologists from Columbia and Stanford Universities in 2000, a booth of jam samples offered shoppers either six jams or 24 jams. The latter attracted a larger amount of interest, but a much smaller percentage of those customers went on to purchase a jam compared to those who'd been attracted by the six varieties of jam. Similar results have been produced in numerous other studies into this topic since 2000.

C Not everyone will give up in the face of too much choice. Some consumers will make a decision, but they'll opt for the choice they always make. This is because the information on which they base their choices is non-existent, too complex or lacking in clarity. One example is mobile phone providers. They provide consumers with information about data plans, length of time, add-ons and so on. The complexity of comparisons makes it easy for consumers to abandon plans to upgrade and simply stick with their existing contract.

c **Read the Focus box to check your ideas. Do you think the article puts forward an effective argument? Why/Why not?**

Evaluating the effectiveness of an argument

It is important to be a critical reader when reading arguments. This means being open to new ideas but unwilling to accept ideas at face value. In order to decide if an argument is good or bad, we can ask a variety of questions.

1 What is the author's argument and the supporting evidence (e.g. examples, statistics, research, reference to experts)?

In a well-known jam study…

One example is mobile phone providers.

2 Does the evidence support the argument, i.e. is it relevant, sufficient, up-to-date and from a trustworthy source?

*As **marketing professor Dr** Harry Shaefer **(2019)** says …*

***Similar results** have been produced in numerous studies into this topic since 2000.*

3 Do the argument and the evidence support the conclusion being made?

Arguments

+ Consumer choice promises freedom and autonomy.

- behavioural paralysis/opt for the choice they always make/fear of missing out

Conclusion

Consumers are clearly both attracted and put off by choice.

4 Is the author biased in any way? Is the argument one-sided?

Marta Iglesias, editor of The Buzz, an independent business magazine.

5 Is the argument logical or poor?

… businesses must take care to offer a degree of choice which entices consumers but allows them to make a satisfactory decision (= logical)

D Another consequence of too much choice is an acute sense of disappointment caused by FOMO, or a Fear of Missing Out. As marketing professor Harry Shaefer (2019) says, 'We're so worried that by making one choice we'll miss out on another, that the choice we make never quite lives up to our expectations.' In theory, increased choice should intensify levels of satisfaction. In practice, it diminishes it.

E Consumers are clearly both attracted and put off by choice. This means that businesses must take care to offer a degree of choice which entices consumers but allows them to make a satisfactory decision without feeling that it involves too much effort.

4 a **Read the article *How to avoid choice overload*. In which paragraphs, A–D, can you find the arguments 1–4?**

1 When companies sell fewer products, consumers feel less overwhelmed.

2 When consumers know exactly what a product stands for by its label, they can make better choices.

3 Having too much choice can have an impact on a company's earnings.

4 Internet retailers can make choice less daunting by providing consumer-created advice.

How to avoid choice overload

A Choice overload occurs when consumers feel overwhelmed by the amount of choice they are given and this outweighs the benefits they may receive, such as greater individual responsibility. While researchers are still examining the impact of choice overload, I believe it could harm a business's profit margins. For that reason, it is something business leaders should take seriously.

B One way to eliminate choice overload and keep consumers happy is to reduce the number of lines a business offers. There can be a marked difference between the number of products that supermarkets offer, for example. One supermarket chain offers around 30,000 products compared to just 10,000 offered by a competitor. Similarly, if you examine one shelf of products in a supermarket, the choice can be staggering. 'There can be up to 30 different varieties of tomato ketchup in one store alone' says Mark Brownlow.

C Making a company's brand clear to consumers can also help. Branding helps consumers quickly become aware of what makes one product different to another. Is the ketchup organic? Are there any added ingredients? Does its flavour set it apart from the rest? When customers associate their brand with particular features and these features are clearly described on the packaging, they can make a quick and informed decision.

D Online retailers often offer consumers a lot more choice than bricks and mortar equivalents. However, they should consider whether their offering is indeed too much. Many say they avoid choice overload through customer reviews and search options, but this may not always be effective. A 2005 study found that few online purchasers write reviews.

E Consumer choice has grown exponentially over the last few decades. Businesses need to recognise that even more choice will become available in future, especially as we move business onto the internet more and more, and that this is an issue which will not go away. That's why we at Bigger Better Marketing are here to help.

b **Read the article again. Is the supporting evidence for each argument in paragraphs A–D effective? Use these questions to help you decide.**

1 Does it justify or exemplify the author's argument?

2 Is it sufficient?

3 Is up-to-date?

4 Is it from a reliable source?

c **Work in pairs and discuss the questions. Give reasons for your answers.**

1 Who is the author? Might he have any biases?

2 What conclusions do you think can be drawn from the author's arguments?

3 Do these match the author's conclusion? Is his conclusion logical?

4 How might you sum up the article overall?

4A Master your reading

› **Goal:** understand a narrative or biography
› **Focus:** recognising foreshadowing of events

Remarkable letters

The blog devoted to the lost art of letter writing.

Nobel Prize winner Richard Feynman's extraordinary letter to his wife.

1 In October 1946 Richard Feynman penned an extraordinary letter to his wife, Arline. In it, he wrote:

2 *It is such a terribly long time since I last wrote to you – almost two years but I know you'll excuse me because you understand how I am, stubborn and realistic; and I thought there was no sense to writing. But now I know my darling wife that it is right to do what I have delayed in doing, and that I have done so much in the past. I want to tell you I love you. I want to love you. I always will love you.*

3 The letter was extraordinary for two reasons. The first is that it was written by Richard Feynman, one of the most influential theoretical physicists in history. He revolutionised the fields of quantum mechanics and superfluidity and was a pioneer in quantum computing and nanotechnology. In 1965 he won the Nobel Prize for Physics and was voted by other eminent scientists as one of the ten greatest physicists of all time. Such a romantic letter from such a scientific mind is remarkable in itself, but the letter was extraordinary for another reason, too.

1 Work in pairs and discuss the questions.

1 When was the last time that you wrote a letter on paper (if ever)? Explain the circumstances.
2 Compare and contrast the experience of receiving a letter versus receiving an email.
3 Why is letter writing sometimes called 'a lost art'?

2 a Work in pairs. Read the first two paragraphs of the blog post and discuss the questions.

1 Why do you think it had been two years since Feynman last wrote?
2 Why might there be 'no sense in writing'?

b Quickly read the whole blog post and put the events in the correct order (1–5).

a ____________ Arline became ill.
b ____________ Richard won a Nobel Prize.
c ____________ Richard married Arline.
d ____________ Richard met Arline.
e ____________ Richard proposed to Arline.

3 Read the blog post again. Are the statements true (T) or false (F)? Which phrase or sentence supports your answer?

1 Richard changed how scientists understand certain subjects.
2 He grew up in New York.
3 From the moment she fell ill, Arline got steadily worse.
4 When Arline was diagnosed with TB, she was expected to remain seriously ill or die.
5 From 1600 to 1900, TB killed more people than all other illnesses combined.
6 For a while Richard told Arline that she would recover.
7 They married with the support of Richard's university.

4 Find words or phrases in the text with these meanings:

1 wrote (paragraph 1)
2 changed radically (paragraph 3)
3 someone who leads the way for others (paragraph 3)
4 well-known and respected (paragraph 3)
5 experienced or felt by two people towards each other (paragraph 4)
6 the likely outcome of a medical condition (paragraph 5)
7 convinced not to do something (paragraph 6)
8 failed to resist – or died – as a result of something negative happening to you (paragraph 8)

4 Richard met Arline in the 1930s at Far Rockway in his native New York. While he was a passionate scientist, she was a passionate philosopher and artist. At first suspicious of each other, they soon grew closer and their mutual respect grew too and while still a teenager he proposed to her and she accepted. They decided to wait to marry. As a brilliant young couple they appeared to have an incredibly bright future ahead of them, **but it was not to be**.

5 As World War II broke out, Arline suddenly fell ill. She experienced a variety of symptoms including swellings in her neck that came and went, violent fevers and a bad cough. She was hospitalised and began to recover but her recovery was short-lived and her symptoms returned. In 1941, at the age of twenty-one, she was diagnosed with tuberculosis. The **prognosis was bleak**.

6 Even today in the twenty-first century, tuberculosis (TB) still kills around 1.5 million people every year but it is easy to forget how much worse it used to be. From the beginning of the seventeenth century to the end of the nineteenth, TB killed more people than any other illness and took the lives of more people than all wars combined. In 1941 it was still incurable (there were no antibiotics at that time) and Richard realised that Arline's disease was probably fatal. Although he wanted to be open and honest with her, he was talked out of it by her parents and against his better judgement he agreed to tell her it was only a mild illness. **The deception couldn't last** and when Arline overheard her mother crying, Richard told her the truth. At the same moment he asked her again to marry him.

7 Getting married was not easy. Richard's parents were set against it and his university, where he was doing a PhD, threatened to withdraw his funding because they felt he should focus on his studies. Arline's health also deteriorated and she was moved to a sanatorium[1]. The couple, however, could not be dissuaded and in 1942, as war raged, they married. They asked two strangers to be their witnesses and no family or friends were present. Richard could only kiss Arline on the cheek for fear of infection. **Their marriage would not last long**.

8 Richard began working on a top secret military project but just as the war came to an end, Arline finally succumbed to her illness. She was just twenty-five years old. And that brings us to the second reason that the letter was so extraordinary …

[1] sanatorium – a place to care for the long-term ill, often patients with tuberculosis

5 a Work in pairs. What do you think is the second reason that the letter is extraordinary?

b Go to page 190 and read the last part of the blog post. Was your answer to Exercise 5a correct?

6 Work in pairs and discuss the questions.

1 Why do you think Richard needed to write the letter?

2 Do you agree with the strapline of the blog that letter writing is 'a lost art'? Why/Why not?

7 a Look at the sentences and phrases in bold in the blog post. What do they have in common? What is their purpose?

b Read the Focus box and check your answers to Exercise 7a.

Recognising foreshadowing of events

When we read a text, we are constantly making guesses about what is going to happen. Writers often help readers in this process by foreshadowing future events. They refer to future events without giving details about exactly what happened and how. This makes the reader wonder what exactly happened, why it happened, how it happened and so on.

… an incredibly bright future ahead of them, but it was not to be.

In 1941, at the age of twenty-one she was diagnosed with tuberculosis. The prognosis was bleak.

When reading, look out for foreshadowing and notice how it builds suspense and keeps you engaged with the story.

8 a Work in pairs. Read the extracts from a different blog post about Richard Feynman. What future events do you think the sections in bold foreshadow?

1 Feynman spoke with a thick Brooklyn accent and loved storytelling. He, more than anyone, was responsible for making physics popular, cool even, **something that was reflected after his death in Apple's *Think Different* advertising campaign**.

2 As a child, Feynman was curious and restless and also a bit of a troublemaker. He hated formality and boredom, and showed himself to be an independent mind who refused to bow before tradition, **a fact exemplified years later by his last words**.

b Go to page 182 to check your ideas.

9 Work in groups and discuss the questions.

1 Have you read any biographies or autobiographies of well-known people? If so, which ones? What did you think of them?

2 Which famous people would you like to read about? Why?

3 If someone were to write a biography about you, how would it begin?

5B Master your reading

› **Goal:** understand a story

› **Focus:** distinguishing between literal and allegorical meaning

1 **Work in pairs. What does the picture show? What do you think the hidden message is?**

2 a **Read the story and write a one-sentence summary. Work in pairs and compare your answers. Are they similar?**

b **Read the story again and answer the questions.**

1 What is the protagonist's reaction to the cabin on first sight?
2 What prompted the protagonist to go in search of the cabin?
3 How does the protagonist feel when seeing their reflection? Why?
4 Why didn't the protagonist return home after the first night away?
5 What kind of support did the hikers provide?
6 How do you think the protagonist felt about their reaction to the bear?
7 Did the protagonist feel they had selected the right path when faced with a choice?
8 What do you think the protagonist notices about their eyes?

c **Find words in the article that match definitions 1–12.**

1 in a way that comforts you (paragraph 1)
2 possibly not real; from a legend (paragraph 1)
3 boring because of always being the same (paragraph 2)
4 making you feel unhappy and dissatisfied (paragraph 2)
5 protect (paragraph 3)
6 spread over a surface carelessly or messily (paragraph 3)
7 the most important parts (paragraph 4)
8 when you imagine you can see or hear things which aren't really there (paragraph 5)
9 experienced (paragraph 6)
10 left quickly (paragraph 6)
11 the feeling that your abilities are not good enough (paragraph 7)
12 look quickly (paragraph 8)

1 I push open the door. It feels reassuringly heavy against my shoulder and creaks as it opens. The room it reveals is dark and I pause while my eyes adjust. When they do, I take in the cosy furniture and consider the 23 long days and nights it's taken me to find this fabled cabin. I can't help but feel both satisfied and disheartened.

2 I think back to the first time I'd heard about this place. 'It's meant to be incredible,' my cousin had said. 'No one knows exactly where it is, but if you find it, you're allowed to stay there as long as you want. Everyone who managed to get there all came back a changed person.' Having been numbed by the monotony of life, something about the mystery and promise of the cabin called to me. One survival course later, I left my unfulfilling job, stuffed what I thought I'd need into a backpack and headed out towards the lush mountains in search of something more.

3 Back in the present, I walk across the room and look out of the tiny window. The tall pines packed densely outside shield the cabin from the world. Only the name on the door revealed this as my destination. I enter the tiny bathroom, turning on the dim light above the mirror and look at myself. Dirt smeared across my face, hair tangled. It's a face I have a hard time recognising.

4 I remember the first day of my trip and how smooth and pale my skin was; how green my skills were. I knew the basics, but nothing can prepare you for putting up a tent in pitch black with a 40 mph gale. I'd woken up the next day soaking wet and with the tent in the branches of a nearby tree, flapping about as if asking me to join it. I'd almost given in and gone home, but I couldn't face the 'I told you so' I'd get, so I kept going. The intrigue of what I might find at the cabin helping me.

5 A week later, I woke up sick as a dog and lay for two days in my tent trembling, hallucinating and falling in and out of consciousness. As I lay shivering, my stomach cramping, dark shadows passed over the tent. I was convinced they were hooded figures in dark cloaks coming for me, but eventually they disappeared and so did my fever. That day, two hikers stopped by my tent. They cooked me dinner and this act of support gave me the strength to continue.

6 On day 10 of my explorations, I finally encountered the thing I feared the most – a bear. I'd heard cautionary tales and was prepared, but you never know how you'll react to such a situation in reality. Luckily, as soon as I saw it rear up, instinct kicked in and I whipped my bear spray out and pressed down the button. The bear took one smell and fled.

7 By day 16, I was beginning to think I'd never find the cabin. The path I was on suddenly forked. Paralysed with indecision, I went from one to the other and back again until I realised that any decision was better than none. I went left and forced myself not to look back, despite the tickle in the back of my mind filling me with self-doubt. The path didn't take me to the cabin, but I'm not sure the other one would have either. I pushed on with urgency, barely even stopping to enjoy the breath-taking views. Finally, after another seven days I came across my destination.

8 I examine the cabin behind me in the mirror. It's nice but I'm puzzled about how this place is supposed to change me. I glance back at my reflection and lean in. I reach up to touch the wrinkles embedded around my eyes, and notice the scratches across my hands. I look back at my eyes and see what lies behind them. Then, I smile.

3 a Read the Focus box and answer the questions about *The Quest*.

b Use your answers to Exercise 3a to help you work out *The Quest's* allegorical meaning. Compare your ideas with a partner.

Distinguishing between literal and allegorical meaning

An allegory is a part of a story or a whole story which has a hidden meaning. A story may have literal meaning e.g. the devastation that happens when a storm hits, and an allegorical meaning e.g. the devastation caused by war. Allegories usually highlight a social or political issue or convey a moral message. Sometimes, they represent a historical event. While the exact allegorical meaning can be debatable, we can ask these questions to help identify it:

1 What message does the story try to convey in its literal meaning?
2 Does the story relate to events or trends in the real world, either now or historically?
3 Can the characters, locations and other things in the story be related to these real life events or trends?
4 How might the actions in the story mirror real life (past or present)?

c Which of these do you think best matches the hidden meaning in *The Quest*?

1 We should always take care of our environment.
2 It's the journey that's important, not the destination.
3 Adventure should be everyone's goal in life.

4 Work in pairs. What do you think events 1–8 might represent in the story?

1 the cabin
2 the tent experience
3 the fever experience
4 the shadows outside the tent
5 the hikers
6 the bear experience
7 the forked path
8 the protagonist's wrinkles and scratches

5 Read the story summaries below. They give the story's literal meaning. What do you think their allegorical meanings are?

- *Moby Dick* tells the story of one man's desperate, failed attempts to catch and kill a giant whale.
- The *Tortoise and the Hare* is about a failed attempt by a hare to win an unequal race with a tortoise.
- *Lord of the Flies* tells the story of a group of boys stranded on a desert island and their failed attempts to create a society and survive.
- *The Hunger Games* tells the story of a wealthy capital city which forces neighbouring districts to give up one boy or girl to compete in a televised show where they compete to be the last to survive.

6B Master your reading

› **Goal:** understand an article on finance

› **Focus:** refining understanding of word meaning

1 a Read the personal finance question and the two bank adverts. Then answer the question.

TEST YOUR FINANCIAL KNOW-HOW

You have £5,000 and you want to save it in a bank account for two years. Which account is better for you?

Open an account online in minutes.
Free luxury pen and diary when you open an account.
Putting your money first.
* on first £1,000; 0.5% thereafter.

ABC BANK

Open a **Super Saver savings account** and earn up to 5% interest* p.a.

Introducing the **SMART SAVER** savings account

[XYZ Bank]

- 2% interest p.a. on all savings.
- Open an account online or in branch.
- You can trust us with your money.

b Work in pairs and compare your answers. Then check on page 191.

2 a Read the introduction to the personal finance blog. What is 'financial illiteracy'? Choose the correct answer(s).

Not knowing enough about:

1 how much we earn from our savings and how much we spend.
2 how our money is invested and how we can invest it elsewhere.
3 how much our bills are and why they are so high.

b Work in pairs. Decide on the approximate meaning of each word or phrase in bold in the blog. Avoid asking someone or checking in a dictionary. What clues help you decide on an approximate meaning?

I think 'rate of return' has something to do with savings and how much money you get from them.

3 a Think of three pieces of advice about how to manage your finances that you expect the blog to give.

b Read the rest of the blog. Did it give the advice you expected?

THE THREE KEY SKILLS OF FINANCIAL LITERACY

Let's face it, most of us are financially illiterate. We don't really know what [1]**rate of return** we're getting on our savings because we assume we're still getting the now-expired [2]**headline rate**. We don't really know what our monthly expenses are or whether our salary even covers them. Many of us don't even know what our current [3]**bank balance** is. Rather than [4]**pay up front**, we buy our beloved shiny new objects on [5]**instalment plans** that involve a small [6]**down payment**, but we don't know what the real interest rate is and hence how long it will take to repay the [7]**principal**. As a result, some of us end up [8]**defaulting** on our loans. We are, in short, not clued up enough. So, to drag ourselves out of this state, here are the three key financial skills we need to develop.

1 Be Saving Savvy

It's advisable to put a bit of money aside every month, even if it's only a small portion of your salary. In a world where small actions over a long period provide big results, getting into the saving habit early on is the best thing you can do, and the first rule of choosing a savings account is: don't fall for the headline rate. It's easy to be tempted by promises of a high rate of return, but look carefully and you will see that that interest rate only applies to a certain portion of your money or for a certain period of time, or perhaps it contains the words 'up to' which means you may not get the full rate being advertised. Work it out and you will usually see that the headline rate is there to mask a much lower interest rate that applies to the rest of your savings. So always do your homework and make sure that you choose an account based on the real interest rate rather than the headline rate.

2 Be a Smarter Spender

Saving for a rainy day is obviously a lot better than spending on things you can't afford, but if you do have to make a major purchase, you need to be savvy about how you pay. Paying by instalments can be an expensive option, particularly those instalment plans which involve making a small initial down payment and then paying off the principal (plus interest of course) over a long period of time. These schemes with their high rates can be damaging to our bank balance, and it's not uncommon for people to default on their loans (paying by instalments is essentially the same as taking out a loan) because they didn't realise the true cost. Much better to pay up front if at all possible, but if you've decided to borrow, for example on your credit card, then rule number one is only borrow if you have a realistic repayment plan in place. Hoping that things will work out is equivalent to hoping that your fairy godmother will appear and repay the loan for you. She won't and without a plan, things rarely work themselves out.

3 Be Brilliant at Budgeting

According to certain sources, less than half of all adults follow a budget. This means that most people don't know how much they can spend each month because they don't know how much they have available to spend, or to put it another way, they lack the most basic financial literacy. Imagine a person getting into a car and starting to drive without having any idea of where they are going or how much petrol is in the tank. Most of us would regard this as a sign that someone is a few slices short of a loaf, but when it comes to personal finance it seems to be standard behaviour. Instead, calculate your monthly expenses and then assign the remaining amount to various budgets, for example, savings, holidays, going out, clothes, etc. Then keep a regular eye on your bank balance to check that you are keeping within budget.

Have you got more personal finance tips? Add them to the comments below.

4 a Underline the phrase *rate of return* in section 1 of the blog, *Be Saving Savvy*. What do we learn about the connotation and collocations of this phrase?

b Read the Focus box and check your answer.

Refining understanding of word meaning

The first time we meet a new word or phrase, we can usually make a rough guess as to the meaning. This rough guess is usually enough to allow us to keep reading. When we meet that word or phrase again, we can refine our understanding by noticing context, collocations and connotations.

For example, in the first paragraph we read:

*We don't really know what **rate of return** we're getting on our savings.*

From this we understand that *rate of return*:

- comes from our savings.
- collocates with *get*.
- is generally connected to finance.

In the rest of the blog we read:

*It's easy to be tempted by promises of a high **rate of return**.*

This sentence tells us more about the phrase. We learn that it:

- has a positive connotation (because it is 'tempting').
- collocates with *high* (and hence probably with *low*).

Working with a rough understanding at first and refining it over time allows us to read more fluently and widely.

5 a Phrases 1–8 from the introduction also reappear in the rest of the blog. Find the phrases and underline them.

b What new information about context, collocation and connotation do you learn for each phrase?

So a high 'rate of return' is an attractive thing because you can be tempted by it. It collocates with 'high' and probably 'low'.

6 Read the blog again and answer the questions.

1 In your own words, explain the three ways in which a savings account headline rate might be misleading.
2 What is often the purpose of the savings headline rate, according to the writer?
3 What is preferable to paying by instalments?
4 What must you have if you borrow on your credit card?
5 What is the most basic financial literacy, according to the writer?
6 How do you ensure that you are not exceeding your budget?

7 Work in groups and discuss the questions.

1 How can people's financial literacy be improved?
2 What are some of the reasons people often go into debt?
3 What is the government's role in helping people to avoid debt?

7B Master your reading

› **Goal:** understand correspondence
› **Focus:** identifying a writer's tone

1 Work in pairs. What do you do when you receive emails that offer you the chance to earn a lot of money? Why?

2 a Read David's email. What do you notice about his tone?

Attention Kindest Sir!
My name is David Richards and I am an expert in family law at Thomas and Associates here on one of the glorious islands of the Bahamas.
It is with deepest regret that I inform you that our client and your dearest relative passed away here in March. As she did not complete a Will prior to her death, we must find out who her nearest living relatives are. We have hunted the entire Earth high and low and can now be sure that you are the only living benefactor of our client's crazy wealth of $2.5m. However, before we are able to hand over the money to you, you must contact us so that we may ensure this is organised lawfully.
I strongly suggest you do this AT ONCE.
Message me immediately.
David Richards
Attorney at law
Email: davidrichardslaw@email.eu

b Read Michael's reply below and the Focus box, then answer the questions.

1 How would you describe the tone of Michael's reply?
2 Does Michael's reply surprise you in any way? Why/Why not?
3 What do you think will happen next?

Dear David,
Well, that came out of the blue. $2.5m eh? Woo hoo! I was not expecting that. Of course, I'm very sad to hear that my relative has died. Who was it? My great aunt Bessie? Always knew she was squirrelling away lots of money under her mattress the cheeky old girl. Had no idea she was in the Bahamas though.
OK, so let's get the ball rolling then. What happens next?
Yours excitedly,
Michael

Identifying a writer's tone

A writer can adopt many different tones to convey their attitude, e.g. apologetic, critical, frustrated, light-hearted, pessimistic, sarcastic, serious. To identify a writer's tone, we can look at their choice of language e.g. their choice of vocabulary, their level of formality and the grammatical structures they use.

*It is with **deepest regret that I inform you** that …* (formal, sympathetic)

*… we **may ensure this is organised** lawfully.* (formal, serious)

Woo hoo! (informal, joyful)

… let's get the ball rolling. (informal, light-hearted)

*(I) Always knew she was **squirrelling away** lots of money …* (informal, humorous)

In some situations (e.g. spam emails), inconsistencies in tone might be an indication that the writer is not who they say they are.

*I am an expert in family law at Thomas and Associates **here on one of the glorious islands of the Bahamas**.* (informality of the words in bold are inconsistent with the formality of the first part of the sentence).

3 Look at the sentences below and decide if they are formal (F), informal (I) or a mix of both (M).

1 Hi! I am writing with regard to an opportunity you may wish to take advantage of.
2 With the greatest respect, I do not feel that it would be advisable to accept this offer.
3 Sorry I haven't got back to you, I've been all over the place this week.
4 I would appreciate it if you could get a move on with sending the information.
5 The recently deceased king was a lovely old chap.
6 Had I been aware of the situation, I would have made efforts to rectify the issues.
7 I've got to get my head down at work for a bit. Talk to you soon.

4 a **Read the rest of the email correspondence between David and Michael. Is David successful in helping Michael claim the money?**

[1]**Dearest Michael,**
I was very happy to get your email and again, I am sorry for your loss. Yes, it was your great aunt Bessie. She was a very sweet lady.
So, there are loads of laws that try to stop you from getting the money, but [2]**the GOOD NEWS is that it is not too difficult with me if you allow me to help you**. If you send me $5000, I can get through all of the red tape and collect the inheritance on your behalf, after which I will of course forward it onto you. I should say that by law here I keep 10% of the inheritance as my fee. [3]**Please send the money to my bank account (details attached) AS SOON AS POSSIBLE. We cannot delay**.

David

Dear David,
THANK YOU FOR YOUR EMAIL. Phew, $5000. It's not easy to get that kind of money when you're just a lowly office assistant like me. I've put together all my life savings, including coins from the back of the sofa, but [4]**it's hopeless. I just don't have enough**. Unless I can send you my stamp collection. Some of those stamps cost me an arm and a leg when I was a kid. I'm sure you'll find worth in them.

Michael

Dearest Michael,
I think you have got the wrong end of the stick. [5]**I need MONEY not stamps. Stamps can't help me at all**. Please send the MONEY as soon as possible.

David

You seem awfully keen on getting the money fast, David. But you see, it's a bit of a problem. I wanna send you the MONEY but I just don't have that sorta cash. How about if I spend the savings I do have flying out to the Bahamas next week? Then, I can help you fill out all the paperwork and save you the bother of doing it all yourself. You'll still get your 10% so we'll both be in the money. [6]**Hurrah!** Seems like a fair solution to me.

Michael

Dearest Michael,
[7]**I assure you that my keenness is simply to get you the money, no more**. You see, you must transfer the funds to me before the end of this week, or the government will claim the inheritance. Any delay at your end is simply reducing or getting rid of any chance of obtaining the money. To cut a long story short, inheritances must be claimed by benefactors within six months of death or the money reverts to the government. Six months ends on Friday.

David

Dear David,
Well, ain't that a pain in the neck. Strange you didn't mention that before. Still, GOOD NEWS! My boss has given me the rest of the week off so I'm gonna get on a plane tonight. I dunno exactly when I'll get there, but I'll come straight to your offices so that we can get cracking on the paperwork and submit it by the end of the week.
[8]**I know it won't be easy, but I also know I'll be in safe hands with you**.
Looking forward to putting a face to your name. Until tomorrow!

Michael

Hello David, are you there? Hello? Anyone there?

b **Match the parts of the correspondence 1–8 with the writer's tone a–h.**

- **a** urgent
- **b** mock joy
- **c** frustration
- **d** optimistic
- **e** affectionate
- **f** mock appreciation
- **g** mock pessimism
- **h** defensive

5 a **Look at the different tones that David uses in Exercise 4b. How might they help him achieve his goal?**

Urgent - push Michael into action before he realises it's a con

b **Find at least four inconsistencies in tone which suggest David is not authentic.**

Dearest Michael (not a formal greeting)

6 a **Answer the questions.**

1. Why does David put some words in capital letters?
2. Why does Michael do the same in his emails?
3. What do you think Michael's intention is in responding to David in the way that he does?
4. At what point do you think David suspects that Michael is suspicious of his intentions?

b **Find words and phrases in the emails in this lesson that match definitions 1–10.**

1. was very unexpected
2. get started (x2)
3. bureaucracy – official rules that seem unnecessary
4. were very expensive
5. misunderstood
6. avoid involving someone in pointless work
7. goes back to
8. inconvenient

7 **Work in pairs. Do you think it is ever a good idea to respond to a scammer? Why/Why not?**

8A Master your reading

› **Goal:** understand an authentic novel

› **Focus:** recognising humour

1 a When you read a novel or watch a film, what sort of main characters do you prefer? Choose from the list of adjectives in the box.

charismatic competent cowardly cynical eccentric flawed heroic impatient incompetent ordinary self-aware virtuous

b Work in pairs. Who is your favourite main character from a novel or film? Describe him or her to your partner.

2 Read the extract from *The Colour of Memory* by Geoff Dyer, a novel set in London in the 1980s. Choose words from Exercise 1a to describe the main character.

In the novel the protagonist recounts details of his daily life in London in the 1980s. Here he is talking about his unreliable car.

I couldn't go out in it without getting lost and I couldn't get lost without losing my temper in sympathy. I often lost my temper almost as soon as I'd folded myself into the driving seat – only a few seconds after it had broken down, in other words. The only time it didn't break down was when it wouldn't start.

As luck would have it, on the night of Fran's visit it was working perfectly – so perfectly that the kids who stole it made barely a sound as they drove off. I must have only missed them by five minutes, which is a shame because I would like to have thanked them personally.

While I got changed, Fran went down to get the A-Z[1] to work out where we were heading. When we left the house a few minutes later the car was gone. It's odd, that elusive sense of non-presence when something just disappears. It takes time to establish that something's not there and for a couple of minutes we paced up and down the street as if the car had just been mislaid – Fran even peered beneath another parked car as though it had rolled under there like a lost coin. Maybe the car was around somewhere and we couldn't see it. Maybe it had never been there. Maybe it was somewhere else.

'It's been stolen,' said Fran eventually and we set off for Brixton police station to report it. Only a few minutes from the house we ran into a policeman who put out an APB on the missing vehicle. I started to explain that it was unlikely that the culprits could travel more than a couple of miles in it …

[1] *An A-Z is a map in a book form.*

3 Read the extract again. Are the statements true (T), false (F) or not mentioned (NM)? Correct the false statements.

1 On the evening of the theft, the narrator lost his temper because the car broke down.
2 The car broke down a lot because it was very old.
3 The narrator found the people who stole his car and thanked them.
4 Fran looked for the car under another car.
5 The police caught the thieves.

4 a Work in pairs and discuss the questions.

1 Did you find the novel extract humorous?
2 Do you think it was intended to be humorous?
3 If so, what makes the extract humorous?

b Read the Focus box and check your answers to Question 3 in Exercise 4a.

Recognising humour

The humour in the novel extracts comes from a variety of techniques including irony, understatement and the techniques below.

Upturned expectations

The author tells us the opposite of what we were expecting.

I must have only missed them by five minutes which is a shame because I would like to have thanked them personally.

Repetition

Repetition is one of the cornerstones of humour and here the author repeats certain words and phrases to create a humorous effect.

*I couldn't go out in it without **getting lost** and I couldn't **get lost** without **losing my temper** in sympathy. I often **lost my temper**…*

Amusing comparisons

Actions or events are compared to other actions or events in an amusing way.

*Fran even peered beneath another parked car **as though it had rolled under there like a lost coin**.*

5 a **Read a later extract from the same novel. Answer the questions.**

1. What make and model of car did Fran arrive in?
2. Who lent Fran the car?
3. What was Fran not allowed to do with the car?
4. What difference does the narrator describe between himself and Fran?

Fran came round the next day in an expensive-looking car. I didn't know what model it was and she wasn't sure either. 'I think it's called a Vauxhall Courgette or something like that,' she said, kicking one of the front tyres as if to suggest casual familiarity with the world of pistons, cross-plys and sump oil.

'Whose car is it?' I asked as we hummed noiselessly past the new riot-proof[2] Tesco's on Acre Lane – it had the look of a place which could be air-lifted out to neutral Vauxhall[3] in under fifteen minutes in the event of trouble.

'It belongs to the guy who goes out with Sal in my house. He lent it to her and she lent it to me on the strict condition that I don't have a prang in it. Apparently, that's what motorists call an accident: a prang.'

Fran wore her glasses to drive. They had big plastic frames that made her look almost comically scholarly. She clutched the wheel like she was steering a ship in heavy weather. We moved very slowly in dense traffic; I groaned, complained and swore but Fran, showing no sign of irritation, tapped the steering wheel to the rhythm of a pop song that played on the radio. Over the years my own impatience had become so extreme that I was in danger of becoming incapable of enjoying anything: every activity was an obstacle to the next. This accelerating impatience had nothing to do with being late or in a hurry; it was a condition not a response. I was even in a hurry when I had nothing to do.

I blame my father. As kids we often used to go for holidays in the car. Our father drove incredibly slowly and every time someone overtook us he would say: 'Ooh, he's in a hurry'. It used to drive me crazy, but Fran would continue looking out of the window and sucking her boiled sweet. (I'd already chewed and swallowed mine.)

[2] *In the early 1980s there were riots in Brixton, where the protagonist lives*

[3] *There were no riots in Vauxhall which is an area close-by*

b **Underline examples in the extract above of the humorous techniques listed in the Focus box.**

6 **What is the author inferring in the phrases in bold?**

1. ... almost as soon as I'd **folded myself** into the driving seat
   - a The car is small.
   - b The car is not modern.
   - c The driving seat needs to be repaired.
2. [Fran was] kicking one of the front tyres **as if to suggest casual familiarity with** the world of [cars].
   - a Fran knew the car well and liked it.
   - b Fran didn't really know much about cars.
   - c Fran was an expert on cars.
3. '**Apparently** that's what motorists call an accident: a prang' [said Fran].
   - a Fran didn't consider herself a motorist.
   - b Fran had never had an accident.
   - c Fran was an experienced driver.
4. Fran would continue looking out of the window and sucking her boiled sweet. (**I'd already chewed and swallowed mine**.)
   - a The author liked boiled sweets more than Fran.
   - b The author disliked boiled sweets.
   - c The author was very impatient.

7 **Work in pairs. Read the extracts from *The Hitch Hiker's Guide to the Galaxy* by Douglas Adams and answer the questions.**

1. Which extract do you find funnier? Why?
2. What techniques does Douglas Adams use to create humour?
3. Would you prefer to read the whole of *The Colour of Memory* or *The Hitch Hiker's Guide to the Galaxy*? Why?

'You know,' said Arthur, 'it's at times like this, when I'm trapped in a Vogon airlock with a man from Betelgeuse, and about to die of asphyxiation in deep space that I really wish I'd listened to what my mother told me when I was young.'
'Why, what did she tell you?'
'I don't know, I didn't listen.'

'So this is it,' said Arthur, 'We are going to die.'
'Yes,' said Ford, 'except... no! Wait a minute!' He suddenly lunged across the chamber at something behind Arthur's line of vision. 'What's this switch?' he cried.
'What? Where?' cried Arthur, twisting round.
'No, I was only fooling,' said Ford, 'we are going to die after all'.

9C Master your reading

› **Goal:** understand arguments in a newspaper article

› **Focus:** identifying flaws in an argument

Conservation: WHAT IS THE WAY FORWARD?

We only have one world

There's only one argument when it comes to the concept of conserving our planet and protecting endangered species, and that's the simple fact that it's our duty. **1After all, it's our fault that species have become extinct.** Chemical fertilisers have reduced the number of insects responsible for pollination; farming and urbanisation have led to a loss of habitat for many species, and the demand for materials such as ivory has been responsible for an increase in hunting. All of these activities have caused thousands of species to be lost over the last century, and continue to wreak havoc on our world.

2Maintaining a balanced eco-system is a goal for all of us. When endangered animal and plant species face extinction, that balance is seriously affected, and biodiversity is reduced. It is our duty to ourselves and to future generations to prevent this from happening. While we cannot completely eradicate our impact on the world due to our need for natural resources to survive, we can work towards using those resources in as sustainable a way as possible, so that we, and other species, can survive.

It's not just the planet that we risk when we live unsustainably. We also risk our own health. Without nature, we don't have access to oxygen, clean water or the food we need to sustain us. When habitats are lost and animals are forced to live closer together, diseases spread more quickly across species and humans are also endangered. Nature provides us with the medicines we need to combat existing and potential future diseases. When nature dies, our hope for medicinal cures die, too.

Admittedly, conservation is costly but taking care of our planet is not something we should ever put a price on. **3Those people who say that conservation is too expensive care only about economics.** There's no point making lots of money if we have no planet to provide for us. **4Making conservation our main priority and protecting all living things is the only way we can ensure a sustainable planet for future generations. If we don't do that, we may as well just not bother.**

1 Work in pairs. Do you agree or disagree with the statements? Why?

'Conservation is a never-ending endeavour.'

'Taking care of a forest is like looking after your well-being.'

'The key to a sustainable future is the balance between nature and industry.'

'Nature can look after itself.'

2 a Read the article *We only have one world* quickly. What is the author's main point?

b Read the article again. Which of statements 1–5 does the author state or imply?

1 Animal extinction over the last century is down to human activity.
2 Humans are able to have zero impact on our planet.
3 Urbanisation can cause epidemics among species.
4 The life expectancy of a human will increase with greater conservation.
5 Providing funding for only some conservation is pointless.

3 **Read the Focus box. Then decide which flaws exist in arguments 1–4 in the article.**

Identifying flaws in an argument

When reading an author's point of view, it is important to be able to identify any flaws in their argument in order to evaluate its effectiveness. Here are some common flaws in logic.

Hasty generalisations

An author makes overgeneralisations or assumptions that cannot be supported by evidence.

People only care about themselves.

Faulty cause and effect

An author states a cause which does not guarantee the effect they claim.

Without the use of chemicals in farming, insect life would flourish.

Either/or

An author suggests there are two options when there are actually further possibilities.

Either conservationists protect all animals, or they protect none.

Personal attacks

An author personally attacks another author rather than attack that author's arguments, or they attack an argument that another author hasn't actually made simply because it's easy to criticise and makes their argument look stronger.

Only someone who has no understanding of animal conservation would suggest such action.

4 a **Read the article *Making harsh decisions*. What is the writer's overall view on conservation?**

MAKING HARSH DECISIONS

Conservation is an issue which may appear clear cut to some but is actually a very challenging, complex issue. On the one hand, we are fully aware that we need to protect nature from harm in order for us to be able to survive here on Earth for generations to come. On the other hand, we have limited financial resources. It has been estimated that we need $76.1bn to protect all endangered species – every single year. This amount is simply not sustainable and requires us to prioritise.

The first thing we need to do is recognise our true role in extinction. We all feel responsible when we hear about animals in danger of becoming extinct, and extinctions have increased over the last hundred years, possibly hundredfold. However, animal species die with or without human interference. It's predicted that 99.9% of all creatures which have lived on Earth have died out. Species therefore come and species go, and it is a natural part of life. We need to focus our efforts on preventing our impact on biodiversity from getting worse, and protecting already affected species whose extinction would jeopardise the planet and our existence on it.

Prioritising means making harsh decisions. Cute animals which attract donations are unlikely to be at the top of the protect list. It would be distressing to see pandas and gorillas go, but if they did become extinct, the impact to us would be minimal to non-existent, whereas the loss of other creatures would be far more devastating. Insects which cross-pollinate crops, for example, must be saved to enable food sources to grow, and squiggly worm-like creatures that live underground may be ugly, but they may also hold the key to cures to currently incurable diseases.

It is understandable that conservationists want to rescue as many species as possible, but they are led by their hearts and not their heads. In a context where it simply isn't possible to save them all, making priorities is the only way forward.

b **Find these points in the article and decide if there are any logical flaws in them.**

1 limited financial resources
2 feeling guilty about losing species
3 prioritising animals which we need
4 how conservationists make decisions about conservation

5 **Work in pairs. How effective do you think these solutions might be in protecting nature in the future? Outline the pros and cons of each.**

- Eat insects to reduce the need to cut down forests to create farmland.
- Introduce laws to ban further urbanisation in industrialised countries.
- Measure the success of a country by things other than economic growth.
- Increase punishment for people who kill wildlife illegally.
- Work towards the reforestation of industrialised countries.
- Add a high tax to all products which are made with unsustainable products or processes.

10c Master your reading

› **Goal:** understand an article
› **Focus:** understanding metaphors

1 a What are the English mistakes (or mistakes according to some people) in pictures A–F?
A – 'breath' is a noun. The correct spelling of the verb is 'breathe'.

b Which 'mistakes' do you find most serious or annoying?

c Are there grammatical or spelling mistakes in your own language which annoy you? If so, explain the mistake and why it annoys you.

2 a Read the article. Which pictures illustrate 'mistakes' 1–3?

b Complete the details below for each mistake.
1 the mistake
2 the rule
3 arguments against the rule

A

B

LANGUAGE WARS:

the greatest linguistic spats of all time

Words are ever evolving – but not without controversy. From creative applications of an apostrophe to the overuse of 'literally', what makes you rage?

What is it about language that gets people so hot under the collar? That drives them to spend hours arguing with strangers on the internet, to go around correcting misspelt signs in the dead of night, or even to threaten acts of violence? The languages we speak are central to our sense of self, so it is not surprising that their finer points can become [1]**a battleground**. Passionate feelings about what's right and wrong extend from the use of 'disinterested' to when and when not to use an apostrophe. Here are some of the most memorable rows, spats and controversies.

1 Apostrophe catastrophe

A so-called 'grammar vigilante' has been correcting shop fronts in Bristol, England, for more than a decade. His pet peeve is the confusion of plain old plurals with possessives, which in English are usually marked by an apostrophe followed by an *s*. Confronted with a sign advertising 'Amy's Nail's', he will [2]**obliterate** the second apostrophe with a sticker. Addressing the potentially illegal nature of his mission in a BBC report, he said: 'It's more of a crime that the apostrophe is wrong in the first place'. Linguist Rob Drummond disagrees: 'Fetishising the apostrophe as if its rules are [3]**set in stone**,' he writes, 'and then fostering an environment in which it is acceptable to take pleasure in uncovering other people's linguistic insecurities is not OK.'

2 Are you really disinterested?

Use this word at your own risk. If what you want to say is 'lacking in interest' then brace yourself, because there's [4]**an army of people** who will point out that it should be 'uninterested', and that 'disinterested' must mean 'impartial'. They are sticklers for what they regard as the correct meaning, and have taken up columnist William Safire's command to '[5]**rear up and rage**, against the dying of an enlightening distinction'. The problem is that if a word is more frequently used to mean one thing than another, then that's effectively what it means: you can't fight a linguistic consensus. The news for pedants gets worse, however. The OED tells us that the use of 'disinterested' to mean not interested or unconcerned has been around since at least the seventeenth century, used by no less a stylist than the poet John Donne.

3 Splitting hairs

You may have been told that it's bad to split your infinitives in English – that you should never put anything between 'to' and the verb – meaning a sentence like: 'She wanted to fully support him' would be wrong. This was certainly a tenet of prescriptive works (like Strunk and White's *The Elements of Style*) and classroom instruction for much of the twentieth century. But the *Chicago Manual of Style* dropped its objection in 1983, and there are relatively few pedants now [6]**prepared to die on a hill** to keep the infinitive [7]**joined in matrimony**. The origins of the 'rule' are [8]**shrouded in mystery**, with perhaps its earliest appearance in an 1803 grammar guide. But in reality, English speakers have been splitting their infinitives for hundreds of years. For an edict that's never been properly observed, it has loomed surprisingly large in the grammatical consciousness.

3 **Read the article again and answer the questions.**

1. What reason does the writer offer for why language can make people so angry?
2. What justification does the grammar vigilante give for his actions?
3. Why does Rob Drummond dislike the vigilante's actions?
4. What is the linguistic consensus regarding 'uninterested' and 'disinterested'?
5. What do we learn about John Donne's reputation?
6. What kind of books used to insist on not splitting the infinitive?

4 a **Work in pairs. Look at metaphor number 4 in the article. What is the effect of describing a group of people in this way?**

b **Read the Focus box and check your answer.**

Understanding metaphors

A metaphor is a way of talking about one thing as though it is something completely different in order to make a point or to paint a more vivid picture.

*There's an **army of people** who will point out that it should be 'uninterested'*

This metaphor compares a group of people to an army (metaphors don't use *as* or *like*). It helps us to understand:

- the size of the group.
- their common commitment to an idea.
- their willingness to act strongly to defend the idea.

Some metaphors continue for several sentences. These are called 'extended metaphors'.

'All the world's a stage,
And all the men and women merely players;
They have their exits and their entrances ...'

(*As You Like It*, William Shakespeare)

There is no clear distinction between metaphors and expressions and often a phrase can be both. For example, to say *she's a bubbly character* is both a metaphor and an expression.

5 **Match metaphors 1–8 in bold in the text with meanings a–h.**

- **a** unclear or unknown
- **b** a large group of people committed to an idea
- **c** destroy
- **d** connected to each other
- **e** can never change
- **f** willing to argue over something whatever the cost and to never compromise
- **g** a subject that people fight over
- **h** protest

6 **What is the metaphor in these extracts and why do you think the author used it?**

1. 'But soft, what light through yonder window breaks? It is the east, and Juliet is the sun!' (*Romeo and Juliet*, William Shakespeare)
2. 'Let us be grateful to people who make us happy, they are the charming gardeners who make our souls blossom.' (*Les Plaisirs et Les Jours* Marcel Proust)
3. 'When love beckons to you, follow him, Though his ways are hard and steep.' (*On Love* Khalil Gibran)

7 **Choose two of these things and think of a metaphor to describe them.**

1. your life
2. learning English
3. the youth of today
4. traffic

My life is a rollercoaster ride. It's exciting with its ups and downs but sometimes it makes me feel ill.

1A Master your writing

Goal: write a blog post

Focus: using hyperbole to enhance impact

1 a Look at pictures A–D. Put the experiences in the order of most irritating (1) to least irritating (4).

b Work in pairs and compare your ideas. What other experiences do you find irritating?

2 a Read the blog post and answer the questions.

1 Who is the writer talking to?
2 What is his main point?
3 How does he make this point?

b Read the blog post again. Are the statements about the writer true (T) or false (F)?

1 He understood his manager's selection of the new skill to learn.
2 He says that he had previously very much enjoyed dancing in front of people.
3 He feels his relationship with his partner has been permanently damaged.
4 He suggests that lunch was an organised event.
5 He felt that time passed in the afternoon at the same speed it had in the morning.
6 His manager asked him to sit out of the final activity.
7 He enjoyed listening to his colleagues' views of him.
8 He believes that the team-building day had an impact on the team.

3 Which techniques does the writer use to make the post engaging and/or dramatic?

1 using rhetorical questions
2 complimenting the reader
3 exaggerating the quantity of things
4 saying something is worse than it is
5 using rhyme

A

B

MAKE A TEAM? MORE LIKE BREAK A TEAM

Dear Managers everywhere,

I know that managing a team isn't straightforward and you're endeavouring to do the best you can. Your team can sometimes be unaccommodating, fall out over the most trivial of things or just plain refuse to cooperate. When that happens, you definitely need to step in and take action. But let me tell you something – nothing, and I mean NOTHING, can break a team more than a team-building day. And here's why.

Last month, my team manager decided my co-workers and I lacked cohesion as a team, so she organised a team-building day. It got off to a flying start with coffee and doughnuts at a high-class hotel. **1 However, it was soon transformed into our worst nightmare**. The first part of the day was dedicated to acquiring a new skill. For some reason known only to herself, our manager had decided that dancing would be that skill. As someone completely lacking in any sense of rhythm, my heart literally stopped at the prospect. Except for a few obligatory and extremely awkward moves on the dance floor at weddings, I'd never actually danced in public before. Not only that, but I was paired with the most naturally gifted dancer ever to grace the dance floor. Lucky me.

For hours, I slipped and stumbled through the routines, breaking all my partner's toes in the process and **2 apologising a million times**. I felt like we'd got on before the team-building day. Now I felt sure we'd never speak again.

Lunch was a welcome respite. I was both parched and ravenous. However, we were led to the kitchen and instructed to conjure up our own meal in some kind of collaborative exercise. Let me tell you that it was less collaboration and more like a free for all for starving animals. I ended up with a few wilted lettuce leaves and one tomato.

My body ached where I didn't know I even had muscles, so I was glad to hear that the afternoon activity would involve sitting down. That delight didn't last long. For 90 interminable minutes, we sat cross legged on the floor in a circle, holding hands as part of a group meditation activity. The room was sweltering at around two hundred degrees and **3 sweat dripped from our hands like a leaking tap**. Nice. Within the first three seconds, my legs had died and I could no longer feel below my knee. Relaxation? More like torture.

The final activity was the icing on the cake. We all had to tell each other something we didn't like about them. That's right – didn't like. I refused to participate, **4 earning me a look from my boss so fiery that I thought I'd combust on the spot**. Of course, I did get to hear about all the things that my colleagues loathe about me so that was great fun!

So, what was the effect of our team-building day? We've basically gone from a team which used to get on to a decent degree, to one that reluctantly communicates through email when only absolutely essential. It's literally broken our team. So, managers, think about that the next time the words *team* and *building* go through your head at the same time.

C

D

4 a Read the Focus box and decide if the examples in bold in the blog post exaggerate quantity or quality.

b Identify two more examples of hyperbole in the blog post.

Using hyperbole to enhance impact

Hyperbole (extreme exaggeration) makes texts (e.g. blog posts, articles and stories) more engaging and dramatic, increasing the impact it has on the reader. Hyperbole usually involves exaggerating quantity and quality.

1 Exaggerate quantity

Say there is considerably more of something.

For hours and hours, …

The room was sweltering at around two hundred degrees.

2 Exaggerate quality

Say something is bigger, easier, wetter, better, worse than it is.

… the most naturally gifted dancer ever to grace the dance floor.

… breaking all of my partner's toes in the process.

Note that the original meaning of *literally* is to indicate a word is being used with its correct meaning.

It's literally broken our team. (*broken* = damaged)

However, it is now often used to exaggerate a quantity or quality.

… my heart literally stopped at the prospect. (*stopped* is an exaggeration)

5 Work in pairs. Complete each phrase with your own idea to create examples of hyperbole.

1 The queue went on for …
2 The party was as dull as …
3 We weren't just a bit thirsty, …
4 My phone alarm was so loud that …
5 There's absolutely nothing worse than …
6 It was so crowded that we felt like …
7 My heart was beating so fast that …
8 The meeting stretched on …

6 Rewrite the sentences in bold using the techniques in the Focus box to make the text more engaging and dramatic.

[1]**I remember one team-building day very clearly**. The first activity was that well-known trust game where you fall backwards and a partner is supposed to stop you from falling to the ground. Well, my partner got a text message just as I began to fall. Rather than waiting to look at it, [2]**he did something stupid**. He took out his phone and looked down at the screen. I landed on top of him and [3]**we both fell to the ground**. [4]**We lay there for a few seconds** tangled together while [5]**a couple of colleagues looked at us**. [6]**I was very embarrassed by the whole thing**.

Prepare

7 a You're going to write an engaging blog post about an irritating experience you have had (e.g. poor customer service, rude passengers on transport). Think of an irritating experience and make notes about:

- what the experience was, where you were and why.
- what happened.
- what exactly irritated you and why.
- how you felt about it.

b Plan your blog post. Decide what you will say in each part of the text:

Paragraph 1: description of the problem

Middle paragraphs: your experience of it and how you reacted/felt

Final paragraph: your conclusion and/or advice to readers

c Think about how you can make your post engaging and dramatic. Write down a few expressions you could use to exaggerate quantity and quality.

Write

8 a Write your blog post. Use examples of hyperbole to make the post engaging and dramatic.

b Exchange your blog post with a partner. Identify examples of hyperbole. How well do they enhance the impact of the text? Are there any examples which could be improved? How?

c Using your partner's feedback, make changes to your own blog post where appropriate.

2c Master your writing

Goal: write project communications

Focus: rejecting ideas and asking for changes

1 Work in pairs and discuss the questions.

1 Have you ever complained about a product or service in writing? If so, what happened as a result?

2 Do you think it's better to be direct or indirect when complaining about something in writing?

2 Read the three exchanges between a project manager (Althea Ocampo) and different people who are working for her. Answer the questions.

1 What is the project?

2 What work or service is each person supplying?

3 What is the problem in each situation?

1

On Trend magazine music article illustrations
Wednesday 09.46 a.m.

Hi Althea,

Please find attached the illustration to accompany the article on the changing music tastes of teenagers. I also attach my invoice.

Thanks!

Bobbi

Re: On Trend magazine music article illustrations
Wednesday 10.03 a.m.

Hi Bobbi,

Thanks very much for the first draft artwork and your invoice.

The artwork has a unique style that really stands out. We will, though, need some changes. As per the brief, our magazine is trying to appeal to a late teenage/ early 20-something audience and that means that we will need a revised version of the artwork with older characters and a more age-appropriate artwork style in order to appeal to our target demographic.

It's great that you could meet the deadline, so fortunately we still have time left to create a new draft. Could you confirm that you'll be able to get this to me by the end of the week? I look forward to paying the invoice when the final artwork is signed off.

Kind regards,

Althea

2

3.18pm
Hey @Althea – photos uploaded to the cloud. You've got access to them, right? They've come out really well I think – I hope you're as happy with them as I am. Invoice coming via email. It all took a bit longer than expected and that's why the invoice is higher than we agreed. Henryk

3.59pm
@Henryk – blown away by the photos – I really like them! Re: fee, we have to stick to the agreement, I'm afraid. We're working to a tight budget and that's why we always agree the fee in advance. Could you resubmit your invoice for the agreed amount?

Once again, great work and hopefully we can work with you again in the future. Althea

3

On Trend magazine print schedule
Monday 3.22 p.m.

Dear Ms. Ocampo,

I wanted to update you on the schedule. We originally agreed to deliver the first print run of 2000 magazines on Friday 14th of next month. Due to a scheduling error, we have had to push this date back to Tuesday 18th. We would like to offer you a 5% deduction to the invoice to compensate you for this inconvenience.

I trust that this will be acceptable to you and please accept my sincere apologies for the delay.

Kind regards,

Noah Wright

Re: On Trend magazine print schedule
Monday 3.44 p.m.

Dear Mr Wright,

Many thanks for your email and for taking the time to update me.

I appreciate your kind offer of a discount, however, I'm afraid that the new delivery date is unworkable for us. We have a stall at Wonderlands Music Festival on Saturday 15th and Sunday 16th of next month in order to promote and sell our magazine, and having copies of the latest issue is absolutely crucial.

I sincerely hope we will be able to find a way to achieve the originally agreed date. Could you confirm that this is possible? If not, please let me know as soon as possible as we will need to make alternative arrangements with a different printer. This would be a matter of regret for us because your services have been highly recommended to us and we were looking forward to working with you.

Kind regards,

Althea Ocampo

3 **Find a word or phrase in the communications with these meanings.**

Email to Bobbi

1 this was mentioned in the brief
2 the kind of people we are trying to attract
3 accepted as finished

Instant message to @Henryk

4 with reference to
5 we don't have much money for this project
6 the sum of money that we both said yes to earlier

Email to Noah Wright

7 Could you tell me in writing that …
8 find a different way to get the job done
9 we would be sad about this

4 a **Read Althea's communications again. How does she tactfully ask for changes or reject ideas?**

When she asks for a change she includes a reason.

b **Read the Focus box and check your ideas.**

Rejecting ideas and asking for changes

When rejecting an idea or asking for a change, it's important to keep the other person 'on board' and not alienate them. Otherwise, their willingness to work with us or the quality of their work might suffer. There are various techniques that we can use to do this.

1 Use *we* rather than *you* or *I* in your message

Using *we* rather than *you* or *I* reinforces the message that you share the same goal and are working together to achieve it.

We will, though, need some changes.

2 Sandwich requests for changes between compliments

It is usually difficult for someone to hear that they need to make changes because it implies that they didn't do their work well enough. Putting the request between two compliments, however, makes the message easier to accept. This is sometimes called 'the sandwich technique'.

Blown away by the photos … Could you resubmit the invoice for the agreed amount? Once again, great work …

3 Include reasons

Forgetting to mention a reason can make the request or rejection seem whimsical and unnecessary, so it is important to explain why we don't like the idea or want the change.

We're working to a tight budget … Could you resubmit your invoice for the agreed amount?

4 Adapt language to suit the recipient

Matching the language used to the recipient (and our relationship with him or her) will help to make the message appropriate.

The artwork has a unique style that really stands out. (professional relationship)

Blown away by the photos. (more personal relationship)

c **Find more examples of each technique in the emails and messages from Althea.**

Prepare

5 **You're going to write emails and messages to people as a project manager. First, read the communications you have received from various freelancers and the comments you have written on their work. What problem is there with each message or piece of work? What changes are required?**

1

Dear Lex,

Please find attached the garden design for Borneo Drive with costing as requested. I also attach my invoice as agreed.

Kind regards,

Trudy

2

Dear Mr Eliades,

As discussed, pleased find redesigns for the Borneo Drive house.

We have created a look which is unique and stunning. It is slightly over-budget but it is, we hope you will agree, worth the extra cost.

Kind regards,

Patricia van Wit

Write

6 **Write a response to each communication in Exercise 5.**

7 a **Exchange your messages with a partner. Give your partner feedback on their messages.**

b **Revise your messages to make them more effective. Use your partner's feedback to help you.**

3B Master your writing

Goal: write a proposal
Focus: using persuasive language

1 **Work in pairs and discuss the questions.**
1 What kind of green spaces do you have where you live?
2 How are they generally used?
3 What are the benefits of having green spaces in urban areas?

2 a **Read the proposal. What problem does the writer describe? What is her proposal? What reasons does she give to support it?**

b **Read the proposal again. Are the statements true (T) or false (F)?**
1 A proposal is designed to persuade readers to follow a course of action.
2 A proposal is made up of continuous text.
3 A proposal has a very formal, academic tone.
4 A proposal describes advantages and disadvantages of an idea.
5 A proposal begins with a summary of the problems and solution(s).

c **Find two or three examples of persuasive language in the proposal. Compare your ideas with a partner.**

3 **Read the Focus box. Match phrases a–f in the proposal with categories 1–4 in the box.**

Using persuasive language

The purpose of a proposal is to persuade the reader to accept an idea. This means providing effective reasons and using persuasive language to do so. Use these persuasive techniques:

1 Highlight the severity of the problem.
a blot on the landscape of the area
seriously detrimental to people's health.

2 Be clear about the positive impact of the idea.
The park is sure to attract further development in the area.
It's sure to be well received by local residents.

3 Provide evidence to support your idea and sound authoritative/knowledgeable.
There is clear evidence that they can ...
It has been proven time and time again that ...

4 Appeal to the reader's sense of what is right.
... a disadvantage that I am sure you will want to address.
The council can be relied upon to do the right thing.

Proposal to create more green spaces

Introduction

The purpose of this proposal is to highlight an issue in Hemston that [a]**council members surely recognise needs to be addressed:** the lack of green spaces in the eastern district. As this district is currently undergoing some development, it creates an amazing opportunity to provide a green space that will benefit everyone in the vicinity.

Understanding the issue

Green spaces are a necessity for a city in that they help people escape the noise and pollution associated with life in a built-up area. Green spaces provide a vital respite from everyday life. [b]**As someone who has worked in healthcare for over twenty years**, I recognise the profound impact on mental and physical health that green spaces can have. There is clear evidence that they can reduce blood pressure and help to lower stress. They also provide opportunities for people to exercise and get in touch with nature.

There are environmental considerations, too. [c]**Green spaces are known to provide**:

- space with a lower temperature than the rest of the city.
- reduced levels of CO_2.
- an area for wildlife to thrive.

The lack of green spaces in the eastern district mean that people are unable to gain the advantages described above, putting them at a distinct and very unfair disadvantage to people elsewhere in the city; a disadvantage that I am sure you will want to address.

A simple solution

The old train line which once ran from the eastern district to Portown has been closed for almost 35 years. Left abandoned, this line is [d]**both unsightly and a magnet for crime and vandalism**. However, if transformed, it has the potential to become as spectacularly successful as the High Line Trail in New York. I would therefore like to propose that two kilometres of the disused train line be turned into a green space for local residents. This park is sure to attract further development in the area. In New York, the High Line brought over $2bn in investment for the area, followed by almost $1m in additional taxation as demand to live in the area skyrocketed. [e]**The impact of this kind of money in the eastern district would be tremendous**.

The practicalities

The costs will not be insignificant. However, the project is worth the investment as the social, environmental and health benefits will be enormous. As has happened with this kind of project before, local and national companies could be asked to contribute to the project in the form of sponsorship in exchange for advertising. In a survey carried out by the local newspaper in the eastern district, local people expressed a desire for a green space as well as a willingness to work on what some described as an inspiring project. Several volunteer groups I have spoken to have promised to contribute a significant number of hours to the project at no cost.

Executive summary

In summary, the eastern district of the city is in need of a green space. By converting the old train line, we can allow residents to enjoy the same opportunities that residents receive in other parts of the city and remove what is currently a blot on the landscape of the area. Since residents' health will flourish, development will transform the area and the district will ultimately prosper, [f]**I am certain that you will see the value in such a worthwhile and necessary goal**.

4 a Complete the sentences with the words in the box.

beneficial	confident	dire	flourished	known
surge	undeniable	worsening		

1 The air in a park is ______ to be cleaner than air elsewhere in the city.
2 Residents are in ______ need of help.
3 The need to provide a green space for people to relax in is ______ .
4 Three impoverished areas which implemented similar projects subsequently ______ .
5 This solution will lead to a huge ______ of interest in the city.
6 I am ______ that you will recognise the fairness of such action.
7 The situation is ______ day by day.
8 Evidence shows that parks are highly ______ .

b Could the words and phrases in the box describe a problem (P) or the suggested solution (S)?

a cause for concern	daring	distressing	inferior
magical	perplexing	phenomenal	revolutionary
troubling	uplifting		

Prepare

5 a Work in pairs. Read the email below and discuss the questions.

1 What kind of open-air events might be held at a community space like the one suggested for the wasteland?
2 How might this space and the events benefit the local community? Make a list of as many ideas as possible.

Hi, have you heard this? Finally, they're going to turn that unsightly, neglected bit of land into something useful. We've been talking about how we need a community space for open-air events for ages – now's our chance! Can you write a proposal and send it to the council? You're much better at that kind of thing than me!

b Select the best ideas from Exercise 5a that you would like to include in your proposal.

c Plan your proposal. Make notes about these things.

- your heading and sub-headings
- the key points you will make under each sub-heading
- what information you might bullet point
- persuasive language you can use

Write

6 a Write your proposal, using your plan in Exercise 5c to help you.

b Exchange your proposal with a partner. What makes their proposal persuasive? Are there any places where the persuasion is too strong or could be stronger? Why?

c Revise your proposal in light of your partner's feedback.

4B Master your writing

Goal: write a letter of application for an internship

Focus: putting a positive spin on limited experience and skills

1 Work in pairs. Look at the photos and discuss the questions.

1 What is the difference between an internship and a normal job?

2 What are the possible advantages and disadvantages for both sides?

2 Read the advertisement for an internship. Would it appeal to you? Why/Why not?

NEW CULTURE GENERATION

We are a leading TV channel and website for the late teen/early 20s market. Our goal is to showcase the most interesting and inspiring cultural events going on today. We aim to appeal to and represent a new generation which is culturally curious and determined to make the most of life's opportunities.

We are seeking a young and very enthusiastic intern with experience of cultural events and/or organisations for a nine-month placement in our marketing team. Punctuality is a must!

Salary: no salary but all travel and expenses are paid
Duties: helping with all the latest digital marketing techniques
Duration: 9 months
Contact: Mr Jenkins
Application: Piotr.Jenkins@newculturegeneration.com
Send email – no CV required

3 a Read Rachel's email. Do you think she's a good candidate for the job? Why/Why not?

Mailbox Inbox VIPs Drafts

1 I would like to [1]**apply for** the marketing internship that was listed on internhunt.net. I believe that my academic achievements and extra-curricular experience mean that I am the [2]**right person for** this exciting internship opportunity.

2 Over the last three years at Mortington College, I've completed a great deal of coursework on the latest marketing techniques and best practices, including social media influencer marketing and content marketing. I know that these areas of marketing are a component of the internship so I am confident that I can help your company [3]**do well** in this area. In addition, much of my coursework has been focused on the young adult market so I believe I have a good understanding of this demographic.

3 Last summer I spent my holiday period volunteering with a local theatre group. I was instrumental in raising awareness of the group through digital marketing. Being up to date on the latest website building software, I was also able to rebuild their website and [4]**introduce** a much more active online presence.

4 As well as studying full time, I have an occasional evening job as a waitress in a café. There, I am not only responsible for serving customers but also for cashing up at the end of the evening shift. This job has taught me the value of good time-keeping.

5 I believe that I would be [5]**valuable for** your organisation and this internship would provide me with the ideal opportunity to gain real-world experience in my chosen field of marketing. I hope to schedule an interview with you at the earliest opportunity and I look forward to speaking with you.

Thank you for your consideration.

Sincerely,

b Look at the extracts from Rachel's email. How does each one link back to the internship job advert?

1 this exciting internship opportunity
We are seeking a young and very enthusiastic intern

2 including social media influencer marketing and content marketing

3 much of my coursework has been focused on the young adult market

4 I spent my holiday period volunteering with a local theatre group

5 raising awareness of the group through digital marketing

6 taught me the value of good time-keeping

4 **In which paragraph(s) does Rachel do these things?**

a describe her relevant work experience
b describe how her studies match the position
c mention the next step
d show that she sees things from the company's perspective
e explain the purpose of the email
f show enthusiasm
g describe relevant extra-curricular experience
h summarise why she is the right person
i provide specific examples

5 a **Match phrases 1–5 in the email with the more business-oriented phrases a–e.**

a achieve its goals
b a big asset to
c the ideal candidate for
d put myself forward for
e kick start

b **What is the effect of using phrases a–e in a letter of application?**

6 a **Rachel hasn't yet worked in marketing. What phrases does she use to put her academic experience in a positive light?**

b **Read the Focus box and check your answers.**

Putting a positive spin on limited experience and skills

When applying for an internship we are unlikely to have much experience in the job field that we are applying for, so it is important to make the most of our coursework and extra-curricular activities in the application letter. Certain phrases help us to do this.

For subjects that you have studied you can say:
***I have completed a great deal of coursework** on the latest marketing techniques.*

For concepts and ideas that you have studied you can say:
*I believe **I have a good understanding** of this demographic.*

For software and programs that you know how to use you can say:
***I am up to date on/proficient in** the latest website building software.*

For principles that you learnt through experience you can say:
*This experience **taught me the value of** positive customer engagement.*

For goals that you helped achieve in a project you can say:
***I was instrumental in** building a strong link to the community.*

7 a **Rephrase the extracts from an application email using one of the phrases from the Focus box.**

1 It took three months to finish the project and this experience showed me that patience is important.
2 During the project, I helped the team to stage an exhibition in a local theatre.
3 Because of my experience in this role, I now know how to design a mobile application.
4 During my first year at college I learnt about various aspects of commercial law.
5 I know how to use spread sheets.

b **Write three true sentences about yourself using the vocabulary in the Focus box.**

Prepare

8 a **You're going to write a letter of application for an internship. Choose the position in the box that interests you most or think of your own job.**

digital marketing assistant junior screenplay writer
management trainee trainee cook trainee teacher
video game designer

b **Complete the advert for the internship position. Add the details that suit you.**

Selios Regent is a _____ company focused on _____. Our goal is to _____. We aim to be number one and we are looking for a keen intern with _____ experience to join us for a _____-month period.
Salary: no salary but all travel and expenses are paid
Duties: _____
Application: Sheila.Fitzsimmons@seliosregent.com
Send email – no CV required

c **Make notes on the studies, experiences and jobs that you have which match the advert.**

Write

9 **Write the first draft of your email. Make sure that you put a positive spin on your relevant experience and studies.**

10 a **Exchange emails with a partner. Use the checklist in Exercise 4 to give your partner feedback on their email.**

b **Read the feedback on your email and write a second draft to improve it.**

5c Master your writing

Goal: write an essay

Focus: synthesising information from a number of sources

1 a **Work in pairs. How much plastic waste do you think you generate every day? Do you think this is a problem? Why/Why not?**

b **Read the extracts from articles and journals and answer the questions.**

1 What is the ocean clean-up project?

2 Why do some people think it is important?

A A project to clean up our oceans is underway. Set to cost millions of dollars, the project will aim to capture plastic in the Pacific Ocean over a ten-year period. It is supported by many people around the world, although there are still some concerns about the specifically-designed equipment's ability to withstand strong currents and poor weather.

B Cleaning up our oceans is a laudable goal, but we must decide whether it's the right focus right now. With a lorry load of plastic being dumped into the ocean each minute of the day, it's clear that the onus needs to be on preventing further damage. Thousands of animals consume plastic and die each year. More plastic in our oceans will make this worse.

C Plastic that could take hundreds of years to decompose has now been found in all four corners of the world and beyond, with scientists saying they've discovered it in the ocean in Antarctica, and on the floor of the deepest part of the ocean, The Mariana Trench, 10,000 metres below sea level. This has caused outrage among the public who have become much more aware of the plastic problem in recent years.

D Work is starting on an effort to clean up in The Great Pacific Garbage Patch, an area of the Pacific Ocean roughly the size of Texas, where 1.8 trillion pieces of plastic have collected according to National Geographic. 94% of this is microplastics, but it has now entered our food chain. It is hoped that the clean-up project will get rid of much of this, although environmentalists are worried that it will cause further harm to sea life.

2 **Read the essay and answer the questions.**

1 What is the writer's argument?

2 What three reasons does the writer give in support of this?

3 How does the writer dismiss the opposing point of view?

1 **There are currently 1.8 trillion pieces of plastic in one part of one ocean alone, with plastic having been found as far as Antarctica and 10,000 metres under the ocean.** While cleaning up this plastic is desirable, in this essay I will argue that the prevention of an increase rather than an eradication of what is already there is more desirable in the short term.

2 Resources are finite, which means that when they are being used to clean up the plastic problem, they are not being used to prevent further disposal of plastic. **It is claimed that one truckload of rubbish is deposited into the ocean every minute of every day. Some of that will be plastic that takes centuries to biodegrade.** If the resources we have were used on prevention first, it would make cleaning up our oceans significantly easier in the future.

3 Public support is a key factor, too. **The concept of cleaning up our oceans has garnered significant public support in recent years as awareness of the plastic problem has increased.** However, while the public focus is on the cleaning up of our oceans, the problem of curbing damaging practices is ignored. Public support and indeed public pressure are both required if agreements to stop dumping plastics in the ocean are to be obtained.

4 The main reason that resources and public support should be focused on prevention is the fact that wildlife and human life are under threat now. Currently, **thousands of animals are thought to die each year as an indirect consequence of plastic consumption, and it is likely that humans are digesting toxins from plastics in the food chain.** By ensuring the situation does not become worse, the effects can be curbed prior to an ocean clean up.

5 Finally, it could be argued that the cost of cleaning up our oceans is insignificant compared to the cost of implementing treaties and laws, and policing them, and therefore the clean up is the better option. However, it is not guaranteed to be a success. **Scientists are concerned that adverse conditions could prevent the clean up project from being a success and the process itself may in fact cause damage to the environment.**

6 It is evident that attention needs to be paid to the issue of plastic in our oceans, and both approaches discussed in this essay are not just worthwhile, but absolutely essential. However, in order to ensure that the problem does not get worse while resources are focused on an ocean clean-up, it is vital that the people of the world come together to stop plastics from getting into the ocean in the first place. Without this, the problem cannot truly be solved.

3 **Look at the parts of the essay in bold that mention each topic below. Identify which two sources in Exercise 1b the information came from.**

1 the amount and location of plastic in the ocean
C and D
2 the amount of rubbish put into the ocean and why it's an issue
3 the focus of public support and the impact of this
4 the impact of rubbish on human life and animal life
5 worry regarding the project to clean up the ocean

4 **Read the Focus box. Look at what you did in Exercise 3. Which step (1–4) was it?**

Synthesising information from a number of sources

Synthesising information means bringing information from different sources to create a new idea in one text. This means following these steps:

1 Read different sources of information and note down the themes and ideas.

2 Look for connections between ideas. This could be similarities but also differences.

Plastic … has now been found in all four corners of the world and beyond, with scientists saying they've discovered it in the ocean in Antarctica, and … 10,000 metres below sea level.

The Great Pacific Garbage Patch, an area of the Pacific Ocean … where 1.8 trillion pieces of plastic have collected …

3 Use the information you've gathered to decide what point(s) you want to make.

The cleaning up of plastic is desirable.

4 Organise the ideas that you have noted down into new coherent ideas, making sure you paraphrase the information rather than use the same wording.

There are currently 1.8 trillion pieces of plastic in one part of one ocean alone, with plastic having been found as far as Antarctica and 10,000 metres under the ocean.

5 a **Look at the article and journal extracts below. In which extracts can you find information about these topics?**

1 the current consumption of plastic
2 plastic waste
3 the recycling of plastic
4 biodegradable plastic alternatives

b **Write a sentence for topic 1 in Exercise 5a that brings together information from the different sources. Paraphrase the ideas.**

A A shocking million plastic bottles are sold every minute around the world. Many are not recycled by users, with some plastic items, such as disposable coffee cups, not recyclable.

B Biodegradable plastics are a great alternative to plastic, as they degrade more easily than other plastics which can take centuries to fully break down. However, they should be used with caution as they will only degrade when heated and pose problems if dumped in the ground.

C Twice as much plastic is produced today than it was 50 years ago, with significantly more waste produced per item. This is particularly worrying as over 90% of plastic is currently not recycled by individuals or organisations. However, other products, such as glass, can have an even bigger impact on the environment.

D Biodegradable products can contaminate other recyclable materials if they come into contact with each other, according to a new report. This can mean the recyclable materials can no longer be recycled, increasing the chances of them ending up on landfill sites.

Prepare

6 a **You're going to write an essay using the topics and text extracts in Exercise 5a. Make a note of your answer to the essay question and your reasons.**

Should we focus our attention on using technology to solve our single-use plastic problem or changing our habits?

b **Use your notes to plan your essay. Include the main point of each paragraph and what ideas from the extracts you can use to support it.**

Introduction:
Main paragraph 1:
Main paragraph 2:
Dismiss opposing viewpoint:
Conclusion:

Write

7 a **Write your essay. Use your plan to help you. Synthesise and paraphrase information from the extracts.**

b **Exchange your essay with a partner. Use the checklist to help you review their work.**

- Has the writer supported his/her ideas with information from the excerpts?
- Is the information paraphrased?

6A Master your writing

Goal: write a summary of a scientific experiment

Focus: maintaining a neutral scientific tone

1 a Work in pairs. Student A: Turn to page 189. Student B: Turn to page 191.

b Write down all the items you remember in the correct order from 1–9. Do not check the list or ask your partner. You have exactly one minute to do this.

c Check your answers. You get one point for each correct item and another point if it is in the correct place on the list, so the maximum total is 18 points.

2 a Ask the rest of the class. Who usually got the higher score, Student A or Student B? Why?

b Work in pairs and discuss the questions.

1 What was the aim of this experiment?
2 What do the results prove?
3 Do you know any other psychological experiments?

3 Look at the pictures of the Asch Conformity Study, a famous psychological study from the 1950s. Describe the procedure in your own words.

4 a Read a summary of the experiment. Put stages A–E in the correct order.

A Later, however, the actors were instructed to give an incorrect answer and the effect on the participant and their willingness to give the correct answer was monitored.

B In the final stage of the experiment, four of the five actors gave the same incorrect answer and just one gave the correct answer. Again, the effect on the participant was monitored.

C Initially, the actors were instructed to give the correct answer.

D As each card was shown, the participant and the actors were asked which of three lines on the card was the same length as a fourth line.

E The participant was placed in a room with five other people and shown a series of cards with lines. The participant was not aware that the other people were actors.

Results

It was observed that when an obviously incorrect answer was given by all the actors, the participant also gave an incorrect answer 1____% of the time. Further, it was observed that when a correct answer was given by just one of the five actors, the participant gave an incorrect answer just 2____% of the time.

b Work in pairs and discuss what percentages you expect to see in the *Results* section of the summary. Then check your answers on page 186.

5 a Work in pairs. How does the summary maintain a neutral scientific tone?

b Read the Focus box and check your answers.

Maintaining a neutral scientific tone

When writing up a summary of an experiment, it is important to maintain a neutral, scientific tone throughout. This is achieved in the following ways:

1 Use the passive voice rather than the active voice where possible.

The actors and the participant were shown another card.

2 Use more formal and precise verbs, rather than informal and general verbs.

The experiment ~~was done~~ was carried out in a research laboratory.

3 Avoid personal judgments and emotive language.

The experiment was ~~cleverly~~ designed to test the theory that …

4 Avoid making general claims.

~~Like everyone~~, the participants reported using their mobile phones for news, games …

5 Avoid vague words.

~~A few~~ 25% of the participants refused to press the button.

6 Avoid making bold claims about what the study proves.

The study ~~proves that~~ suggests that individuals are willing to lie about their actions.

Prepare

7 a Work in pairs. You're going to write up a scientific experiment. Look at the pictures below and answer the questions.

1 What is happening in each picture?
2 What does the experiment prove?

b What vocabulary will you need to write a summary of this experiment?

6 a Cross out the words that make the sentences sound unscientific.

1 The participants completed the assignment quickly in an average time of 54 seconds.
2 The participant was totally unaware that the other people in the room were actors.
3 It was noted that around 85% of people avoided making eye contact.
4 The study examined why people always smile when they greet a stranger.
5 The participants were placed in a lovely room and left alone for ten minutes.
6 The results of the experiment were obviously not shared with the participants.

b Rewrite the sentences to make them sound more scientific.

1 My colleague, Richard, asked all the participants five very simple questions.
2 The research proves that people love to get rewards, even if they are not earnt.
3 The researchers showed the participants a very funny film.
4 We noticed that all the participants did the task without complaint.
5 Researchers told the participants not to touch the envelope at all.

Write

8 Write up a summary of the experiment. Use the summary in Exercise 4 to help you.

7C Master your writing

Goal: write a review

Focus: creating vivid imagery

1 a Work in pairs and discuss the questions.

1. What app – apart from social media apps – do you use the most? Why?
2. There's a saying that 'there's an app for everything'. How true do you think this is?
3. Do you think the apps you use enhance your life or detract from it? Why?

b Read the app blurbs. Which one would you most like to try? Why?

Meditate Today will help you to sit down and switch off from the world around you, giving you the chance to relax, recuperate and feel refreshed ready for the day ahead.

Learn your lesson is an app which brings new ideas into your life. Take micro-courses on topics of your choice and develop useful, valuable and/or fun skills. Choose topics from the arts to technology.

Animate-me! is an app that lets you add animations to your photos. Select which part of your photo you want to move and how, and bring your pic to life.

Develop your skills on the go?

Lifelong learning is a joy, but who has the time to dedicate hours to an evening course these days? That's why I was attracted to new app *Learn your lesson*. It promises the opportunity to learn a little and often through micro-courses on a variety of topics, but does it deliver?

The app's free one-month trial is a great way to peruse the content. The monthly fee for full access is then £5. Be warned though – trying to find the subscription cancellation option is a bit **[1]like searching for the proverbial needle in a haystack**. There are FAQs to help you, but getting hold of a real living person is nigh-on impossible.

Registering is easy and having given preferences as to topics, you'll immediately see a list of recommendations. I generally found these to be useful, although the system did throw up a few odd recommendations – why would a woman interested in fine arts want a course on horse management?! It felt as if the course in question felt so unloved, **[2]it leapt up of its own volition and yelled 'pick me!'**.

With over 30,000 micro-courses on offer, entering the app was **[3]like being a kid walking into a candy store**. However, the abundance of choice soon became overwhelming. I stuck to my recommendations list and avoided the search engine altogether. This stopped me wasting hours drowning in a sea of possibilities.

Each course is made up of several short videos with accompanying tasks. Because each video is **[4]a bite-sized snack**, it can easily be consumed in a single sitting. I watched one each lunchtime and can say it was often **[5]a ray of light in an otherwise dismal day**. Of course, watching a video doesn't actually develop your skill – you need to go away and practise that yourself – but it does equip you with the right knowledge.

So, how exactly is *Learn your lesson* different to all those 'how to' videos you can find online already? Well, the app owners guarantee that the course creators are experts in their field, and vet the content. The app also provides a community space where users share ideas. I personally found this invaluable. Other tools may have comments sections, but they can be **[6]as helpful as a chocolate teapot**, and as friendly as a bear having a bad day.

So, would I recommend this app to others? Yes, but with caution. Use the trial to check it out first before you commit to a regular expense, and make a note to cancel your membership before the month is up if it isn't for you. Otherwise, the app will be eating into your bank account forever more.

2 a Read the app review on page 138. What positive and negative points does the reviewer mention? What is her overall recommendation?

b Read the review again and put the information in the order it appears.

a ______ a comparison to similar tools
b ______ how well it does what it says it does
c ______ cost
d __*1*__ what it claims to do
e ______ a recommendation
f ______ how easy it is to access

c What style does the writer use in her review? Tick the items you notice.

- addresses the reader directly
- uses language to bring images to life
- uses formal language
- uses technical language
- uses only short sentences

3 Read the Focus box. Then match expressions 1–6 in bold in the review with the types of imagery in the Focus box. Do they express a positive or a negative point of view?

Creating vivid imagery

We can use metaphors, similes and personification to create vivid imagery in writing. In a review, these can highlight or even stress the writer's point of view. A writer may use common expressions, or they may be creative with language to avoid clichés (a phrase which is so overused that it loses its impact).

Metaphor

A metaphor is an expression used to describe a person or thing. It refers to something different but with similar characteristics.

drowning in a sea of possibilities

Simile

A simile is a comparison of two things which begins with *as* or *like*.

as friendly as a bear having a bad day

Personification

Personification describes the act of giving an object human characteristics or qualities.

Otherwise, the app will be eating into your bank account forever more.

4 a Which sentence in each pair provides a more vivid image?

1 **a** The homepage is as confusing as a barking cat.
  b The homepage confused me from beginning to end.
2 **a** A selection of random images appears on the page.
  b A bundle of images have been thrown randomly onto the page.
3 **a** The game is pretty monotonous to play.
  b The game is about as fun as watching paint dry.
4 **a** The help pages stand up and demand to be counted.
  b The help pages are one of the best things about it.

b Do the images in Exercise 4a express a positive or negative point of view?

5 a Complete each sentence. Be creative and use your own ideas.

1 The app costs far less than __*a cup of coffee*__ but will last much longer.
2 I'd rather ____________ than use this app again.
3 Accessing the content is as easy as ____________.
4 The app is as smooth as ____________.
5 The app's name doesn't call out and say 'Don't I look interesting?'. It says '____________.'

b Work in pairs and compare your ideas. Which images do you think are the most vivid? Why?

Prepare

6 a You're going to write a review of an app that you use. Think of an app and make notes on these things. Decide if you would recommend it or not.

- what the app does
- what it does well
- what it does less well
- cost
- ease of use
- comparison to similar tools

b Decide what ideas from your notes to include and organise them into a logical order. Use the order in Exercise 2b to help you.

c Think of three ways that you could bring imagery into your review to emphasise your point of view.

Write

7 a Write your review. Use your plan to help you.

b Review your text and answer the questions. Make improvements where necessary.

- Is it clear and useful to readers?
- Did you include the features of a review as outlined in Exercise 2b?
- Did you create imagery to highlight a point of view?

c Exchange your review with a partner. If you use the app in your partner's review already, do you agree with the review? If not, would you use it? Why/Why not?

8C Master your writing

Goal: take part in an online discussion

Focus: dealing with rudeness online

1 **Work in pairs and answer the questions.**

1. How often do you comment on things in writing online or contribute to discussion forums?
2. What rules do you try to follow when posting comments online?
3. Have you ever experienced rudeness from someone online? Explain what happened and how you dealt with it.

2 a **Read the question posted online. How would you answer it?**

dazedandconfused | five hours ago

How do I choose which career path to take?

Help! I'm just about to graduate and I still have no idea which career to choose. My degree was a general one in English and philosophy. How can I choose the right career path?????

b **Read the comments in response to the post and answer the questions.**

1. In what ways are *ashley* and *bishop* rude?
2. Why do you think *boyd* doesn't reply to *malarkay*?
3. What do you think motivates *ashley, bishop* and *malarkay* to take part in the online discussion?

1

clemence | three hours ago

Most people these days seem to believe that you should follow your passions when choosing a career. Unfortunately, I have to disagree. For most people their passion lies in art or sport or music but only 3% of jobs are in those fields. Following your passion will probably make you unemployed.

ashley | four hours ago

Well have you got a better idea? Or perhaps you're one of those people who shoot down ideas but never offer any of their own …

clemence | three hours ago

I think your suggestion for me to put my own ideas forward is very valid. I agree with the website 80000hours.org (named after the number of hours the average person spends working in their lives) which has concluded that it's better to choose a career based on how you can have a positive impact on the world.

2

selly | one hour ago

It's all about thinking which global problems need solving and then deciding where and how you can help solve them. That should direct your choice of career.

bishop | one hour ago

Oh not another do-gooder! It's hard enough to work out how to choose a career path without trying to solve the problems of the world!

selly | one hour ago

I agree that it's not easy, either to choose a career path or to solve the problems of the world. When I talk about positive impact, I'm actually thinking about making a difference rather than solving the world's problems.

3

boyd | one hour ago

Do you have any specialised skills?

malarkay | one hour ago

Of course he doesn't have any specialised skills – he did English and philosophy. Didn't you even read the question, genius?

malarkay | one hour ago

Well? Nothing to say???

3 a Read the extracts below. What techniques do the contributors use to deal with online rudeness in 1 and 2?

1 … I think your suggestion … is very valid.

2 I agree that it's not easy.

b Read the Focus box and check your ideas. What other techniques can you think of?

Dealing with rudeness online

When people disagree, online discussions often descend into rudeness and accusations, however, there are ways to lessen the chances of this happening and so to appear more convincing to other people reading the discussion.

Note the points we agree on

Even in a heated argument, there may be things that both sides agree on. Mention those things to establish common ground.

Reframe rudeness as thoughtful argument

Even when someone is rude and unreasonable, respond as though they have been thoughtful and reasonable.

Avoid the trolls

There are some people who will never listen to reasoned argument and their only aim is to make you (or anyone) angry. They are called 'trolls' and research shows that trolls understand the emotions of other people very well but don't feel them personally. For this reason they often enjoy causing disruption online. If you spot a troll, it's usually best to avoid engaging with them in the first place.

4 Match statements 1–5 with responses a–e. What techniques from the Focus box is the contributor using?

1 I don't understand your point. Do you even understand your point?

2 I just completely disagree with you. I basically couldn't disagree more if I tried.

3 I think you're just cherry-picking evidence to suit your particular point of view.

4 This is a stupid argument. There's so much more in the world to worry about.

5 Most people with common sense would disagree with you.

a I don't agree that I'm being selective but I do agree that we should look at all available research.

b Yes, I understand what I'm trying to say but I'm sorry if it came across as overly complex.

c I'm not sure about that but I do agree that there are two sides to the argument.

d Actually, I agree. There are plenty of other topics that deserve our attention.

e It's a shame that our views are so far apart on this.

5 Think of a suitable response to these challenging online comments.

1 You're not looking at both sides of the argument. Try to be more open-minded.

2 Just go online and do some research. There's plenty of evidence for my point of view if you bother to look for it.

3 Most scientists would disagree with you.

Prepare

6 Choose a topic below for an online discussion. Make brief notes on your opinion on the topic.

- It's better to spend any money that you earn. Who knows what will happen tomorrow?
- Sometimes you have to betray your colleagues to get ahead at work.
- People don't have just one career nowadays – they have several careers over the course of their working life. That's a good thing.

A – TUBE DRIVER

C – BOXER

B – FLIGHT ATTENDANT

Write

7 a Work in pairs. Write your opinion as though taking part in an online discussion. Your partner should respond in a challenging way on the same page. Continue the discussion for at least four turns.

b Discuss which attempts to deal with rudeness were the most successful. Why?

c Work with a different partner and repeat the activity.

9A Master your writing

Goal: write a narrative

Focus: using emotive language

1 Work in pairs. Look at the photos and answer the questions.

1 What do you think they show?

2 To what extent can you relate to this?

2 a Read the title of the story. What story genre do you think it might be? What might happen in it?

b Read the story and check your ideas.

c Read the story again and put the structure in the correct order.

a ______ describe the climax of the story

b __1__ briefly introduce the setting

c ______ describe how the character reacts to the story ending

d ______ develop the storyline towards a climax

e ______ briefly introduce the main protagonist and his character

f ______ introduce the main character's problem

Life: a reboot

1 Guy pushed open the heavy factory doors, taking care not to let them swing back and hit the person behind him. He edged forward and joined the throng of workers shuffling their way along the sidewalk. Snow had fallen during the day and it crunched under his heavy work boots. He pulled his collar up around his neck and hung his head low. At a good head taller than those around him, he stood out; a feeling he could never seem to shake.

2 The sun had already dipped below the horizon, leaving only street lights to show him the way. The crowds began to thin around him as he trudged further and further from the central district. Eventually, the crowds dissipated and he found himself on his own. He pulled his car keys from his pocket and pressed the button, the lights on his car flashing up ahead. He saw the snow on his windscreen and sighed. 'There must be more to life than this,' he thought, knowing that he'd be here doing the same thing tomorrow and the day after that.

3 Guy opened his door, felt around the glove compartment and pulled out a scraper. Moving back towards the windscreen, he noticed a flyer tucked under one of the wipers. Surprisingly, it was dry. He looked around. There were no flyers on any other cars. Strange. He picked it up and looked at it.' Are you tired of life? Sick of feeling like something is missing? Do you want an experience of a lifetime? Visit us and find out more.'

4 As Guy stared at the words, he felt a surge of something he hadn't felt for a considerable amount of time. Hope. Perhaps change was possible. He stood there for some time before he finally pocketed the flyer, wiped away the worst of the snow and got into his car. The address wasn't too far from here, maybe he should check it out. He pulled out into the road, turned on his radio and set it to a pop channel. As his car rolled down the icy street, he began to tap his finger on the steering wheel and a hum came out of his mouth, shocking him.

5 As Guy pulled up outside the address on the flyer, he noticed lights coming through cracks in the darkened windows. Someone was there. He stepped out of the car and eagerly strode towards the door of what looked like an abandoned warehouse. He knocked on the door loudly. No answer. He pushed the door and felt it give, so he leant on it harder and it flew wide open. He stepped into the building and blinked as his eyes adjusted to the light in the room. When everything came into focus, his legs gave way and he stumbled back. His mouth fell open. Along the wall in front of him stood dozens of men with their eyes closed. Him. They were all him. 'Ah,' said a woman in white. 'Our curious creature has finally returned.' A man walked behind Guy and closed the door behind him, locking it. 'It takes time, but they always take the bait,' he drawled. 'You've had quite the adventure, haven't you? Don't worry, we'll make sure you don't slip out again.' In that moment, a saying popped into his head. 'Be careful what you wish for.' Then, his mind and his world went black.

3 **Work in pairs. Read the Focus box and discuss which emotion(s) sentences a–c evoke through word choice.**

Using emotive language

We select particular words in a story in order to create an emotional response in readers. These words might describe the following:

1 A person's movements, e.g. walking (*stroll*), face (*wide-eyed*).
2 A person's voice, e.g. clarity (*mumble*), volume (*yell*), pitch (*squeal*).
3 A person's feelings, e.g. positive (*deliriously happy*), negative (*desperate*).
4 A crowd of people, e.g. their attitude (*hostile*), their movement (*pushing and shoving*)
5 A description of an object, e.g. its size (*massive*), its attractiveness (*sparkling*).
6 A description of a place, e.g. size (*vast*), appearance (*contemporary*), atmosphere (*gloomy*).

The words in bold in sentences a-c exemplify how different words can evoke different emotions.

*The boy **walked** across the playground with his bag in his hand. (=neutral)*

a *The boy **bounded** across the **noisy**, **chaotic** playground, **swinging** his bag back and forth.*
b *The boy **trudged** across the **derelict** playground, **dragging** his bag along the ground beside him.*
c *The boy **crept** as silently as he could across the **eerie** playground, **clinging** onto his bag for dear life.*

4 **Underline words in the story that create a sense of the emotions below. What do each of these words describe?**
1 hopelessness (paragraphs 1–3)
2 hope (paragraphs 4–5)
3 fear (paragraph 5)

5 a **Complete the table with the words and phrases in the box.**

bleak creep quietly (be) ecstatic exuberant hostile plod roar furiously scream hysterically shiver squeal in delight

Happiness	Sadness
	bleak
Fear	**Anger**

b **Complete sentences 1–4 with the correct form of the words and phrases in Exercise 5a. More than one answer is possible.**
1 When we saw what was in front of us, we all ___________ .
2 I'd never seen a more ___________ crowd than the one in front of me.
3 As soon as the first firework went off, we ___________ .
4 He ___________ along the corridor.

6 **Work in pairs. Rewrite the sentence below four times. Each sentence should express one of the four emotions in Exercise 5a.**
The woman read the message on her phone and then said, 'It's happened.'

Prepare

7 a **Work in pairs. You're going to complete the story of *Life: a reboot*. Answer the questions and make notes.**
1 What does the protagonist see when he regains consciousness?
2 How does he escape his capture?
3 What happens to his captors?
4 What happens to the other clones?
5 Where does the protagonist end up?

b **Plan your story using your notes. Make a list of possible emotive language that you could use in your story.**

Write

8 a **Write your story. Use your plan to help you. Use appropriate language to get an emotional response from your readers.**

b **Exchange your story with a partner. What do you enjoy about the story? Which words/phrases in particular create an emotional response from you?**

10A Master your writing

› **Goal:** write attractive brochures and websites

› **Focus:** writing a problem–solution text

1 **Work in pairs and look at the pictures of high-tech mini homes. What specific problem is each one designed to solve? What kind of person might each one appeal to?**

2 **Read the brochure and website. Which pictures in Exercise 1 do they relate to?**

Raft©

A new kind of home for an uncertain future

Do you worry about rising sea levels and flood risk? Wouldn't it be nice to know that your home was built to last, whatever happens? Raft™ is the home you have been waiting for. It is a new kind of micro-house that will provide you with a long-term home, whatever the future holds. It is a self-sustainable, flood-proof pod which pushes back the boundaries of future-proof living. Its trailblazing design and use of virtually indestructible plastics allows you to live anywhere and survive anything. It can serve as city-centre accommodation, rural retreat or floating escape pod. It is engineered for survival and heralds a new era in affordable accommodation.

Contact us now and take the first step to a more secure, survivable future.

2DAYHOME©

Your first affordable step on the housing ladder

Are you fed up with paying rent but unable to afford your own place? Do you fear never getting a foot on the housing ladder? What if there were an affordable solution to this problem? What if there were a way onto the ladder without being saddled with decades of debt? What if that solution were available now, today, right this minute?

Welcome to the 2DAYHOME© – the revolutionary self-assemble micro-home. Delivered in parts and assembled in under two days, this wonder home offers an affordable first step on the housing ladder and the ground-breaking design means each 2DAYHOME© can be internally configured to suit your needs.

Why wait to get a foot on the housing ladder?
Email us now.

1

2

3

3 **Both texts have a similar six step structure. Can you tell what that structure is?**

1 a strapline which summarises the benefits (e.g. 'a new kind of home for an uncertain future')

4 a Read the Focus box and check your answers in Exercise 3.

b Look at the 2DAYHOME website and identify the different parts of the six-step structure used. Compare your answers with a partner.

Writing a problem–solution text

One way to make products or services sound attractive on websites or brochures is to write a problem–solution text. The text, which works a bit like a narrative, describes a problem that the reader will identify with and then explains why the product or service is the solution. The text can often be broken down into six steps.

1 The text often begins with a strapline, which is a short memorable way to describe the advantages of your product or service.

A new kind of home for an uncertain future.

2 The problem is often written in the form of a question.

Do you worry about … ?

3 Then the text asks the reader to imagine that there is a solution to this problem.

Wouldn't it be nice to know that … ?

4 Then the text introduces the product or service.

Raft is the home you've been waiting for.

5 The text describes the features and benefits.

Its trailblazing design … allows you to live anywhere.

6 Finally, the text finishes with a call to action, an invitation to the reader to take the next step in the process, often expressed within a sentence which summarises the key benefits.

Contact us now and take the first step to a more secure, survivable future.

Structuring text as problem–solution makes the product or service seem relevant to the reader and avoids simply listing features in a dry, uninspiring manner.

5 a Complete the problem–solution text below to describe picture 1 in Exercise 1.

Sustano Home©

1 A self-sustainable micro-home that …
2 Do you worry about …? Do you wish that …?
3 Wouldn't it be nice if …
4 Introducing …
5 a With built-in wheels, the Sustano Home allows you to …
  b It can serve as a caravan, a mobile office or …
  c The highly-efficient, built in solar panels and wind turbine mean that …
  d The revolutionary rain water collection system allows you to …
6 Contact us now and …

b Work in pairs and compare your ideas.

Prepare

6 a Choose one of the products or services below, and think of any phrases from the brochure and website in Exercise 2 that might describe it.

b Make notes on the features and benefits that you might talk about in a website or brochure for your chosen product or service.

c Think about who your product or service might appeal to. What problem do you solve for this person? What strapline might appeal to them?

Write

7 a Write the first draft of your website or brochure. Remember to use the six-step process described in the Focus box.

b Exchange texts with a partner. Make notes on how they could improve their website or brochure. Then write a second draft of your text to improve it.

Language bank

LANGUAGE

1A Present, past and future perfect

We use perfect verb forms (present/past/future perfect simple or continuous) to look back from a particular **point in time** (i.e. *now* or *then*) at an earlier **event or process**.

With **action verbs** (e.g. *try, use*), use perfect continuous forms to refer back to earlier **processes**:

*I've **been trying** to call you for hours.*

Use **perfect simple** forms to refer back to earlier **complete events** (or series of events):

*I'm happy because **I've passed** my test.*

With **state verbs** (e.g. *know, cost*), we don't normally use perfect continuous forms:

*How long **have** you **known** them?* NOT: ~~*How long **have** you **been knowing** them?*~~

There are four main reasons for using perfect verb forms:

1 Measuring time up to a point (usually with *for*, *since* or *how long ...?*):

I'll have had this phone for five years soon.

In negative sentences, the simple and continuous forms have different meanings:

*I **haven't used** this website for years.* (= I last used it years ago)

*I **haven't been using** this website for long.* (= I've been using it, but I only started recently)

2 Direct results of earlier events (often with *so* or *because*):

*I'**d** just **passed** my test **so** I was really happy.*

3 Experiences up to a point (often with *ever, never, before, already, yet* or *times*):

*I didn't want to watch the film again because I'**d already seen** it ten **times**.*

4 Recent news and trends:

*I'**ve just seen** a squirrel ... but it'**s gone** now.*

We can mention a specific earlier time with the past or future perfect, but not with the present perfect:

- *I'**ve hurt** my back ~~last week~~, so I can't carry those boxes.*
- *I'**d hurt** my back **the previous week**, so I couldn't carry the boxes.*

1B Subject raising

Subject raising involves moving the subject of a *that*-clause 'up' to become the subject of the main clause, which is followed by a *to*- infinitive.

***It** seems that **you**'re unhappy*	→	***You** seem **to be** unhappy*

We can use subject raising:

- with *seem, appear, turn out* and *happen*:

*They **appear** to be late.*

- with some adjectives for probability:

*She's **likely** to know.* ▶ See 2B page 148

- with some passive reporting verbs:

*She's **said** to be furious.* ▶ See 9B page 162

In general, the version with subject raising is more natural in everyday speech. There are two ways of making negative sentences:

*She seems **not** to have noticed./She **doesn't** seem to have noticed.*

Perfect and continuous infinitives

Use a **continuous infinitive** (*to be doing*) to refer to actions in progress at a particular time:

It seems (now) *that he's lying* (now).
*He seems **to be lying**.*

It seemed (yesterday) *that he was lying* (at the time).
*He seemed **to be lying**.*

Use a **perfect infinitive** (*to have done*) to refer to earlier states and complete events:

It seems (now) *that he cheated* (earlier).
*He seems **to have cheated.***

It seemed (yesterday) *that he had cheated* (earlier).
*He seemed **to have cheated.***

Use a **perfect continuous infinitive** (*to have been doing*) to refer to earlier actions in progress:

It seems (now) *that he was lying* (yesterday).
*He seems **to have been lying**.*

It seemed (yesterday) *that he had been lying* (earlier).
*He seemed **to have been lying**.*

1C Infinitive phrases

- Most infinitive phrases can come **before or after** the statement they're commenting on:

It wasn't great. To be honest, I hated it.

It wasn't great. I hated it, to be honest.

Other examples: *to give them their proper name/title; not to put too fine a point on it; to be sure; to be honest/frank; to tell the truth; to be fair;* etc.

- A few usually come **before** the statement, in order to show how it relates to earlier information:

*I was worried about visiting my in-laws, but **needless to say**, <u>everyone was extremely kind</u>.*

Other examples: *to cap it all; to add insult to injury; to make matters worse;* etc.

- A few usually come **after** the statement in order to say that something is more extreme than your words suggest or that there is more you could have said:

*<u>The meeting was boring</u>, **to put it mildly**.*

Other examples: *to put it bluntly; to name (but/just) a few; to say the least;* etc.

PRACTICE

1A

1 Choose the correct alternatives.

1 Ricky's upset because somebody has *scratched/been scratching* the side of his car.
2 I haven't *worn/been wearing* a tie for years – they're so uncomfortable!
3 I've *climbed/been climbing* about ten cliffs so far, but I've never *done/been doing* it without safety harnesses.
4 My eyes are red because I've *chopped/been chopping* onions. Don't worry – I haven't *cried/been crying*.
5 Oh, what a nice surprise! We've just *talked/been talking* about the fact that we *haven't seen/been seeing* you for ages.

2 Complete the sentences with the correct form of the words in brackets.

1 Ricky was upset when we saw him because somebody ______ (scratch) the side of his car.
2 I'm going to wear a tie for tomorrow's presentation. It's the first time I ______ (wear) a tie for years.
3 Vera is planning to climb a huge cliff next year. She ______ (climb) about ten cliffs by then, but it'll be the first time she ______ (do) it without safety harnesses.
4 Chris's eyes were all red when we saw him. It looked like he ______ (cry), but in fact he ______ (chop) onions.
5 It was weird to see Freda at the party yesterday, especially because we ______ (just/talk) about her.

1B

1 Complete the conversation with the correct form of the words in brackets.

A: Hey, Emily. Can you help me? I left my jacket here on this chair earlier, but when I came back, my wallet [1]______ (turn out / go) from the pocket. You [2]______ (not / happen / notice) who took it, did you?
B: Well, there was a man who [3]______ (seem / act) suspiciously. He [4]______ (appear / wear) some kind of motorbike helmet. When he approached your chair where your jacket was, he [5]______ (appear / pick) something up.
A: Really? OK, I'm going to call the police. I guess I [6]______ (unlikely / see) my money again.

2 Rewrite the phrases in bold with *it* + a *that*-clause.

1 We didn't manage to buy tickets. **We turned out to have been standing** in the wrong queue.
It turned out that we'd been standing in the wrong queue.
2 **The house appeared not to have been lived in** for years.
3 **There seems to have been** a power cut last night.
4 Do you need some help with your essay? **I happen to have written** one on that topic last week.
5 **They might appear to be ignoring** you, but perhaps they're just waiting for some information before replying.

1C

1 Tick the sentences where the infinitive phrase in bold is in the most natural position. Choose a better position for the infinitive phrase in the other sentences.

1 Sheila can play loads of musical instruments, **to name but a few**, including the guitar, the violin and the saxophone.
2 I know my cooking was a disaster today, but, **to be fair**, it was the first time I'd tried to cook that dish.
3 I've heard worse singers than you, but you're still pretty bad, **to be sure**!
4 That painting is really ugly. **Not to put too fine a point on it**, I think you've wasted your money.
5 Roger took my car without asking to borrow it, **to add insult to injury**, and then he spilt crisps all over the seats.
6 Everything turned out OK in the end, **needless to say**.

2 Choose the correct alternatives.

Good afternoon. My presentation today is about the perils of posting too much personal information online, or oversharing, [1]*to give it its proper title/to make matters worse*. I'd like to tell you what happened to me. For years and years, I posted every tiny detail of my life online. It was great at first, but [2]*to cut a long story short/to give a simple example*, I ended up losing two of my best friends, after revealing details of their personal lives. It was very embarrassing, [3]*to be precise/to put it mildly*. But then, [4]*to give it its proper title/to make matters worse*, some thieves used my personal information to raid my bank account. I was disappointed, [5]*to say the least/to put it bluntly*, but I guess I've learnt a few valuable lessons.

Want more practice? Go to your Workbook or app.

LANGUAGE

2A The continuous aspect

The continuous aspect is used when we want to focus on the action, not the result. We do this for different reasons:

- when we see the activity as **temporary:**

*I've **been living** with my parents while I look for my own place.* (= temporary)

- when we see the activity as **limited** (we are describing 'part' of an activity, not the finished whole):

*I'**m working** on my presentation at the moment, and I've still got loads to do.*

- to describe a **repeated** or **changing** action:

*I'**ve been cycling** to work every day recently.*

- when we describe **trends:**

*Many urban areas **are becoming** more gentrified.*

We also use the continuous aspect with verbs of the senses (*see, hear, feel, understand* and *remember)* to focus on the action rather than the result:

*I **heard** someone **shouting** in the street late last night.*

(This suggests the action was repeated and ongoing.)

*I **heard** someone **shout** in the street late last night.*

(This suggests I only heard them shout once.)

We don't generally use verbs with a **stative** meaning with the continuous aspect:

*I **believed** it was possible.* NOT: *I ~~**was believing**~~ it was possible.*

Some verbs can have both a **stative** or **dynamic** meaning, with no real difference in meaning:

*I **don't feel** well./I'**m not feeling** well.*

Others do change the meaning. Compare:

*I **think** it's a great idea.* (think = believe)

*I'**m thinking** about what to have for dinner tonight.*

(= actively thinking)

2B Probability

We can use a number of different patterns with adjectives to express possibility.

- *It* + *be* + adjective + *that*-clause:

***It's likely that** we'll arrive early.*

- Pronoun + *be* + adjective + *that*-clause:

***I'm sure that** they knew all about it.*

That can also be omitted:

It's likely we'll arrive early.

To emphasise the subject of the sentence, we can use:

- Subject + adjective + *to*-infinitive:

***We**'re **likely to arrive** early.*

With the adjectives *(im)possible* and *bound*, only one form is possible.

*It's **impossible** that we could have finished it on time.*

NOT: ~~We were impossible to have finished it on time.~~

We can modify *(un)likely* with the following adverbs: *highly, quite.*

*She's **highly unlikely** to be there on time.*

We can modify *sure* and *certain* with the following adverbs: *pretty, fairly, absolutely, totally, quite.*

*I'm **pretty certain** that she won't say no.*

2C Cleft sentences

Cleft sentences are used to connect what the speaker and listener already know to what is new information, and to emphasise certain things.

In cleft sentences that begin with *It*, the *It*-clause focuses on the important information in the sentence, and the following clause links *it* to what is already known:

***It's** Jamie **who** plays tennis, not Jane.*

We can focus on any information in the sentence, depending on what we want to emphasise. Compare with example above:

*It's **tennis** that Jamie plays, not **badminton**.*

We can also use negative structures in the *It*-clause:

*It **wasn't** Sally who stole your watch.*

We can include information other than nouns in the *It*-clause, depending on what the new information is:

It was ***because of her hard work*** that she won.

In cleft sentences beginning with *What*, the *What*-clause refers to the known information, and the following clause introduces the new information. They add emphasis to the verb in the *What*-clause:

***What** I love most **are** horror movies.*

When we substitute the main verb with *did*, we use an infinitive. We can omit the *to* from the full infinitive with no real change in meaning:

*What she **did** was **(to) ask** them for more money.*

If the main verb is usually followed by a gerund, then the cleft is also followed by a gerund:

*What I **hate** is **being** ignored.*

If we want to emphasise one thing above all else, we can replace *What* with *All*:

***All** I need is another two weeks.*

PRACTICE

2A

1 Choose the correct alternatives.

1 Maddie *works/is working* from home this week.
2 They're late. They *must have missed/have been missing* the bus.
3 Can you see Graham *wave/waving* from the top of the building?
4 I've *sent/been sending* over a hundred emails today.
5 I won't be in today, I've *got/been getting* the flu.
6 The situation *definitely gets/is definitely getting* better for them.
7 How long *have you known/have you been knowing* Clara?
8 I heard my neighbours *argue/arguing* for hours last night.
9 I've *thought/been thinking* a lot about you lately.

2 Find the five sentences with mistakes and correct them.

1 Eco-friendly travel is generally becoming more and more popular in my country.
2 What will you do this time next week?
3 We've lived with my in-laws while our house is being decorated.
4 The organisation is believing in its staff.
5 I'd lie on the beach if I wasn't in class at the moment.
6 I haven't been doing much work lately.
7 They'd talked about Chris when he suddenly walked in the room.

2B

1 Complete the sentences with one word.

1 It's unlikely ______ they'll agree to this.
2 The finance department are sure ______ reject the budget.
3 She's highly ______ to agree, because it's in her best interests.
4 ______'s possible we'll get there early at this rate.
5 We ______ certain this will get approved.
6 Craig's unlikely ______ have already bought her present.
7 You're bound ______ get the job, I'm sure of it.
8 I'm sure ______ things will get better for you soon.

2 Choose the correct alternatives.

The world of work is changing significantly and rapidly, and this is bound [1]*it will/to* continue into the future. One area of concern is that of automation, and while it's [2]*highly/totally* likely that a small number of jobs will become fully automated, experts are fairly sure [3]*not to/that this will not* mean humans being replaced. A significant number of jobs are likely [4]*to/that they will* become at least partially automated, however, which will mean the need to develop new skills in the workforce.

Polarisation of the workforce [5]*is/that* sure to continue too, with the number of high-skilled jobs and low-skilled jobs increasing, and a fall in the number of medium-skilled jobs. It's also possible [6]*to/that* manufacturing jobs will decrease, while jobs in the service sector continue to rise. This in turn means that workers are quite [7]*likely/possible* to offer their services online, as opposed to more traditional avenues of recruitment.

With all of these changes occurring [8]*it/we* can be quite sure that whatever industry we work in, it's bound to look different to now.

2C

1 Put the words in the correct order to make sentences.

1 enjoy / video / What / is / games / we / playing
2 Janice / was / drank / coffee / your / that / It
3 the / wasn't / who / It / letter / me / wrote
4 that / to / money / we / I'm / All / save / saying / more / is / need
5 Jerry / It / ate / your pear / was / who / not me
6 to / What / investigate / did / we / was / them / ask
7 is / I / What / dishes / the / like / don't / doing
8 to / I / at / was / school / It / sew / learnt / that

2 Rewrite the sentences beginning with the word given.

1 I hate people that don't clean up after themselves.
What ______________________.
2 I didn't call you late last night.
It ______________________.
3 He was arrested because he stole a car.
It ______________________.
4 We just need a bit more money.
All ______________________.
5 She stayed up all night to finish her essay.
What ______________________.
6 My cousins live in Chichester.
It ______________________.
7 We simply want a second chance.
All ______________________.
8 He studied a lot, that's why he passed the exam.
It ______________________.

Want more practice? Go to your Workbook or app.

LANGUAGE

3A Question forms

In spoken English, there are a wide range of question forms we can use.

Negative questions

These include a negative auxiliary, and the speaker usually has a certain response in mind. They are often rhetorical (i.e. they don't require an answer):

Don't you want to see your cousin?

Statement + question word

These are often used to show surprise. We can also use them to check if we haven't heard something clearly:

You spent how much? (= I can't believe how much you spent.)

Indirect questions

These are often used with questions that may be difficult to ask, in order to 'soften' them. They are usually more formal and the word order is the same as in sentences:

Could you tell me what you plan to do about the situation?

In a similar way, we can embed questions in statements. **Embedded questions** are used with adjectives such as *unclear, uncertain*, etc:

*It's **unclear why** she took the documents with her.*

Embedded *yes/no* questions use *if* or *whether*:

*It's not clear **if** they received the order yet.*

Question tags

We use question tags to check or confirm information. In this case our intonation on the question tag falls:

Jake's not really into sport, is he?

Question word + *is it*

Also known as cleft questions, these add emphasis to the thing we are asking about, and are usually more formal:

*What **is it** that you wanted to speak to me about?*

3B Reason clauses

While we often introduce reasons with *because*, there are several words/phrases we can use:

- *Since, As, Given that* and *Seeing as* + clause to describe reasons that the listener already knows, or are common knowledge between the speaker and listener:

__Since__ there's nothing on TV tonight, let's go out.

__Seeing as__ it'll be warm, let's have the party outside.

In that + clause usually comes in the second part of the sentence:

*This product isn't likely to sell well, **in that** it's quite a niche market.*

- *Insofar as*/*Inasmuch as* + clause to justify a comment in a more formal way:

*We don't expect a lot of opposition to the plans, **insofar as** they'll benefit most of the community.*

- *For fear of*/*At the risk of* + object + *-ing* to describe possible outcomes:

*We've ordered twice as many products, **for fear of them running out** during the holidays.*

We can also use *-ing* clauses to express reasons for past actions:

*I've been up all night, **trying** to find a solution.*

3C Ways of modifying adjectives

Gradable and ungradable adjectives

Some adjectives are **gradable**, which means the degree of strength can vary (e.g. *hot, good*). Others are **ungradable**, which means the degree cannot be varied (e.g. *boiling, excellent*). We modify these in different ways.

We can only use certain **adverbs** to modify **gradable adjectives** (e.g. *barely, bitterly, deeply, extremely, fairly, perfectly, rather, somewhat, seriously, very*):

*We were **deeply sorry** to hear your news.*

We can only use certain **adverbs** to modify **ungradable adjectives** (e.g. *absolutely, completely, essentially, nearly, totally, utterly, virtually*):

*I felt **totally overwhelmed** by my workload at the time.*

Really, pretty and *quite* can be used with both gradable and ungradable adjectives.

However, with gradable adjectives quite means 'fairly', whereas with ungradable adjectives it means 'absolutely'. Compare:

*The story was **quite interesting**, but nothing ground-breaking.*

*The story was **quite fascinating**, a real eye-opener!*

Collocations

Certain modifying adverbs collocate with certain adjectives (e.g. *highly recommended/unlikely/successful; utterly ridiculous/wrong; ridiculously cheap/easy; strongly opposed, perfectly open/honest/straightforward; virtually impossible*):

*It seems **perfectly straightforward** to me, I'm not sure what you don't understand about it.*

Classifying adjectives

Some adjectives can be described as 'classifying'. They define something and therefore can't be modified:

*He's **married**.*

However, some adjectives can be both classifying and non-classifying, with a change in meaning:

*She has a slightly **foreign** accent.* (foreign = gradable)

*It's a **foreign** car.* (= classifying the type of car)

PRACTICE

3A

1 Complete the questions with the missing words.

1 ______ you want to go tonight? I thought you liked his music.
2 You don't like potatoes, ______?
3 You think it's worth ______? £300?
4 ______ you tell me how much a new one costs?
5 ______ you going to say hello? Bit rude.
6 Why ______ she's not at work?
7 You went ______? To HIS house?
8 I don't know ______ I should laugh or cry.

2 Put the words in the correct order to make questions.

1 much / how / lost / you ?
2 table / the / broke / who / it / was / that ?
3 difficult / early / up / so / isn't / to / it / get ?
4 at / you / stayed / you / home / tell / could / why / me
5 wanted / talk / what / you / it / is / that / to / about ?
6 available / me / you / tell / could / it / you're ?
7 happened / you / out / what / didn't / find / want / to ?
8 shall / let's / we / it / leave / there ?

3B

1 Put the words in brackets in the correct order to complete the sentences. There is one extra word you do not need.

1 (*as / best / you / Seeing / to / know / Zoe*), you should be the one to ask her.
2 We don't expect too many people to come, (*that / given / a weeknight / it's / is*)
3 July isn't the best time to go, (*peak / in / it's / that / season / is*).
4 I went all around town, (*look / looking / open / somewhere / for / still*)
5 We don't want to buy them too early, (*that / for / of / price / down / the / going / fear*).

2 Correct the mistake in each sentence.

1 Since as there's not much on at the cinema, let's watch something at home.
2 We rang around everywhere, try to find a replacement at the last minute.
3 You need to book early, for fear of them to sell out.
4 I'd love to try the pie, given as you liked it so much.
5 I was lucky in I had lots of people to help me.
6 We should get there early, at the risk for stating the obvious.
7 Keep your money somewhere safe as that you don't want to lose it.
8 The performance was a huge success insofar that the financial side of it was concerned.

3C

1 Choose the correct alternatives.

I hate it when I see people post [1]*very fake/fake* news stories on social media. In my opinion, it's [2]*perfectly/strongly* straightforward to check the facts of a story before you post it, and some of these stories are [3]*bitterly/utterly* ridiculous. The other day I was [4]*somewhat/essentially* disappointed to see a [5]*virtually/really* stupid news story posted by a friend who I respect. The whole thing was [6]*quite/very* impossible to believe, and I really thought they knew better than that. It just [7]*doesn't/does* seem very clever to me. Fact-checking a story before you post is [8]*perfectly/barely* straightforward, and doesn't take a moment to do.

2 Complete the sentences with an adverb from box A and an adjective from box B. Sometimes more than one combination is possible.

A

bitterly perfectly quite rather ridiculously seriously virtually utterly

B

capable cheap disappointed fascinating hurt impossible ridiculous ugly

1 It's ______ to know what they're thinking.
2 I was ______ by the results – they were terrible!
3 Those curtains are ______ . Can we change them?
4 Jan is ______ of doing the job.
5 Several people were ______ in the accident. It was awful.
6 The documentary was ______! I learnt a lot.
7 Ten pounds is ______ for a theatre ticket.
8 It's ______ to suggest she was wrong. Of course she wasn't!

Want more practice? Go to your Workbook or app.

LANGUAGE

4A Non-future uses of *will*

Inferences

We can use *will* to make inferences (guesses) about present states (e.g. with *know*, *be*, *have*, etc.):

*Why not ask David? He'**ll know** the answer, I'm sure.* (= I'm guessing that he knows)

We can use the **future continuous** to infer what is probably happening now:

*You'**ll be wondering** why I'm wearing a suit, I imagine.* (= I bet you're wondering)

We can use the **future perfect** to make inferences about past events:

*Anna's been in a meeting all day, so she **won't have read** your email.* (= I bet she hasn't)

Habits

We can use *will* to talk about long-term present habits. Use *would* to talk about past habits.

*My dad'**ll get up** early every Saturday to go fishing.*

This use of *would* means the same as *used to*. Use *used to* (not *would*) for past states:

When I was a child, my mum used to own (NOT ~~*would own*~~) *a shop.*

Refusals and insistence

We use *won't* to say what people refuse to do. We can also use it to complain about objects, the weather, etc:

*There's something wrong with this door. It **won't open**.* (= it refuses to open)

The past of *won't* for refusals is *wouldn't*:

*When I was a child, I **wouldn't eat** vegetables.*

Stress the word *will* to complain that somebody regularly insists on doing something harmful/annoying:

*I'm not surprised you feel tired, but you **will*** (NOT ~~*you'll*~~) *stay up late watching videos, won't you?*

4B Real conditionals

Conditionals (sentences with *if*, *unless*, *as long as*, etc.) fall into two families:

Real conditionals

About things that **may be true** or are **likely to happen**.

- Real past: *If you missed the last lesson, please take a copy of the worksheet we used.* (= I know some of you missed the lesson. If you're one of those people, please take …)
- Real present (zero conditional): *If you don't have a worksheet, please take one now.*
- Likely future (first conditional): *If you miss the next lesson, you'll probably fail the final exam.*

Unreal conditionals

About things that are **untrue or unlikely to happen.** ▶ See 5B page 154.

Be careful with *if* + past simple. It can refer to the real past (e.g. *If you **missed** the last lesson, …*), the unreal present (e.g. *If I **had** more copies, I'd give you one.*) or the unlikely future (e.g. *if I **failed** the exam, I'd be devastated.*)

Verb forms in real conditionals

In real conditionals, **many** verb forms are possible, including imperatives, modal verbs, continuous forms, perfect forms, *used to*, *be going to*, etc., as long as they refer to real/likely situations:

*When I was younger, I **used to** get stressed if I'**d drunk** too much coffee.* (= whenever I'd drunk …)

However, it is unusual to use *will* in the *if*-clause, except when it contains:

- a prediction:

*I'll drive you to the airport **if it'll save** you time.* (= if you predict that it'll save you time)

- a promise/willingness to do something later:

*I'll drive you to the airport **if you'll fix** my computer later.* (= if you promise that you'll fix it)

- a refusal/insistence (▶ See 4A):

***If they won't eat** vegetables* (= if they refuse to eat them)*, why not give them vegetable soup?*

***If you will tease** the cat* (= if you insist on teasing it)*, don't be surprised if you get scratched.*

4C Giving vague impressions

To communicate that our memories or sensations are not completely clear, we can use a variety of phrases and structures.

Nouns

Use phrases like *something resembling*, *what could almost be*, *what might possibly be*, *kind of like* and *what can only be described* as before a noun:

*We arrive at **what could almost be** an airport, but it's underwater.*

Use *or that kind of thing* or *or something like that* at the end of a sentence:

*It was like a drinks machine, **or that kind of thing**.*

Adjectives

Use *ish* or *-y* with adjectives to make them less precise:

*It was a **pinky** grey colour.*

You can also use modifiers like *somewhat*, *pretty* and *fairly* to make adjectives sound less definite:

*It's **somewhat** cold.*

Also use the adverb *vaguely* with adjectives such as *familiar*, *aware*, *troubling* or *guilty*:

*She was **vaguely aware** of our presence.*

With actions, use phrases like *somehow* and *I don't know how*:

***Somehow**, we got out safely.*

***I don't know how**, but we were suddenly in the mayor's office.*

PRACTICE

4A

1 Match statements 1–6 with the people who made them a–f.

1 'I'll wait for hours for the perfect shot.'
2 'It wouldn't stop.'
3 'Well, you will drive too fast.'
4 'I will not be spoken to like that.'
5 'You won't have heard this one before.'
6 'I wouldn't touch them.'

a Somebody accusing a friend of dangerous habits.
b Somebody introducing a joke.
c A photographer describing his/her hobby.
d A parent addressing a cheeky child.
e Somebody complaining about yesterday's rain.
f Somebody describing his/her childhood attitude to vegetables.

2 Correct the mistakes in each sentence.

1 Whenever I'm feeling stressed, I'll have turned off all the lights and listen to some relaxing music. It always makes me feel better.
2 When I was a child, I would live with my grandparents.
3 Your best shoes are covered in mud again! But you'll wear them for your cross-country walks, won't you?
4 My dog hates the rain. She won't be going outside even if there's just a light drizzle.
5 We should call them to say we've arrived – they'll get worried by now.
6 When I was a student, I remember I'll often spend ages planning each essay, but then I wouldn't have time to actually write it!

4B

1 Choose all the possible options to complete the sentences.

1 If you *didn't/ don't/ won't* stop making so much noise, I'm going to get really angry.
2 You can pay in cash, but you can also pay by card if *you/ you'd/ you'll* prefer.
3 **A:** Apparently Harry studied in Spain for a year.
B: Really? So if he *lived/ used to live/ would live* in Spain, his Spanish must be pretty good.
4 I can lend you my notes as long as *you/ you'd/ you'll* look after them.
5 Hurry up! If *we/ we'll/ we might* miss the bus, we'll be late.

2 Complete the sentences with the most suitable form of the verb in brackets. Sometimes more than one answer is possible.

1 I'm going to check what Gareth's doing. If he ______ (watch) TV again instead of helping us, I ______ (be) really annoyed.
2 If you ______ (enjoy) her last novel, I'm sure you ______ (love) her new one, which is coming out next week.
3 We haven't decided what to do about food this evening. I suppose if everyone ______ (be) really hungry, we ______ (go) to a restaurant, or we ______ (just/get) a takeaway.
4 I ______ (prefer) not to buy a new coffee maker this month unless the old one ______ (be) completely beyond repair.

4C

1 Complete the conversation with the phrases in the box.

kind of like	somehow	that kind of thing	vaguely
verging on			

A: So – it's a winter's day, and you walk into a village. What can you see?
B: Well, lots of people in old clothes, [1]______ .
A: And what can you smell?
B: Hmmm, a fresh smell, [2]______ you get at a fruit market.
A: And how do you feel?
B: Tired, [3]______ exhausted. I've been walking all day. I'm [4]______ aware that people aren't looking at me. [5]______ , I think they can't see me …

2 Put the text in the correct order.

A blue hoody that had seen better days, perhaps from a university sports team, that kind ______
B On that morning at breakfast, I was vaguely __*1*__
C he sensed that we were watching him, and we quickly retreated behind newspapers. ______
D of thing. He was also wearing what could ______
E aware that something wasn't quite right. The stranger had arrived at the hotel wearing a greeny ______
F almost have been those 3D glasses you used to use to watch films in the 80s. Somehow, ______

Want more practice? Go to your Workbook or app.

LANGUAGE

5A Linking devices

Linking devices show how ideas are connected. They fall into three main families. When you know which family a linking device belongs to, you can predict how to use it.

Conjunctions (e.g. *if, because, inasmuch as, now that, provided that, supposing that*) are followed by a clause (e.g. something happened):

I'm disappointed ***because*** *nobody helped me.*

Some conjunctions contain *that*, which you can leave out (especially in spoken or informal English), as long as the meaning is clear:

Now (that) *everybody's here, we can start.*

Prepositions (e.g. *without, apart from, but for, regardless of*) are usually followed by a noun phrase (e.g. *something*). Many prepositions can also be followed by an *-ing* form with or without a subject (e.g. doing something/ **somebody** doing something) or an indirect question (e.g. what happened):

The journey was fine ***apart from*** *a few problems/ the car breaking down/ what happened when we arrived.*

A few linking devices (e.g. *before, since, given*) can be used as both conjunctions and prepositions:

Given (that) *you've worked here before.*

Given *your previous experience, we'd like to offer you the job.*

Linking adverbs show the relationship between two sentences (or two statements joined by *and/ or/ but*). Most linking adverbs (e.g. *however, granted*) come at the beginning or end of the second statement, separated by commas/pauses:

I was worried. ***However****, everything turned out OK.*

Everything turned out OK, ***however****.*

A few linking adverbs (e.g. *still, nonetheless*) can come after an auxiliary verb/before a main verb:

I don't mind helping you, but I'm ***still/ nonetheless*** *not happy about it.*

5B Unreal conditionals

Unreal conditionals are sentences with *if* (or similar words) where the speaker/writer is imagining a different reality in the past, present or future.

- Unreal/unlikely future (second conditional):

It ***would be*** *awful if I* ***lost*** *my job.* (but I don't expect to)

- Unreal present (second conditional):

I'd know *how to use this printer if there* ***weren't*** *so many buttons.* (but there are too many so I don't know)

- Unreal past (third conditional):

The printer ***wouldn't have jammed*** *if* ***I'd read*** *the instructions.* (but I didn't read them so it jammed)

It is possible to mix conditionals about different times:

The printer ***wouldn't have jammed*** (earlier) *if there* ***weren't*** *so many buttons* (now).

Use *If it weren't for/ If it hadn't been for* + noun phrase to highlight the importance of something:

If it ***weren't for/ hadn't been for*** *my sister, I'd never have applied for the job.*

Use *If* + subject + *were to* + infinitive to make it clear you're talking about the unlikely future, not the real past:

If I ***were to offend*** *you, I'd apologise immediately.* (clearly about the unlikely future)

We can remove the word *if* and move *were* or *had* to the beginning, especially in formal English:

Had I known *you were outside, I'd have let you in.* (= if I'd known)

5C Hypothetical language

Wishes

Wishes (with *I wish* or *if only*) about the unreal past and present work in the same way as *if*-clauses.

- Unreal past: *I wish you****'d told*** *me earlier. If you****'d told*** *me earlier, I could have tidied up.*
- Unreal present: *I wish I* ***had*** *more time. If I* ***had*** *more time, I'd write my life story.*

To make wishes about the unlikely future, use *would* when the wish is about other people (or machines, the weather, etc.). This often contains the idea of a refusal (see 4A page 158):

I wish somebody ***would make*** *a film of my life story.* (but I know they never will)

I wish it ***would stop*** *raining.* (but it refuses)

We don't use *would* in future wishes about ourselves. We use *could* instead:

I wish I ***could go*** *to the Oscars one day.* NOT: ~~*I wish I would go*~~ *...*/~~*I wish I went*~~ *...*

Similar structures

Use *would rather* + subject + past simple to talk about present preferences, often in polite refusals:

A: *Do you mind if I open the window?* ***B:*** *Actually,* ***I'd rather*** *you* ***didn't****.* (= please don't)

When the subject is the same in both parts, we use *would rather* (*not*) + infinitive without *to*:

I'd *rather* ***I*** *didn't have to go.* ▶ *I'd rather* ***not go****.*

Use *would rather* + subject + past perfect to complain about a past action (including your own):

I'd ***rather*** *I/ you* ***hadn't told*** *anybody, but it's too late now.* (I'm annoyed that I/you told somebody)

We can say *it's (about) time* + subject + past simple/ continuous to say that something should happen very soon (or should have happened already):

It's about time *they* ***repaired*** *this road.*

We can use *as if/ as though* + past simple/perfect to compare something with an imaginary situation:

Our teacher treats us ***as if/ as though*** *we* ***were*** *children.*

PRACTICE

5A

1 Choose one or two correct options to complete the sentences.

1 Given *that we've got no/ our lack of/ having no* customers, shall we go home early?

2 Supposing we *offered/ offering/ to offer* a hundred more, would that make a difference?

3 Now *sleeping/ I've slept/ to sleep* a little, I feel better.

4 Regardless of *him being rude/ his rudeness/ he's rude*, you shouldn't have reacted like that.

5 Apart from *having been chased/ being chased/ I was chased* by wild dogs, I'm OK, I guess.

2 Complete the second sentence so that it means the same as the first. Use the word in brackets.

1 I don't know how I'd manage if you weren't so generous. (but)
_______ , I don't know how I'd manage.

2 You'll be perfectly safe – unless you do anything stupid. (provided)
_______ , you'll be perfectly safe.

3 Everybody's welcome to join our yoga class. Their age doesn't matter. (regardless)
Everybody's welcome to join our yoga class, _______ old they are.

4 There's no point copying somebody's essay. It won't teach you anything useful. (inasmuch)
Copying somebody's essay is pointless _______ learn anything useful.

5 The acting is terrible. I know the actors are only children, but it spoils the film. (granted)
The actors are terrible. _______ only children, but they spoil the film.

5B

1 Complete the sentences with the phrases in the box.

had I known	if it would	I were to tell you
there were to be	were it not	were we to

1 _______ it was so dangerous, I'd never have gone parachuting.

2 Unfortunately, we cannot accept your application as it does not fulfil all our criteria. _______ make an exception for you, it might set a precedent for the future.

3 I'd speak to your teacher _______ help you get a better mark, but I don't think it will.

4 You think this puzzle's difficult, do you? What if _______ there's a simple solution?

5 If _______ an election this week, who would you vote for?

6 Bees are the unsung heroes of the insect world. _______ for these creatures, we would quickly run out of food.

2 Rewrite the sentences using unreal conditionals with *if*.

1 We didn't win the match, perhaps because I missed that easy goal.

2 We got caught in a traffic jam earlier so we're not home yet.

3 It was raining, so not many people came to the concert.

4 We weren't waiting for you at the airport because you didn't tell us what time you were arriving.

5 Hannah's broken her leg so she can't go dancing.

6 I wasn't looking where I was going so I walked into a lamppost.

5C

1 Complete the conversation with one word or a contraction in each space.

A: You look upset. What's happened?

B: I'd rather [1]_______ say. I'll be fine.

A: Come on, you can tell me. Sometimes when you talk about a problem, it solves itself.

B: Hah! If [2]_______ it were that simple! OK, I'll tell you, but I'd really rather you [3]_______ tell anyone else, OK?

A: I promise. What's up?

B: It's my boss. She treats me as if I [4]_______ stupid. It's been getting me down for ages.

A: Really? Perhaps it's [5]_______ time you told her how it makes you feel.

B: Well, it's too late for that now. This morning I told her I don't want to work for her stupid company anymore. I [6]_______ I hadn't been so rude, but I was really upset.

2 Write wishes about these situations. Start each sentence with *I wish*.

1 I don't have enough time.

2 I shouldn't have spent so much money.

3 Nobody is willing to help me with my project.

4 Why on earth was I wearing that silly hat when they took my photo?

5 My dream is for somebody to write a song about me ... but I know it'll never happen.

6 It's a shame there aren't 25 hours in a day!

Want more practice? Go to your Workbook or app.

LANGUAGE

6A The passive

There are many different reasons why we use the passive in English, such as when we don't know who carried out the action, or when the agent doing the action is not important. Other reasons include:

- to maintain the focus on what we put at the beginning of the sentence (after previously mentioning it):

Temperatures are set to fall again this week. ***The cold weather*** *has been caused by strong southerly winds.*

- when the agent is a long phrase, to avoid the sentence sounding awkward:

We have been overwhelmed by ***the number of thoughtful, caring responses to our appeal****.*

- to avoid responsibility by 'depersonalising' the action or event:

The report hasn't been finished quite yet.

NOT: ~~*I haven't finished the report quite yet.*~~

There are several reasons we avoid using the passive in English. These include:

- we want to avoid the construction *be being* or *been being*:

The government will be investing several billion pounds in education over the next five years.

NOT: ~~*Several billion pounds will be being invested in education over the next five years.*~~

- with intransitive verbs:

It happened to me when I was young.

Some verbs have two objects (a person and a thing). If the focus of a passive sentence is on the 'thing' we add *to*:

They gave the government the information. (active)

The government *was given the information.* (passive)

The information *was given* ***to*** *the government.* (passive)

When a verb has a dependent preposition, the preposition remains directly after the verb:

Over 1,000 people ***applied for*** *the job.* (active)

The job was ***applied for*** *by over 1,000 people.* (passive)

6B Making formal recommendations/The present subjunctive

After certain verbs e.g. *insist, suggest, recommend, propose, request, order, think, demand* we use the infinitive without *to* for all persons. This is known as the **present subjunctive**, and is generally used in formal spoken and written English:

We ***demand*** *the minister apologise for his comments.*

We also use the present subjunctive after certain adjectives e.g. *essential, advisable, vital, crucial, imperative, desirable, best*:

It is ***best*** *he say nothing until the decision has been confirmed.*

We also use it after certain nouns (usually followed by a *that* clause) e.g. *decision, recommendation, proposal, suggestion, advice, insistence, demand, requirement, condition*:

She agreed to give an interview on the ***condition*** *that she not be identified.*

We often use fixed expressions with the subjunctive form. These include:

- *Come what may, ...* = 'whatever happens'
- *Far be it from me to ...* to introduce something that is not intended to disagree, even though it sounds like it might.
- *Perish the thought!* to show, often sarcastically, that something is ridiculous
- *Suffice to say, ...* to show you think something is obvious or to summarise

Me have a holiday this year? ***Perish the thought!***

We also use *It's high/about time* + past simple for urgent recommendations.

It's about time *the council started repairing the city's roads.*

6C Comparatives

We can use adverbs and adverbials to make big or small comparisons, e.g. *much, a lot, just that little bit, way, far, even, a bit*:

Life is ***far*** *better when you have great friends.*

We can also use *anything/nothing like/nowhere near* + *as* + adjective + *as* to describe very big differences.

If her cooking is ***anything like as*** *good* ***as*** *yours, I'd be surprised.*

Some adverbs use a comparative form like adjectives:

We should arrive a bit ***earlier*** *than we thought.*

Adverbs formed from adjectives (with a *-ly* ending) are compared with *more* or *less*:

I did ***more badly*** *than I expected.*

We can use *one of the* + superlative + plural noun:

It's one of the best films I've ever seen.

Use *prefer* + *to* to talk about general preferences:

Janice ***prefers*** *cats* ***to*** *dogs.*

Use *'d prefer/'d sooner/'d rather* + *than* to talk about a specific or hypothetical preference:

I'd sooner *go by train* ***than*** *bus, it's quicker.*

We can also compare things with contrasting adjectives:

I'm not so much amused as dismayed.

There are a number of idiomatic expressions we use to compare things:

- *X can't hold a candle to Y* (= *Y* is much better)
- *X is not (even) in the same league as Y* (= *Y* is much better)
- *X doesn't bear comparison with Y* (= *Y* is much better)
- *X is beyond comparison* (= *X* is the best):

Pop music ***can't hold a candle to*** *the classics.*

PRACTICE

6A

1 Choose the correct alternatives.

The new film, released this week, takes place in the not-too-distant future. [1]*It's set/They set it* on a distant planet which [2]*has been set up by them as/has been set up as* a prison colony for the most violent criminals of the time. While [3]*it had been being built by the new world government/the new world government had been building it*, rich mineral deposits were found, and so the prisoners are set to work mining when they arrive. When [4]*the prison colony opens/people open the prison colony*, a group of new arrivals immediately starts plotting their escape. They begin hatching a plan, but are soon found out, however, and the worst punishment of all [5]*is given to them/is given them*: the Mindflow.

2 Rewrite the sentences using the words given.

1 After only five minutes, United had scored the first goal.
After only five minutes, the first goal ________ .

2 We'll eat your sandwiches if you leave them there.
Your sandwiches ________ .

3 People are talking about the new film.
The new film ________ .

4 They gave the prize to a young student.
The prize ________ .

5 They gave the prize to a young student.
A young student ________ .

6B

1 Choose the correct alternatives. Sometimes both are correct.

1 I suggest she *rethink/rethinks* her plans.
2 Our advice is *that you choose/choosing* your options carefully.
3 Far *be/is* it from me to disagree, but I'm not sure that's the best way forward.
4 It's high time we *leave/left* – we don't want to miss our train.
5 It's essential he *check/checks* his application carefully before submitting.
6 They recommended she *leave/left* the company next week.

2 Complete the conversations with one word.

1 **A:** It looks like the weather's not going to get any better next week.
B: ________ to say, we're going to need to pack some jumpers!

2 **A:** It's ________ we left. Lunch break's nearly over.
B: Yeah, you're right. We should be getting back.

3 **A:** Do you think Jack'll ever manage to get to school on time?
B: ________ the thought! I mean he'd have to get up early.

4 **A:** When should Kayla submit her application?
B: We strongly suggest she ________ it as soon as possible.

6C

1 Choose the correct alternatives.

1 We have made a range of suggestions to make your journey just *that/this* little bit better to plan.
2 Get a move on, could you move any *slowlier/more slowly*?
3 Their performance in the first half wasn't a patch *on/in* their performance in the second half.
4 I prefer their earlier music *than/to* their later stuff.
5 Gina is one of the cleverest *people/person* I know.
6 In terms of nightlife, my town doesn't even bear *comparing/comparison* with London.
7 He's not so much fat *as/than* well built.
8 I'm nowhere near as active *as/than* you.
9 Martina Rudd can't hold a candle *for/to* Beatriz Delanova. She's the greatest dancer of her time.
10 I'd sooner *visit/to visit* the dentist than see him again.
11 It's one of the *harder/hardest* things I've ever had to do.

2 Write comparative sentences using the prompts. Put the words in brackets in the correct form.

1 Shona / nowhere / tall / Ciara.
2 The Greentones / league / Purple Pop.
3 It / one / (funny) / (film) / of this year.
4 We arrived / early / expected.
5 United / nothing / good / Rovers this season.
6 I / sooner / shop at local shops / supermarkets.
7 James / way / (funny) / Chris.
8 His films / candle / those of Bertoletti.
9 I / not so much / angry / confused.
10 Generally / I / prefer / a good film at home / a night out.
11 Tonight / I / prefer / go out.
12 Her muffins / anything like / tasty / mine.

Want more practice? Go to your Workbook or app.

LANGUAGE

7A Determiners

Determiners belong to two families:

Definite determiners: *the*; demonstratives (*this, that, these, those*); possessives (e.g. *my, John's*)

Indefinite determiners: *a/an, another*; quantifiers (e.g. *some, a few, all, half*); numbers (e.g. *one*)

A noun phrase can start with up to three determiners:

[1] indefinite determiner	(of)	[2] definite determiner	'order' adjective	[3] number, few/many	adjective(s)	noun
most	*of*	*the*		*thirty*		*people*
all	*(of)*	*those*			*important*	*facts*
one	*of*	*your*	*first/next/last*	*few*		*journeys*

We don't need *of* after *all, both* and fractions (e.g. *half, a quarter*): *half the time/both the guys*

We can use multipliers (e.g. *twice, three times*) without *of* before a definite determiner: *twice the size*

We can use modifiers to adjust the meaning of determiners: ***almost** all the people*, ***just over/under** half the time*, ***exactly/precisely** those reasons*, ***very** few problems*, ***quite** a few places*, etc.

We can use *quite, rather, such* or *something of* before *a/an* to emphasise an opinion:

*It was **quite/rather an** odd experience.*

Special uses of determiners

In informal English, we can use unstressed *some* with a singular noun to emphasise that we don't know exactly who/what it is. We can stress the word *some* to express amazement.

Unstressed: *There's **some guy** on the phone who wants to talk to you.* (= I have no idea who he is.)

Stressed: *Wow! That was (quite) **some party!*** (= That was an amazing party.)

7B Relative clauses

Defining relative clauses help the reader/listener identify which person/thing we are talking about. The relative pronoun (usually *who/which/that*) can be omitted if it refers to an object, not the subject:

This is the computer (which/that) I bought. (*which/that* refers to the object: I bought **it**.)

Non-defining relative clauses provide extra information, separated from the rest of the sentence with commas/pauses. The relative pronoun (usually *who* or *which*, not ~~*that*~~) cannot be omitted:

This is my favourite website, which I use every day.

Non-defining relative clauses sometimes comment on a whole statement, not just a person/thing:

We got lost, which was annoying. (The fact that we got lost was annoying.)

Relative clauses with prepositions

'Basic' prepositions (e.g. *about, of, with*, and prepositions of time and space) usually come in the same positions as in a full sentence, but they can come before *whom* or *which* in formal English:

*This is the site (which/that) I was telling you **about** last week.* (I was telling you **about** [it] last week.)

Formal: *This is the site **about** which I was telling you last week.*

Longer (or less 'basic') prepositions (e.g. *despite, according to*) are mainly used in non-defining relative clauses. They always come before *whom/which*:

*I had a ticket, **despite which** they wouldn't let me in.* (NOT: ... ~~*which they ... despite*~~.)

7C Reduced relative clauses and similar structures

Reduced relative clauses (RRCs) start with *-ing* forms (for active voice) or past participles (for passive voice). Similar structures start with prepositions, adjectives, etc.

1 Active verb: *The people **waiting** outside didn't look happy.* (= who were waiting)

2 Passive verb: *John and Sue, **made** to wait in the rain, got angry.* (= who were made to wait)

3 Preposition: *The people **outside** the house were getting wet.* (= who were outside)

4 Adjective: *John and Sue, **wet** from the rain, wanted to go home.* (= who were wet)

Most RRCs are defining (e.g. sentences 1 and 3 above), with no commas/pauses. But non-defining RRCs (with commas/pauses) are also possible (e.g. sentences 2 and 4).

We can add *not* at the beginning of an RRC to make it negative:

*Any cars **not parked** in the correct places will be removed.* (= which aren't parked)

When not to use reduced relative clauses

Only use RRCs when the relative pronoun is the subject, and when it is easy to work out the tense of the shortened sentence.

Don't use RRCs with *-ing* forms for short, complete past actions. Use a full relative clause instead:

The thief who stole my bag has been arrested. NOT: ~~*The thief stealing my bag ...*~~

PRACTICE

7A

1 Choose all possible options, a–d, to complete the sentences.

1 After spending ______ unpleasant three days in training, I was totally fed up!
a an b any c another d every

2 When I submitted my application, they told me I needed to sign ______ strange form first.
a any b some c this d a

3 My new flat is almost ______ the size of my old one.
a exactly b quite c half d twice

4 It was an amazing journey and we had ______ an adventure along the way.
a something of b many c twice d quite

5 Wow! That's ______ story! You should write it down in a book!
a much b quite a c some d such an amazing

2 Complete the text with the words in the box.

few half quite some twice

In 1984, Liliana and Emil Schmid set out from Montreal, Canada in their Toyota Land Cruiser, with a plan to spend a year driving around North and Central America. They travelled light: the [1] ______ 'mod cons' they took with them included mosquito nets, a water container and a makeshift bed. Their schedule proved to be [2] ______ challenge! As the end of the year approached, they had only visited just over [3] ______ the seven countries they had intended to visit, so they decided they needed [4] ______ the time to complete their journey. After the second year, they decided to extend their journey by another two years, [5] ______ a commitment!

7B

1 Combine the pairs of sentences using defining or non-defining relative clauses. Choose the best position for the preposition in bold. Omit the relative pronoun, if possible.

1 I need something. I can fix this picture to the wall **with** it.

2 I was trying to help. **Instead of** helping, I think I made the situation worse.

3 Are there any gadgets? Ones you can't imagine living **without**?

4 It was raining heavily. **Despite** this, I decided to go for a run.

5 We need some kind of cabinet. We can put the TV **on top of** it.

6 Is there anything? You have a particular talent **for** it.

2 Complete the sentences using the words in brackets.

1 It took half an hour to get the projector to work, ______ (time) everyone was really bored.

2 We ordered the shoes on the 14th, ______ (three weeks) they still hadn't arrived.

3 Welcome to today's meeting, ______ (purpose) is to discuss last week's conference.

4 It looked like they'd been eating pizza, ______ (remains) were still all over the table.

5 I found many old paintings in the cellar, quite ______ (few) looked pretty valuable.

7C

1 Change the relative clauses in bold into reduced relative clauses. One clause cannot be changed.

1 Several objects **that belonged to the museum** were stolen.

2 The book which **you're looking for** is on the shelf near the window.

3 Anybody **who doesn't want to attend the event** should send me an email.

4 'Logic' is a word **which is derived from the Greek, *logos***.

5 When you arrive at the airport, look out for a woman **who'll be holding a sign with your name**.

6 Please don't turn off any computers **which are being used at the time**.

2 Change the sentence in bold into a reduced relative clause, a *to*-infinitive or a similar structure and combine it with the other sentence.

1 We're staying at the Palace Hotel. **It was designed by a local architect**.

2 Please remember to bring any documents. **They are necessary for your journey**.

3 Prince's Park is my favourite place to relax. **It's near the city centre**.

4 The candidate answered the questions hesitantly. **She felt nervous throughout the interview**.

5 The money should be spent on more trains. **It's currently being spent renovating the road**.

Want more practice? Go to your Workbook or app.

8A Describing habits and compulsions

Use *will* + infinitive without *to* to describe typical behaviour in the present:

*I**'ll say** 'sorry' even if it's not my fault.*

*Whenever I get in late at night, I **won't remember** where I put my keys the next morning.*

We often use *always* with this use of *will*:

*She**'ll always check** she locked the door at least twice when she goes out.*

We can also use *always/forever* + present continuous to describe habits:

*She**'s always going on** about her singing career.*

We can also use *constantly/continually* + present continuous in this way:

*He**'s constantly parking** in front of my car.*

This form can be used to describe very positive or very negative/annoying behaviour:

*He**'s always giving** money to charity.* (positive)

*Helen**'s constantly stealing** other people's food from the fridge.* (negative/annoying)

To describe compulsions, we can use *I have this tendency/(overwhelming) urge/I tend* + infinitive with *to*:

***I have this tendency to walk** in a room and forget what I came in for.*

After *I have this habit of/I find/catch myself/I can't stop myself (from)*, use verb + *-ing*:

*I **have this habit of forgetting** people's names too easily.*

Keep on + verb + *ing* can be used to describe repetitive behaviour:

*I **keep on forgetting** where I left my keys.*

8B The future in the past

There are several ways to describe the future from a past perspective. These forms all have equivalents in the present (which express the future from a present perspective).

- *was/were going to* or **past continuous** describes plans or arrangements we had in the past, which usually didn't come true:

*I **was going to** just relax this weekend, but there's too much to do.*

*We **were meeting** on Friday, but he called to say he couldn't make it.*

- For plans in the past that were certain to come true, we can use *always* + *was/were going to*:

*From an early age, it was clear that Shahla **was always going to** be a teacher.*

We can use *was/were bound to* with a similar meaning:

*The new policy **was bound to** cause us problems.*

- *was/were due to* is used to describe scheduled/formally planned events:

*Initially, the event **was due to** take place in spring, but was delayed until the following year.*

- *was/were (all) set to* and *was/were on course to* describe something that was almost certain because of conditions/plans at the time:

*We **were all set to** leave when we heard the news.*

*The new policy **was on course to** be implemented last month, but last-minute technical problems delayed it.*

- *was/were on the point/verge of* describe changes that had already begun:

*Contestants **were on the point of** starting when an audience member ran on to the stage.*

- *was/were about to* describes thing which were imminent or almost happening:

*I **was about to** leave when they suddenly turned up.*

- *was/were on the threshold of* describes a wider change or situation that was already beginning:

*At the turn of the century, it seemed we were **on the threshold of** a new era.*

We can also use verbs which express perceptions and/or have a future meaning (e.g. *assume, decide, envisage, expect, guess, hope, know, imagine, suspect, think*) + *would* to describe our past perspectives of the future:

*I **suspected** they **wouldn't** accept our proposal.*

8C Emphasising advice

We can emphasise advice in a number of ways.

- *Whatever/However/Whichever/Whenever/Wherever* + *you* + verb, + imperative/*should*:

***Whenever** you visit the city, you **should** bring a map.*

- *Whatever/Whichever* + noun + *you* + verb, imperative/*should*:

***Whichever** one you choose, think carefully about the best place to buy it.*

- *Whatever* is generally used when there is an unlimited range of things:

***Whatever** type of transport you use, stay safe.*

- *Whichever* is generally used to refer to a limited range of things which have already been mentioned:

*You can go by the motorway or by country roads. But **whichever** way you go, make sure you drive carefully.*

- *However/No matter how* + adjective, + imperative/*should*:

***However easy** you think it will be, you should always make sure you're prepared.*

- *No matter* + *what/which/who/where/when/how* + *you* + verb, imperative/*should*:

***No matter where you go**, always **keep** your wits about you.*

For very strong emphasis, use *Under no circumstances/On no account* + *whatsoever* + inversion:

***Under no circumstances whatsoever should you** try to travel without the correct documents.*

A more informal version of this is *No way* + inversion:

***No way should you** try to get in without a ticket.*

PRACTICE

8A

1 Complete the text with the correct form of the verbs in the box.

look say speak talk translate use

Since I moved to Spain I've been trying my best to learn Spanish, but it's difficult. First of all, I'm forever [1]_______ 'uh-huh' or 'Si, si' when I don't understand something, because I don't want to interrupt people. Sometimes when I do this though, people will [2]_______ at me strangely and ask what I mean, and I come unstuck. I keep trying though, and I tend [3]_______ to people in Spanish even if I know the person I'm speaking to speaks better English than my Spanish. It becomes painfully clear when they respond in English, but I keep on [4]_______ Spanish, and I wonder if this is rude. Nonetheless I have this overwhelming urge [5]_______ Spanish (or at least try!). I have this habit of [6]_______ into Spanish directly, too, and then using the wrong words, which can be embarrassing. Once, for example, I tried to say I was embarrassed, but said I was *embarazada*, which means 'pregnant' in Spanish!

2 Rewrite the sentences using the words in brackets.

1 Whenever I watch football on TV, I want to scream at my team. (urge)
2 Any time I bend down to pick something up I make a loud, groaning noise. (will)
3 I throw away food packaging as soon as I open it, every time. (present continuous + always)
4 I always talk out loud when I'm at home alone. (catch myself)
5 I dance when I listen to music in the car. (tend)
6 I walk up and down the room when I'm on the phone. (tendency)

8B

1 Complete the sentences with the correct form of the words in the box.

assume course due have hope set

1 Given the manager's reservations, I just _______ he wouldn't approve our plan, but he actually did.
2 Tina was all _______ to leave for the airport when she saw her flight was delayed.
3 Will was _______ to return yesterday, but storms meant his flight was delayed.
4 I was going to _______ dinner with friends tonight, but I've come down with flu so have to cancel.
5 It seemed Josh was on _______ to get the job, but unfortunately he got rejected in the final round.
6 I _______ I would get a pay rise this year, but deep down I knew it wasn't really going to happen.

2 Complete the second sentence, using the word in brackets, so that it means the same as the first. Write between three to five words.

1 They thought that the introduction of several new companies to the market would drive down prices. (envisage)
It _______ the introduction of several new companies to the market would drive down prices.
2 It was clear at the time that the project would definitely fail. (bound)
It was clear at the time that the project _______ fail.
3 I was sure it wasn't happening. (knew)
I _______ happen.
4 At that point in time, humans were just beginning a new age. (threshold)
At that point in time, humans _______ a new age.
5 Judy was just going to buy the car when she saw a better offer elsewhere. (set)
Judy was _______ buy the car when she saw a better offer elsewhere.

8C

1 Match the sentence halves.

1 You can go by bus or get a taxi. But whichever
2 No matter how
3 No way should
4 Wherever you
5 On no account
6 Under no circumstances whatsoever
a choose to stay, make sure you visit the beach.
b one you choose, make sure you get a receipt.
c tired you feel, keep going.
d whatsoever should you make eye contact.
e you argue with the official. It won't help your case.
f should you travel alone at night.

2 Use the prompts to write sentences.

1 whatever / do / (not) forget / passport
2 however / interesting / think / is / shouldn't / photographs
3 no matter / you meet / polite
4 whatever / day / travel / should / leave early
5 circumstances / carry / valuables / whatsoever
6 whichever / option / choose / (not) pay / too much
7 way / talk / strangers
8 whenever / meet / people / shake / hand

Want more practice? Go to your Workbook or app.

LANGUAGE

9A Narrative tenses

When telling a narrative (e.g. a story, a joke), use the **past simple with action verbs** for the main events in the order they happened:

*The doorbell **rang**. I **opened** the front door and **saw** a strange man standing there.*

Use the **past continuous**, the **past simple with state verbs**, or *could* + *see/hear/tell*, etc., to describe the background situation around the time of the main events:

*I **could see** something was wrong immediately. He **was wearing** dirty old clothes. He **looked** terrible.*

Use the **past perfect simple/continuous** for background events/processes before the main events:

*His clothes looked like he**'d been wearing** them for weeks. Something terrible **had happened** to him.*

Narrative techniques

Previews: We can use the future in the past to preview upcoming twists in the story and to express the characters' hopes and fears: *Things **were about to get** very complicated.*

Creating/relieving suspense: We can use a series of 'background' verb forms to create a powerful impression that something dramatic is going to happen: *He **was staring** angrily at me. He **was holding** something heavy in his hand. I **couldn't tell** what it was at first. Suddenly, he …*

The narrative present: We can use the present simple/continuous for part of a story to make it feel as if it's happening now. This technique is especially common in jokes and spoken anecdotes:

*Suddenly, he **hands** me the object he**'s holding**: a photo album. 'It's been a long time,' he **smiles**.*

9B Reported speech

Backshifting

Reported speech usually involves backshifting (changing present tenses to become past tenses; changing past tenses to become past perfect). We don't have to use backshifting if we want to emphasise that something is still true now.

Direct speech: *'I'm arriving tomorrow morning.'*

→ *Yesterday she told me she**'s arriving** this morning.*
(= I still expect her to arrive as promised)

→ *That's weird. She said she **was arriving** this morning.*
(= but I don't know if it's still true OR it's no longer true because 'this morning' has finished.)

Backshifting and modal verbs

Will, can, may and *shall* backshift to past-tense forms (*would, could, might* and *should*). *Must* and *mustn't* (for obligation) often become *had to* and *wasn't/weren't allowed to*. *Should* can become *was/were* supposed to when we're reporting other people's recommendations:

*'I**'ll** help if I **must**. When **shall** I start? What **should** I do?'*
→ *He said he**'d** help if he **had to**. He asked when he **should** start and what he **was supposed to** do.*

Passive reporting verbs

When we use the passive voice to report what was said, it is normal to start with *It* (e.g. *It was said that* …). With some reporting verbs (e.g. *allege, assume, believe, consider, expect, know, report, rumour, say, think, understand*), we can raise the subject of the reported speech to replace *it* as the subject of the whole sentence. The verb in the reported speech becomes a *to*-infinitive (e.g. *to do, to be doing, to have done, to have been doing*):

*It is alleged that **they stole** the money.* → ***They** are alleged **to have stolen** the money.*

*It was rumoured that **the allegations weren't** true.* → ***The allegations** were rumoured **not to be** true.*

For information on subject raising and infinitive forms, see 1B page 146.

9C Participle clauses and verbless clauses

Participle clauses use **past participles** (e.g. *done*) or **present participles** (e.g. *doing*) instead of normal verbs with subjects and tenses. This enables us to express causes, time and conditions in fewer words than usual, which is useful in written English.

1 **Cause:** ***Not knowing what to do**, I did nothing.*
(= because I didn't know …)

2 **Time:** ***Sitting at the bus stop this morning**, I witnessed a robbery.* (= while I was sitting …)

3 **Condition:** ***Done properly**, a patio can transform a dull garden.* (= if it's done properly, …)

They can also work like **reduced relative clauses** that have been moved to the beginning:

4 ***Written 500 years ago**, this text is the oldest in our collection.* (= this text, which was written …)

However, because they can have several meanings, and because they don't have a subject or a tense, the reader/listener has to work harder to understand them from context.

Present participles have an active meaning (e.g. 1 and 2 above); **past participles** have a passive meaning (e.g. 3 and 4). We can use **complex participles** to refer to earlier events:

***Having seen** the film a few times, I decided to turn off the TV.* (= because I had seen …)

***Having been travelling** all day, they won't want to …*
(= because they'll have been travelling)

You can add *not* or *never* to make a participle clause negative:

***Never/Not** having done it before, I didn't know what to do.*

Common fixed expressions with participle clauses include: *all being well* (= if everything goes well), *all things considered* (= when you consider everything), *bearing in mind that* … (= when you consider that), *given the chance* (= if I were given the chance), *judging by* … (= based on) *speaking of* … (= while we're speaking of) and *that said/having said that* (= although I've said that).

PRACTICE

9A

1 Put the text in the correct order.

A _______ Two hours into my return journey, I was feeling tired. I put some music on to keep me awake.

B _______ The previous day, I'd spent eight hours driving to pay a surprise visit on my cousin, but when I'd arrived, there had been nobody home.

C _______ So after leaving countless voicemail messages, I'd turned around and begun the long journey home.

D _______ Suddenly, a cat dashed out of the shadows right in front of me. I was going to hit it!

E __*1*__ I got out of the cold hotel bed. Drowsily, I looked out of the window and groaned.

F _______ So there I was, driving along in the dark. The music was loud and I was singing along. It had been raining, so the road was slippery. A dark shape was moving by the roadside verge.

2 Choose the correct alternatives.

As I stared out at the snow-covered road, I realised I [1]*hadn't eaten/haven't eaten/wasn't eating* since the previous afternoon. So I [2]*had headed/headed/was going to head* down to the grimy breakfast bar for some food.

While I [3]*had eaten/was going to eat/was eating*, I checked the weather forecast on my phone. A huge blizzard was heading right towards us. It [4]*had hit/was due to hit/was hit* within an hour. If I didn't get away quickly, I [5]*had been/was being/was going to be* stuck there for a week.

I [6]*had run/ran/was running* upstairs, grabbed my bag, paid my bill and dashed out to clear the snow from my car.

9B

1 Report the conversation you had with Angela to your friend Ben. Use backshifting where possible.

1 Angela: 'Do you have any idea what's happened to Ben?' *Angela asked me if …*

2 Angela: 'I haven't heard from him for ages.' *She added that …*

3 You: 'Actually, I'm seeing him tomorrow in the café.'

4 You: 'Shall I send him a message to see if he'd mind if you joined us?'

5 Angela: 'No, I'm afraid I'm going to be tied up all day tomorrow.'

6 Angela: 'There's a meeting at my office that I absolutely must attend. I mustn't be late.'

2 Complete the text with a passive form of the first verb in brackets and a *to*-infinitive form of the second verb.

According to unconfirmed reports, there was a burglary at the City Museum last night. Thieves [1]*are believed to have stolen* (believe/steal) several priceless exhibits.

A rare 12th century vase [2]_______ (assume/be) among the items that were stolen. The vase [3]_______ (consider/be) one of the most valuable items in the museum. According to one source, private collectors [4]_______ (rumour/try) to buy the antique vase for several months, but their offers [5]_______ (say/reject) repeatedly.

9C

1 Complete the sentences with the phrases in the box.

all being well	all things considered
bearing in mind	given the chance
judging by	that said

1 It was a terrible play. _______, the acting was excellent.

2 I don't know the result of the match, but _______ their sad faces, I guess they lost badly.

3 We're making good progress so, _______, we'll finish this week.

4 _______ that it's your first time, you've done a great job.

5 I know I'll never be a Hollywood actor, but _______ I think I'd be pretty good.

6 There are pluses and minuses, but _______, it's a good plan.

2 Complete the second sentence with two words so it means the same as the first.

1 Mobile phones may not be used while you are on the school premises.
You may not use mobile phones _______ the school premises.

2 I pretended not to notice Gemma because I felt embarrassed about my earlier behaviour.
_______ about my earlier behaviour, I pretended not to notice Gemma.

3 I spent all my money on the train ticket so I couldn't afford a taxi from the station.
_______ all my money on the train ticket, I couldn't afford a taxi from the station.

4 We were forced to call the police because nobody had admitted responsibility.
_______ admitted responsibility, we were forced to call the police.

5 *Moby Dick*, which was first published in 1851, didn't become popular until the 1920s.
_______ in 1851, *Moby Dick* only became popular in the 1920s.

Want more practice? Go to your Workbook or app.

LANGUAGE

10A Emphasis and persuasion

There are a number of techniques we can use in a presentation to make it more persuasive and many of these can also be used for emphasis in casual speech.

Using auxiliaries to add emphasis: we often stress the auxiliary when speaking, and to contradict what has just been said:

*We **do** believe in the future.*

Using repetition: we can do this in a number of ways:

- repeating intensifying adverbs:

*They're **really, really** good at what they do.*

- using comparative + comparative:

*With these new advances we will become **stronger and stronger.***

- using statement + repetition + explanation:

It's the best ... it's the best because there's no other like it.

- repeating a key word/phrase you want to emphasise:

All of us** want to see this happen. **All of us.

Rhetorical questions (sometimes including answers):

When do we want this? Now, that's when.

Tripling: making points in 'threes' so that they're more memorable:

*We want to make the company **efficient, hard working** and **adaptive to change.***

Machine-gunning: listing lots of points quickly:

*The way forward is **bright, manageable, ambitious, opportunistic, doable** and **lucrative.***

Contrasting pairs: giving two opposing ideas. The first is usually negative and the latter is what we want:

We don't want to sit there and do nothing. We want to be proactive.

Alliteration: using words with the same first letter or sound next to each other:

*We need to create a **g**reat **g**lobal alliance.*

10B Heads and tails

Heads and tails are common in informal, spoken English (but not in written English). Heads allow us to focus attention on something specific, while tails allow us to clarify something.

Heads: can be **noun phrases** which we want to focus attention on by bringing them to the beginning of the sentence. They are usually followed by a **pronoun** which then refers back to the head. The two parts are separated by a comma:

***Getting up in the morning when it's dark**, I can't deal with that.*

***My sister**, she's a dentist.*

They are often used instead of the possessive *'s* in spoken English.

Compare:

My dad's friend loves tennis.

My dad, his friend, she loves tennis.

Tails: work the other way round. They come at the end of the sentence to qualify what we are talking about, and they make it easier for the listener to follow what we're referring to. They are usually **noun phrases** and refer back to a **pronoun** at the beginning of the sentence. The two parts are separated by a comma:

*We loved it, **that film.***

*He's a clever person, **Danny.***

10C Concession clauses

Concession clauses allow us to contrast two ideas. They reduce the strength of the original idea:

He likes pasta. (original idea)

***Although he likes pasta**, he doesn't like spaghetti.*

- *Although/Even though* + clause. *Even though* has a similar meaning to *Although*, but is slightly stronger. It suggests something is always done or is a fact:

***Even though it's very old**, it's still popular today.*

- *Even when* + clause. This means something happens occasionally:

***Even when the bus was on time**, he was late.*

- *Even if* + clause. This means 'whether or not':

***Even if I studied extra hard**, I couldn't pass an exam.*

- *While/Whereas* + clause. *While* often means 'at the same time'. *Whereas* usually provides an introductory statement:

***While I think you're brave**, I don't think you should go on that trip.*

- Adjective + *as/though* + clause:

***Easy as it may sound**, you still need to make sure you're prepared.*

- *However* + adjective + clause:

***However difficult** you think it might be, I'm sure you can do it.*

- *Much as* + verb of feeling:

***Much as** we might **hate** it now, it's likely to become increasingly popular in the future.*

- *Nevertheless,/Nonetheless,/All the same,/However,* + clause to refer to a previous sentence:

*A lot of people believe it's a valuable approach. **Nonetheless, the evidence is lacking.***

- *In spite of/Despite/*+ noun/noun phrase/gerund:

***Despite the changes**, it still works in the same way.*

We can also use these with the fact that + clause:

***In spite of the fact that it's not popular**, it's important and necessary.*

PRACTICE

10A

1 Complete the sentences with one word.

1 New technology is becoming _______ and cheaper.
2 Nobody wants to see us fail. _______ .
3 _______ do people like this idea? Because it's great, that's why.
4 People _______ love our products. They really do.
5 We don't hate it. We _______ it.
6 It's interesting ... it's _______ because it's unique in the market.
7 It's _______ , way ahead of the competition.
8 It's bad, which makes us _______ , not happy.

2 Read the text and identify eight presentation techniques.

You know the feeling: it's cold, dark and wet outside but you know you need to get out there and exercise. But as winter draws nearer it gets harder and harder to get up off the sofa and go out the front door. Nobody wants to go outside in that weather … nobody.

So what's the solution to all this? The *Multicise*! With over 30 functions in one machine it's effective. It's effective because you can use it at home, even while you watch the TV. With its clever design you can work out, lift weights, strengthen legs, arms and back, do cardio … and much more!

So remember: don't sit, get fit! And *Multicise* really does do what it says. You'll be fit in no time.

10B

1 Match the sentence halves. Is each one a head (H) or tail (T)?

1 Monopoly,
2 That hotel in the photo,
3 It always seem to be full of traffic,
4 He's not very open to new ideas,
5 The house at the end of my road,
6 They're lovely,

a the road in front of my house.
b that's where we stayed last year.
c they always have their lights on.
d my boss.
e my neighbours are.
f that's my favourite game.

2 Put the words in the correct order to complete the conversations. Remember to include commas in the correct place.

1 **A:** Does she work in sales?
B: No, *marketing / Fiona / she / in / works*
2 **A:** *Chris / party / that / That / the / at / guy / was*
B: Yes, that's right.
3 **A:** What's your favourite food?
B: *like / Pizza / I / that's / what*
4 **A:** *back / aunt / That / she's / at / woman / the / my*
B: Oh, she looks a lot like you.
5 **A:** Would you like the steak?
B: *we / No / meat / don't eat / Sarah and I*

10C

1 Choose the option, a–c, which is <u>not possible</u>.

1 _______ she's impatient and abrupt a lot of the time, I like her.
a Although
b Despite
c Even though

2 _______ we might not like it, it's still true.
a Much as
b While
c Nevertheless

3 It's not the best idea. _______ , it's all we have at the moment.
a Although
b Nevertheless
c All the same

4 _______ their limited resources, they've done very well this year.
a Even when
b Despite
c In spite of

2 Find the five sentences with mistakes and correct them. Sometimes more than one answer is possible.

1 Despite they might hate the plan now, once they see it in action I think they'll come round.
2 While it's popular, the science behind it is fundamentally flawed.
3 Difficulty though it is, it's essential that we deliver on time.
4 Although the low fares, people still aren't using public transport in the city.
5 Bright though Kevin was, he didn't do well in exams.
6 However beauty you think it is, most people will disagree with you.
7 While it may be difficult sometimes, all employees must follow company procedure precisely at all times.
8 He drove as fast as he could. Despite, he didn't arrive on time.

Want more practice? Go to your Workbook or app.

Vocabulary bank

1B The internet and social media

1 Match the words in the box with the definitions.

blanking cyberbullying flaming
ranting trolling

1 expressing your strong opinion passionately and emotionally
2 reacting angrily and aggressively to what others have said or written, often turning a formerly calm discussion into an angry battle
3 deliberately and repeatedly trying to spoil something (e.g. a discussion forum), for example by making negative comments and upsetting the participants, without trying to do anything constructive
4 deliberately and repeatedly trying to hurt the feelings of a specific person or group of people online
5 ignoring somebody in order to make them feel bad

2 a Choose the correct alternatives.

1 I hate scrolling through my social media *bookmark/ feed/ navigation* – it's always just full of silly *memes/ portals/ streams* and adverts.
2 I like to keep up to date with current affairs by checking which *bandwidths/ portals/ hashtags* are *feeding/ browsing/ trending* each day.
3 The internet connection in my flat is fairly good, but if everyone is trying to *bookmark/ stream/ trend* videos at once, we quickly run out of *bandwidth/ hashtags/ navigation*.
4 When I go online, I usually begin on my favourite *bandwidth/ meme/ site* and then start *browsing/ feeding/ trending* by following links to other sites.
5 I always *bookmark/ browse/ stream* interesting articles to make them easier to find again later, especially when they're on sites with tricky *hashtags/ memes/ navigation*.

b Which statements in Exercise 2a are true for you? Change the others to make them true for you.

1C Phrasal adjectives

1 Rewrite the sentences using phrasal adjectives.

1 His recommendation wasn't so subtle.
He made a *not-so-subtle* recommendation.
2 The company pays him for recommending its products during his videos.
He makes ____-____ recommendations of the company's products during his videos.
3 This year's results were better than we had expected.
We had ____-____-____ results this year.
4 The saleswoman wasn't prepared to negotiate – she said I could take her offer or leave it.
The saleswoman took a ____-____-or-____-____ approach to the negotiation.
5 My favourite restaurant allows you to eat all you can, and just pay a fixed price for it.
There's an ____-____-____-____ offer in my favourite restaurant.
6 I couldn't say no – it was the sort of opportunity that only comes up once in your lifetime.
It was a ____-____-a-____ opportunity, so I couldn't say no.
7 Despite the flood damage, the shop owners decided to open their business as usual.
The owners adopted a ____-____-____ approach after the flood.
8 You didn't think out the conclusion to your essay very well.
Your essay ended with a rather poorly-____-____ conclusion.

2 Match the phrases in bold with the correct meaning, a or b.

1 Their music is **middle-of-the-road.**
a extreme, unconventional b neutral, safe
2 To be a successful influencer, you need a **larger-than-life** personality.
a calm and disciplined b lively and energetic
3 After the meal, I stood up and gave an **off-the-cuff** speech.
a spontaneous, unplanned b carefully planned and practised
4 She's the **odds-on** favourite to win the award.
a extremely likely b possible but unlikely
5 This process uses **state-of-the-art** technology.
a the latest b well-established
6 The film we saw was just a **run-of-the-mill** romantic comedy.
a low-quality b typical, standard
7 We need to find a way to achieve more with our **ever-dwindling** resources.
a constantly growing b getting smaller and smaller
8 The company is going to make **across-the-board** staff cuts.
a affecting every department b larger than expected
9 The restaurant is popular with **well-to-do** clients.
a rich, high-class b expecting value for money
10 My city is suffering from **unheard-of** levels of pollution.
a unpopular, unknown b record-breaking

2B Work practices

1 Complete the phrases in bold with the words from the box.

appraisal contracts income lieu line manage misconduct pay procedures push rank rata

1 A lot of employers in the fast food industry employ staff on **zero-hour** ______ .
2 I'm sure this will be OK, but I need to check with my ______ **manager** first.
3 Can I have a day off next week **in** ______ of last Saturday?
4 The government is unlikely to ever introduce a **universal basic** ______ .
5 Oh dear, Dan's just been called into the boss's office. Do you think he's likely to be **given the** ______ ?
6 I'm sorry, I see the advantages of your proposal Vanessa, but I'm afraid I'm going to have to **pull** ______ on this and turn it down.
7 Did you hear? Ben's been fired for **gross** ______ . Apparently he stole a computer from the office, which means he won't get any **severance** ______ .
8 I'm going to ask for a pay rise at my next **staff** ______ .
9 We need to start **disciplinary** ______ against Joanne. Her work really hasn't been up to scratch for a long time now, and I'm having to constantly **micro-**______ her.
10 The part-time position pays £12,000 a year (£21,000 **pro** ______).

2 a Complete the questions with the missing words.

1 What types of activities might be considered gross ______? Does it depend on the industry?
2 What types of ______ procedures can a company start against an employee?
3 Have you ever had a staff ______? What happened?
4 Do you know anyone who works on a ______ -hours contract? What do they do?
5 Do you think the government of your country will ever introduce a universal basic ______? Why/Why not?
6 In what ways can a ______ manager help their employees to perform to the best of their abilities?

b Work in pairs and discuss the questions in Exercise 2a.

2C Semantic prosody

1 a Match the words and phrases in bold in 1–5 with the words and phrases in bold in a–e that have a similar meaning.

1 The new system has **caused** us more problems than it's worth.
2 In some countries, the disease **is rife**, with up to 45% of the population affected.
3 Jackie seems to **be hell bent on** implementing the unpopular measures to increase working hours.
4 Residents are busy preparing for the **impending** storm, which is predicted to be one of the worst to hit the area for decades.
5 We need to look into the reasons why young people **commit** crime.

a After a successful conservation programme, fish populations are **abundant** in the lake.
b He has **generated** a lot of new ideas since he's been at the company.
c The council **are committed to** improving public services for city residents.
d She **performs** all her tasks efficiently. We are very satisfied with her work.
e I'm really looking forward to the **upcoming** holiday, we're going to have a great time.

b Which of the words and phrases in bold introduce collocations with a positive connotation? Which introduce ones with a negative connotation?

2 Match the words in bold in Exercise 1 with the words they collocate with.

1 corruption/rumours/ill-feeling *be rife*
2 a goal/an ambition/a result ______
3 a task/an operation/a guitar solo ______
4 problems/offence/damage ______
5 saving something/your plans/investing in something ______
6 release/trip/visit ______
7 conflict/disaster/catastrophe ______
8 resources/wealth/wildlife ______
9 destroying something/ruining something ______
10 murder/a sin/an error ______

3 Use the prompts to write sentences which are true for you.

1 I'm committed to …
2 I'm really looking forward to the upcoming …
3 I don't like it when people are hell bent on …
4 I think … can cause …
5 … is abundant in my local area at the moment.
6 In the next year I'd really like to achieve …

3A Prefixes with similar meanings

1 a Match the pairs of prefixes in the box with the words they complete in 1–6.

bi-/multi-	hyper-/hypo-	inter-/intra-
macro-/micro-	over-/under-	re-/pro-

1 economics/biology/level
2 critical/tension
3 national/net/state
4 -duce/-ject/-nounce
5 lateral/part/ polar/lingual
6 paid/achiever/rated/done

b Match the meanings 1–6 with the prefixes in Exercise 1a.

1 between or among/within
2 backward/forward
3 two/many
4 above/under
5 too much/not enough
6 on a very large scale/on a very small scale

2 Complete the sentences with a word formed from a prefix and word from Exercise 1.

1 ____ is the study of organisms that are too small to see with the naked eye.
2 Most people feel they are seriously ____ and should earn a lot more money.
3 It's vital that we ____ carbon emissions in the next ten years, they are far too high at the moment.
4 A special commission is to investigate ways of boosting ____ commerce within California, irrespective of what's happening in other states.
5 I thought my boss was being ____ of my ideas – they weren't great, admittedly, but they weren't that bad.
6 The two countries are resuming ____ talks in order to try reach some form of agreement between themselves.
7 Caitlyn is a real ____. She consistently exceeds her targets.
8 The doctor said I'm suffering from ____ and need to take things easy for a while.

3 a Choose six words made with prefixes from Exercise 1 and write a definition for each one.

b Work in pairs. Read out your definition for your partner to guess the word.

3C Verbs related to reporting

1 Match the words in bold with definitions 1–12.

I'm an investigative journalist for a national newspaper. It involves lots of different things, but writing will usually start when my editor **briefs** me on a story. This is an important starting point as I need to know what kind of story it's going to be. For example, we might have received information which we want to **disclose** to the public. In this case, we need to fact-check everything in order to **substantiate** the information we've received, because it's important we remain unbiased and don't **misrepresent** the facts, **smear** anyone, or damage their reputation. Sometimes I might have an idea for a story which I want to investigate, in which case I'll **pitch** the idea to my editor. If they approve it, I'll **probe** people and try to **unearth** or **expose** activities which I think the public should know about. Once I've written my story, I'll **proofread** it carefully – not just to make sure it's error free, but also because I don't want to unduly **sensationalise** the story. I also need to check I'm the first person reporting it, as I want to make sure I don't **plagiarise** anyone else's work.

1 deliberately give a wrong description of someone's opinions or of a situation
2 instruct or inform someone in preparation for a task
3 find out hidden information or the truth about something or someone
4 deliberately make something seem more shocking than it is
5 reveal information that has not been widely known
6 prove the truth of something someone has said
7 take words or ideas from someone else's work and pretend they're yours
8 make the truth about a secret public
9 read something carefully to make sure there are no mistakes in it
10 try to persuade someone to accept an idea or proposal
11 ask questions to find things out, especially things the people concerned don't want you to know
12 damage someone's reputation with false information

2 Work in pairs and discuss the questions.

1 Do you always proofread your writing carefully? What kinds of things do you look for? Does it depend on what you are writing?
2 In what ways can the news misrepresent the facts about a story?
3 Can you think of any famous people who have been smeared by the media? What happened?
4 What types of media tend to sensationalise stories? Newspapers? Social media? TV news?
5 How can journalists probe people to unearth the facts?
6 Have you ever pitched an idea to someone? What was it? Were you successful?

4A Words with *self-*

1 a Complete the sentences with the words in the box.

self-conscious self-contained self-control self-effacing self-esteem self-explanatory self-indulgent self-inflicted self-made self-pity self-reinforcing self-reliant self-righteous self-sacrificing

1 Phobias can be ____ when you become afraid of fear itself.
2 I get very ____ when I'm speaking in public and everyone is looking at me. I hate it!
3 His ____ acts allowed his companions to escape, even if he himself could not.
4 She's a ____ millionaire – she built her business from scratch.
5 Harry is so ____ – he criticises the flaws in everyone else's character, but never his own.
6 My flat isn't completely ____ – there's a shared kitchen with the other flats.
7 Your problems are completely ____ – they're the result of your own reckless behaviour.
8 I used to suffer from low ____, but I feel a lot more positive about myself now.
9 I've drawn you a map to find my house. Hopefully it's ____, so I won't need to tell you what everything means.
10 It's hard to become ____ when you leave home, after depending on your parents for so long.
11 Roger is very ____ – he hates talking about all his amazing achievements.
12 I know it's a bit ____ of me, but I'm going to treat myself to a week in a luxury spa.
13 Stop wallowing in ____ – there's no point sitting around feeling sorry for yourself.
14 I have no ____ – I'll happily eat a whole packet of sweets one after the other till they're gone.

b Which words from Exercise 1a have a generally positive or negative meaning? Which could you use to describe yourself?

4C Describing the senses

1 a Look at the words in the box. Decide whether they relate to vision (V), sound (S), feel (F) or taste (T).

blare bloodcurdling blotchy bristly crinkly clank clatter ear-splitting fleecy piquant starlit willowy

b Match 1–12 with a–l to make sentences.

1 The bloodcurdling
2 The music blaring
3 It was supposed to be a smooth paint job, but it came out
4 She'd wrapped the present in crinkly
5 He scratched his bristly
6 The explosion was
7 He lay down on the fleecy
8 The gates
9 The railway line was so near that when a train went past
10 The fish was quite bland
11 The starlit
12 Her husband was short and heavy

a brown paper, which rustled as I removed it.
b sky was the most beautiful he'd ever seen.
c clanked as they were pushed hard together.
d ear-splitting, and woke people for miles around.
e but the lemon sauce was quite piquant.
f scream from the castle alarmed the villagers.
g beard, which was beginning to irritate him.
h all the dishes would clatter on the shelves.
i while she was willowy and graceful.
j from the car stereo kept everyone awake.
k rug and immediately slept.
l a blotchy mess.

c Look at the words in the box in Exercise 1a. Which ones:

1 are verbs?
2 are adjectives?
3 have a positive meaning?
4 have a negative meaning?
5 have a fairly neutral meaning?

5A Adjectives with dependent prepositions

1 a Complete the sentences with a suitable preposition after the adjectives in bold. Sometimes more than one word is possible.

1 Most of us are **blind** ______ the fact that without their hard work, our cities would be **overflowing** ______ rubbish.
2 When Jack joined the company, he was quite **peripheral** ______ the project, but now his contributions are **vital** ______ its success.
3 Some people are just **famous** ______ being famous – they're completely **superfluous** ______ society.
4 Hospital cleaners are **invisible** ______ most people, but they play a pivotal role in keeping hospitals **free** ______ infections.

b Match the sentence halves. Pay attention to the adjectives and prepositions in bold.

1 I love the smell of cinnamon – I find it **reminiscent**
2 The film was boring and completely **lacking**
3 Ruth is so absent-minded – she's **prone**
4 Hopefully the concert will go ahead, but it's **contingent**
5 I've been **engrossed**
6 I don't have the right qualifications so I'm not **eligible**
7 There's no hope any more – we need to be **resigned**
8 You sometimes make me feel like my views don't **count**
9 When you're cold and tired, you're more **susceptible**
10 I don't know what's happened. Please **acquaint**

a **to** illnesses.
b **in** this book recently. I just need to know the ending!
c **to** the fact that there's nothing more we can do.
d **for** anything.
e **to** forgetting what she's saying in the middle of a sentence.
f **of** winter afternoons as a child.
g me **with** the facts.
h **in** any sense of character or plot.
i **on** the number of people who pre-book tickets.
j **for** the job.

2 Complete the questions with a preposition. Then work in pairs and ask and answer the questions.

1 What would you like to be famous ______ ?
2 What smells/sounds do you find reminiscent ______ your childhood?
3 What are you prone ______ doing when you're tired?

5B Compound adjectives with *-ing* forms

1 a Match the words and phrases in the box with the words in bold with a similar meaning.

dangerous depressing eternal important for many people
non-criminal spectacular stressful terrifying and exciting

1 The roller coaster is a **hair-raising** ride for all the family.
2 Frank had been a **law-abiding** citizen all his life until he decided to avoid his taxes.
3 The decisions we make today will have **far-reaching** consequences for all of us.
4 The job interview was a **nerve-racking** experience but I made it to the end somehow.
5 I feel like I'm fighting a **never-ending** battle with the weeds in my garden.
6 The audience gasped as the acrobat performed **death-defying** stunts.
7 Writing reports is **soul-destroying** work, but it's got to be done.
8 The views from the mountaintop were absolutely **breath-taking**.

b Complete the second sentence so that it means the same as the first.

1 I didn't agree with everything he said, but his arguments certainly provoked me to think.
I didn't agree with everything he said, but his arguments were certainly *thought-provoking*.
2 There's an exhibition at the gallery which has won some awards.
There's an ______ exhibition at the gallery.
3 The good thing about failure is that it builds your character.
The good thing about failure is that it can be a ______ experience.
4 I love jogging, although it consumes an awful amount of time.
I love jogging, although it's awfully ______ .
5 I spent the morning carrying heavy boxes, which felt like it was going to break my back.
I spent the morning carrying heavy boxes, which was ______ work.
6 My jaw drops open when I remember the mistakes I made when I was younger.
I made some absolutely ______ mistakes when I was younger.
7 We are so grateful for your generosity, which inspires a sense of awe in us.
We are so grateful for your ______ generosity.
8 I'm thinking of his pies, they make my mouth water.
I'm thinking of his ______ pies.

6A Social issues

1 a Complete the statements with the pairs of words and phrases in the box.

austerity/breadline	downtrodden/disaffected	food banks/safety net	glass ceiling/discriminatory
multicultural/racism	outreach/marginalised	squatters/entitlement	taboo/politically correct

1 It's undeniable that there's a ____ in most industries, which prevents women from reaching the highest positions. This is clearly because of ____ policies.
2 ____ measures introduced by a government (such as reducing public spending), while aiming to reduce national debt, simply don't work and leave many living on the ____.
3 ____ play an important role in society, providing a ____ for those who can't afford to feed their families.
4 It's important to avoid ____ subjects during public debate, in order to ensure such debates are ____.
5 Some people think ____ who take over derelict buildings play a useful role in raising awareness of homelessness. Others think they just have an exaggerated sense of ____.
6 In any ____ society, there is always going to be the danger of the rise of ____.
7 There needs to be an effective ____ programme to assist the most ____ in society, otherwise they are unlikely to seek help.
8 The most ____ in society are always the most ____ voters.

b Work in pairs. Do you agree with the statements? What are the most important social issues for you?

6B Marketing and advertising

1 Match the words and phrases in bold with definitions a–j.

1 I really hate the catchy **jingles** a lot of adverts use. They get stuck in my head all day!
2 Some companies use **celebrity endorsements** to help promote their products so you buy more.
3 The film was so popular that they created a whole range of **tie-ins** to sell, from books to children's toys.
4 If you can't face the supermarket crowds, but you can't wait for delivery, then **click-and-collect** offers the perfect solution.
5 I love **scan-and-shop**. I get to pick the products I want at the supermarket, but I don't have to then stand in a long queue. In some places you can even use an app on your phone for this!
6 **Viral advertising** is often seen as very effective because people don't often realise it's an advert that they're watching.
7 **Promos** such as buy two, get one free may seem attractive, but it's often cheaper just to buy one.
8 **Niche marketing** can be extremely cost effective in specialised markets.
9 Most **slogans** use predictable linguistic formulas, such as listing ideas in 'threes'.
10 It's normal for companies to offer a **no-quibble returns policy**, as long as you keep the receipt.

a a product connected with a new film or TV show
b a short song used to promote products, designed to be easily remembered
c offers or special deals
d you order something online then pick it up from the shop
e offering a refund without challenging it
f a short phrase that is easy to remember and is used to describe products in adverts
g a system where you use a handset to scan goods as you shop, then pay for them at the checkout
h advertising to a small, specific market
i a type of advertising which uses social media, email, etc. to promote a product
j a statement made by a famous person saying that they like and use a product

2 a Choose five of the words and phrases in Exercise 1 and think of a real example of each.

Slogans: 'Go to work on an egg.'

b Work in pairs. Share your examples with your partner for them to guess which word or phrase it's an example of.

7A Travel problems

1 a Complete the sentences with the words in the box.

capsized	colliding	congested	gridlock	grounded	impassable	jetlag
puncture	~~seized up~~	shipwrecked	stranded	write-off		

1 I was driving through the desert when my car's engine _seized up_ – some sand or dust must have got into the mechanism.
2 I'm still suffering from ____ three days after my long flight – my body just can't cope with crossing so many time zones so quickly.
3 My bike's front wheel has a ____, so I'll need to take it off and buy a new inner tube.
4 The roads round here can get pretty ____ in the mornings, when everyone's trying to drive to work at the same time.
5 The last bus leaves in three minutes. If you miss it, you'll be ____ here all night.
6 There was total ____ in the city centre during the morning rush hour – nobody could move.
7 After they were ____, they survived for three years alone on a desert island.
8 We had to swerve sharply to avoid ____ with a kangaroo in the middle of the road.
9 All planes were ____ for three hours because of the severe fog and high winds near the airport.
10 Luckily, no one was in the car when the tree fell on it, but the car itself was a total ____ – it'll need to be scrapped.
11 The route through the mountains is ____ for cars during the winter – the only way through is on horseback.
12 The sea was so rough that our small boat nearly ____.

b Which words from the box can describe problems with:

1 cars/driving/roads?
2 planes/flying/skies?
3 boats/sailing/waterways?
4 all forms of transport?

2 Work in pairs and discuss the questions.

1 Which travel problems in Exercise 1 have you experienced?
2 Which problems are the most/least serious?

7B Finance and investment

1 Complete the texts with the words and phrases in the boxes.

collateral creditor credit rating ~~debtor~~ default depreciates repossess

Perhaps the best-known example of a secured loan is a mortgage, which uses the [1] _debtor_'s house as [2] ____ (i.e. the guarantee that the loan will be repaid). Although it's a good way of borrowing large sums of money, it has its risks: if you [3] ____ on your obligations in any way (e.g. by missing repayment deadlines), the [4] ____ (usually a bank) has the right to [5] ____ your house. Even if they decide against such a drastic step, your [6] ____ may be downgraded, making it much harder to borrow money in future. Another risk is that your house [7] ____ (i.e. goes down) in value, and you end up owing more than your house is worth – a situation called 'negative equity'.

appreciate assets hedge speculating write off

In general, investors can make the most money by [8] ____ – buying high-risk [9] ____ that might [10] ____ sharply if you're lucky, but might also collapse in value. They may even become worthless, in which case the investor will have to [11] ____ the investment. For this reason, many investors prefer to invest in [12] ____ funds, which contain a mix of high- and low-risk investments.

bonds commodities derivatives stocks and shares

Two of the most popular forms of investment are [13] ____ (i.e. certificates to prove you've lent money to a government or a large company) and [14] ____ (i.e. certificates to prove you own parts of companies). Investors also often buy and sell [15] ____ (e.g. oil, gold), the price of which is set by the market, not individual companies. However, a lot of modern investment involves [16] ____ – complex financial tools involving (for example) the right to buy or sell something at a certain price in future.

8A Emotions and personality

1 a Read the sentences. Do the words in bold have a positive or negative meaning?

1 She's so **officious**. She just loves bossing people around with that rule book of hers.
2 Don't be so **defeatist**. You can actually do this if you apply yourself.
3 I don't feel I was being **discourteous**, in fact they were being rude, not me.
4 He was a little **disconcerted** to find his ex girlfriend at the party.
5 He kept talking over me, I was absolutely **incensed**.
6 He's quite good fun to be around, although he can be **hot headed** when people don't agree with him.
7 These **grasping** landlords are always thinking of new ways of putting rents up.
8 Brian, I've had a bad day and I'm not in the mood for any of your **jocular** remarks, OK?
9 The driver was the only one who survived the crash, but was **guilt ridden** for years afterwards.
10 Oh, here comes **do-gooder** Claire with another charity for us to contribute to. Shame I left my wallet in the office ...
11 No, you didn't get it this time, but there's no need to get **downhearted** about it just yet.
12 If he wasn't a **megalomaniac**, he wouldn't have wanted to be the president in the first place.

b Match definitions a–l with the words in bold in Exercise 1a.

a too eager to tell people what to do
b confused or unsettled
c depressed
d hungry for power in an obsessive way
e person with good intentions but who may be naive or unrealistic
f joking, humorous
g consumed by feelings of responsibility for an action
h expecting failure
i greedy
j very angry
k impolite, unpleasant
l prone to quickly losing their temper

2 Work in pairs. Discuss whether you know any people who can be described with the words in Exercise 1a.

8B Noun forms

1 Look at the nouns and identify which adjective or verb they derive from.

1 grumpiness adjective: *grumpy*
2 greyness adjective: ____
3 petulance adjective: ____
4 moodiness adjective: ____
5 grimness adjective: ____
6 nonchalance adjective: ____
7 coarseness adjective: ____
8 eradication verb: ____
9 implementation verb: ____
10 thoughtlessness adjective: ____

2 Rewrite the sentences using the noun form of the words in bold.

1 I just don't like how **grey** it is here in England.
I just don't like the greyness here in England.
2 I think she was put off by how **grim** the town was.
3 It makes me mad how **thoughtless** people can be.
4 He attempted to be **nonchalant**, but he didn't fool me.
5 We've waited a long time to **eradicate** this disease.
6 I'm **moody**, which can be seen as a bad thing.
7 It's easy to think about it, but difficult to **implement**.
8 Her **grumpy** attitude at breakfast time didn't help matters.
9 His **coarse** language wasn't to everyone's taste.
10 Some of my colleagues' **petulant** behaviour can be a little tedious.

9A Adverbs for stories

1 a **Choose a phrase, a or b, which matches the meaning of the adverb in bold.**

1 The boy **sullenly** threw his books on the floor.
 a in a careless way
 b in an angry or unpleasant way

2 'Well, it's just a job', she remarked **flippantly**.
 a in a supportive way
 b in a way that was not serious

3 How soul destroying to be so **tantalisingly** close but not reach the summit.
 a in a way which arouses desire for something that cannot be obtained
 b in a way which teaches you how to improve the next time

4 You have to admit it, you behaved **monstrously** towards her.
 a very badly
 b in a boring repetitive way

5 Sadly, the marriage ended **acrimoniously** after a string of rows in public.
 a surprisingly quickly
 b in a bitter way, full of anger

6 When I told him the news, he just looked at me **vacantly**.
 a showing no interest
 b showing that he was open to new ideas

7 'Might I sit next to you?' he asked **daringly**.
 a with a bright smile
 b bravely

8 Rather **heartlessly**, he left her on their wedding day.
 a sadly
 b cruelly

b **Complete the sentences with adverbs in the box.**

acrimoniously	daringly flippantly	heartlessly	tantalisingly	vacantly

1 ________, they crossed the rope bridge between the two mountains.
2 ________, they got rid of their old dog and bought a younger one.
3 When the promotion had seemed so ________ near, it had suddenly slipped away from him.
4 He stared ________ out of the window during the whole lesson.
5 The game finished ________ with players from both teams fighting with each other.
6 He ________ remarked that she'd find another boyfriend, and not to worry about it.

9C Landscape adjectives

1 **Match the words in bold with definitions a–k.**

1 The garden was absolutely **parched** after three months without rain.
2 This roadside verge is totally **overgrown** – all those weeds need cutting urgently.
3 The tundra is the **bleak** belt of land in the far north, where it is too cold and dry for trees to grow.
4 The taiga is the huge **forested** belt of land just south of the tundra, stretching across Siberia, Canada, etc.
5 The region is known for its gently **undulating** landscape consisting of gentle hills.
6 What a **picturesque** view! I've got to take a selfie!
7 Don't go near the cliff edge – there's a **sheer** drop down to the sea far below.
8 I went hiking over the **windswept** moorlands – and nearly got blown away!
9 The city centre is completely **barren**, without even a single patch of grass or tree.
10 These hills and valleys are too **craggy** to grow crops, so they're used for grazing sheep and goats.
11 When the river dried up, this region became an **arid** desert.

a extremely steep *sheer*
b empty of vegetation or wildlife
c beautiful
d cold and unattractive, with no interesting features
e with only plants that can survive strong winds
f damaged as a result of extreme heat and dryness
g extremely dry
h covered in (too many) wild plants
i uneven and covered in large rocks
j covered in trees
k gently rising and falling; neither flat nor mountainous

10A Collocations with *idea*

1 **Match the sentence halves.**

1 **The very idea of**
2 **I like/love the idea of**
3 Having to work in the evenings is
4 What's **the big idea**,
5 Whose **bright idea**
6 Believing in ghosts
7 I wonder, could you **give me an idea**
8 We've been **toying/flirting with the idea**
9 This meeting is just a chance to **bounce**
10 The belief in learning styles **stems from**
11 I haven't got **the faintest/foggiest idea**
12 We need to **come up with**

a never having to work again.
b is a truly **crackpot idea**.
c what Tony was talking about in the meeting.
d **ideas** for what to do for Simon's birthday.
e telling the boss we don't need an hour for lunch?
f staying out until 1 a.m. on a weeknight seems ridiculous to me.
g **not my idea** of fun.
h **of** moving house.
i **ideas around/off each other**.
j was it to leave the front door open?
k **as to** how long you expect the project to take?
l **the idea** that we all learn in different ways.

10B Phrasal nouns

1 **Rewrite the sentences with the phrasal verbs in bold as phrasal nouns.**

1 On my way to work this morning, my car **broke down**.
On my way to work this morning I had a *breakdown*.

2 A member of the public anonymously **tipped off** the police with information about the burglary.
Police received an anonymous ______ from a member of the public about the burglary.

3 Carbon dioxide has steadily **built up** in the atmosphere.
There has been a steady ______ of carbon dioxide in the atmosphere.

4 Let's **get** all the family **together** for Dad's birthday.
Let's have a family ______ for Dad's birthday.

5 The audience **burst out** laughing at his joke.
There was an ______ of laughter from the audience at his joke.

6 We **set out** to make this a non-profit organisation.
This has been a non-profit organisation from the ______ .

7 The government intends to **crack down** on people who don't pay tax.
The government is planning a ______ on people who don't pay their tax.

8 I think our coats got **mixed up** at the party.
I think there was a ______ with our coats at the party.

9 The government were forced to **climb down** over their position regarding the virus.
There was a government ______ over their position regarding the virus.

10 There are several features you can **add on** to this car.
This car comes with several ______ .

2 **Complete the sentences with the phrasal nouns from Exercise 1.**

1 The company is implementing a ______ on people arriving late.
2 The basic price is £100, but this increases with any ______ you purchase.
3 There's heavy traffic on the M25 this morning because of a ______ .
4 Let's get to the stadium early, so we can enjoy the ______ before the match starts.
5 Right from the ______ , Celia knew that her new boss was going to be difficult to work with.
6 Police have raided an illegal bookmaker's after a ______ from a member of the public.
7 Last weekend we had a big family ______ to celebrate my gran's 80th birthday.
8 It was only when she opened the bag and realised it wasn't hers she realised there'd been a terrible ______ .
9 The minister's embarrassing ______ was all over the front pages.
10 Later on Jamie regretted his sudden ______ when she'd told him the news.

3 **Work in pairs and discuss the questions.**

1 Have you ever bought anything with add-ons? What was is and what were the add-ons?
2 Can you think of the last time you were involved in a mix-up? What happened?
3 What was the last get-together you went to? Who was there? What was it for?

Communication bank

Lesson 1A

Exercise 10

You're on the second day of a team-building weekend with your English class, and the organiser has asked for feedback. You've had some issues with various aspects of the weekend. Make notes on what the problems were.

- the activities
- the accommodation
- the food
- the location
- the participants

Lesson 2A

Exercise 10

1 Trends in sport

- Attendance at Women's cup final matches

Year	2013	2014	2015	2016	2017	2018	2019	Future
Attendance	4,988	15,098	30,710	32,912	35,271	45,423	52,000	set to continue to rise

- Growth of e-sports – events where video gamers compete: 121 million players in 2016, 165 million players in 2018, predicted to grow to 250 million players in 2021.
- Use of Video Assistant Referee (VAR) technology – video used to review referees' decisions in real time. First used in full at the 2018 World Cup, subsequently used at the 2019 Women's World Cup. Very likely to be used in the future.
- In future, possibility of wider use of Virtual Reality (VR) and Augmented Reality (AR) when watching sport. For example, the use of a headset to make you feel like you're in the game.

2 Trends in education

Past	Sources of information: teacher, textbooks Strict discipline Focus on administrative skills
Present	Greater use of technology: computers, internet, blended learning (a mix of online and face-to-face teaching) Virtual Reality (VR) and Augmented Reality (AR) to encourage exploration Focus on exploration and work skills
Future	The end of teachers? More gamification More interacting in simulations

Lesson 2D

Exercise 10a

Student A

Start the conversation, using the notes you made in Exercise 9. After a while, try to end the conversation.

Lesson 1D

Exercise 10

You're going to attend a conference for language learners from around the world. The conference starts with a face-to-face welcome reception, where you're expected to mingle with the other conference participants. Before the conference, help your partner to plan one or two simple stories to tell at the event. You don't need to write your stories – just plan what you'll say. Use these ideas and your own ideas:

- your best/worst experience as a language learner
- your best/worst experience of trying to network with strangers
- anything else that will grab people's attention – see the ideas in the 'Useful phrases 2' box for inspiration

Help you partner to work out a 'hook' for each story – a line to make others desperate to ask you about it.

Lesson 2C

Exercise 11

Group A: Prepare arguments for the items on the agenda. Group B: Prepare arguments against each item.

City Council meeting agenda

1 Proposal to install speed bumps/traffic calming on every residential road.
2 Proposal to pedestrianise the city centre.
3 Proposal to increase the number of cycle lanes around the city.
4 Proposal to build 100 new affordable homes on green land in the south of the city.
5 Proposal to reduce rubbish collection from weekly to twice-weekly.
6 Proposal to introduce free public transport for under 18s and over 60s.

Lesson 2D

Exercise 10a

Student C

Listen to the conversation and make a note of how many Useful phrases from the lesson they use.

Lesson 3C

Exercise 11

Story A

www.stealthtricks.com/ATM/police

Use this simple trick to stay safe when withdrawing cash. It's a little known fact, but one that might save you money – and possibly your life.

You're alone, late at night, in a quiet part of town, and you need cash to get a taxi home. You approach the ATM, put your card in, but then you hear footsteps and a cruel voice in your ear, 'Take out the maximum amount, give it to me, and don't look round,' your potential attacker says calmly in your ear.

What do you do? Well, not many people know this, but if you enter 999 into the machine, the bank will automatically alert the police, who will arrive within minutes. As long as you can stall the potential robber during that time, you'll be safe.

Be smart, and don't get caught out!

Story B

WELCOME TO CAT ISLAND

Nomination Island, in the Indian Ocean, is home to hundreds of cats. Thought to have been left by early explorers, the cats have bred and multiplied, and taken over the island.

Story C

Over 75% of adults now get their news from social-media websites.

According to a recent survey carried out by the leading national polling company *YourVyu*, 78.3% of adults say they now use social media as their main source of both national and international news.

This figure has increased from 43.7% three years ago, in a similar survey carried out by the same polling company. The figure is highest among those under 30, while those polled over 60 still claim to use traditional sources such as print newspapers and television as the main source of their news.

Story D

New smartphone design to feature holographic projection

A small San Francisco based tech company have announced plans for a new smart phone with the capacity for holographic projection, which they're calling Trufon 1. This amazing new technology will enable owners to watch movies in true 3D, on the go.

It comes with a whole host of other features, including a year's free subscription to their own media-streaming service, allowing you to wow your friends and put on a real show – all from your own mobile phone.

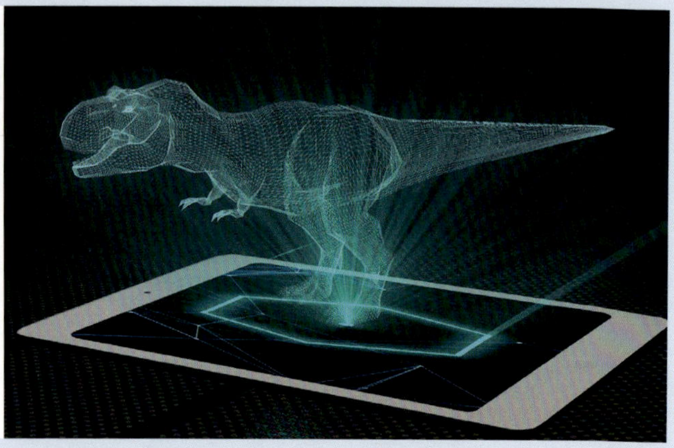

Lesson 3D English in action

Exercise 5a

Hip hop best bet for a cheese that will please: Swiss study

BURGDORF, Switzerland (Reuters) 'Exposing cheese to round-the-clock music could give it more flavour, and hip hop might be better than Mozart', Swiss researchers said on Thursday.

Nine wheels of Emmental cheese, weighing 10 kilos (22 pounds) each were placed in separate wooden crates last September to test the impact of music on flavour and aroma.

The cheese was exposed 24 hours a day to A Tribe Called Quest's hip hop track *We Got it From Here*, Mozart's *Magic Flute* opera or Led Zeppelin's rock classic *Stairway to Heaven*. One wheel was played the throbbing techno of Vril's *UV* and another Yello's dark ambient piece *Monolith*.

Soundwaves at low, medium and high frequencies were played for three others, while one wheel was left in peace.

'The most obvious differences were observed in strength of flavour, smell and taste,' Bern University of Arts researchers said in reporting the findings of a culinary jury, which did blind tasting. 'The hip hop sample topped the list of all cheese exposed to music in terms of fruitiness ... (it) was the strongest of these in terms of smell and taste.'

Benjamin Luzuy, a Swiss TV chief and jury member, told Reuters TV, 'The differences were very clear, in terms of texture, taste, appearance – there was really something very different.'

The experiment, instead of using loudspeakers, used mini transmitters to conduct the energy of the music into the cheese. 'All the energy is directly resonating inside of the cheese,' Michael Harenberg of Bern University of Arts told Reuters.

Beat Wampfler, the cheesemaker behind the project, said the cheeses were tested twice by the jury and both times the results were more or less the same. He said the experiment would now focus on hip hop.

'The idea is now to take 5 or 10 cheeses and put hip hop on them and then compare.'

Lesson 2D

Exercise 10a

Student B

Let Student A start the conversation. Be an active listener and try to keep the conversation going for as long as possible.

Lesson 3D

Exercise 9

Student B

World's biggest gathering of Nigels and all things Nigelness attracts 433 Nigels

Never, in all that is Nigel, have so many Nigels been gathered in one place at the same time. Some 433 people with the same name gathered at a pub over the weekend to 'celebrate Nigelness'. The party, at the Fleece Inn in Worcestershire, is believed to have set the record for the number of Nigels gathered, and was organised by landlord Nigel Smith, 56.

He hopes he has done his bit to help put the name back on the map with his event in the village of Bretforton, which also raised money for the British Heart Foundation. He said, 'I've always felt that the name's much maligned – people would say to me when I was young, "Nigel, that's got to be a joke name, hasn't it?". So it was really just to get a few Nigels together in the same room, to share Nigel stories and celebrate our Nigelness – that was the original intention.'

Mr Smith first started making plans for a Nigel-themed get-together a couple of years back when he was 'a bit shocked' to find Office for National Statistics data suggested there had been no babies named Nigel in 2016.

He finally got round to arranging the event this year and, after a Facebook page advertising went viral, he was delighted with the turnout. He said, 'We got some 433 Nigels there last night, plus about another thousand non-Nigels who'd just come along for a laugh.'

All Nigels were required to prove their credentials with a passport or driver's licence, and anyone who did was rewarded with a free pint and a Nigel badge. Everyone else was given a non-Nigel badge. Mr Smith said, 'We had a singer, a busker – both called Nigel – and a comedian called Nigel. We had Nigel awards for the furthest travelled, the youngest and the oldest. We picked a collective noun for Nigels, which is *a niggle of Nigels*.'

Lesson 3D

Exercise 9

Student A

Woman dreams of swallowing engagement ring and wakes up to find she has

Jenna Evans says she woke up and was relieved to realise it had been a dream until she discovered she wasn't wearing the ring.

A woman dreamt she had swallowed her engagement ring and when she woke up she realised she had.

Jenna Evans was on a high-speed train when she had a dream in which some 'bad guys' were getting on and the best way to protect the 2.4 carat diamond ring was to gulp it down. 'I popped that sucker off, put it in my mouth and swallowed it with a glass of water,' Ms Evans said in a Facebook post.

Ms Evans, of San Diego, California, woke up and was relieved to realise it had been a bizarre dream – until she discovered she was no longer wearing the ring. She said, 'When I woke up in the morning, there was no ring on my finger. I couldn't help but laugh at it, and then I had to wake my fiancé up and tell him that I had swallowed my engagement ring.'

Ms Evans, 29, went to an urgent care clinic where doctors decided not to allow the ring to pass through naturally and referred her to a specialist. An upper endoscopy was carried out, in which a small camera and device is inserted down the throat. Ms Evans said she began to cry as she signed the forms for carrying out the procedure because she feared she might die and not live to marry her fiancé Bobby Howell.

Doctors located the ring in Ms Evans' intestines and Mr Howell presented her with it again. In her Facebook post, Ms Evans wrote, 'Bobby finally gave my ring back this morning – I promised not to swallow it again, we're still getting married and all is right in the world. I'm so grateful that everybody can laugh about it, because it truly is a very funny story.'

Lesson 4A

Exercise 4

Suggested answers

1 It might come from a traumatic childhood or teenage experience of being laughed at (by friends or peers) for dancing in an embarrassing way.

2 People interpret the physical fear (e.g. from dangerous sports) or social fear (e.g. from the embarrassment of losing) as exhilaration. Even non-dangerous sports like running might trigger our 'fear' reactions (like running to escape from danger). In a similar way, people can get a buzz out of films (e.g. thrillers), music (e.g. heavy rock) and video games.

Lesson 4C

Exercise 11

Student A

Read the following script to your partner, pausing and waiting for his/her responses.

OK, I want you to imagine you're on a beach. What can you see? What can you feel? What can you smell? What can you taste? What can you hear?
You start to walk along the beach. Where do you come to? What can you smell or hear there? How do you feel?

Lesson 4A

Exercise 11

Work in pairs to plan a two or three minute description of a phobia like the one in Exercise 10. Use these ideas:

- Will you talk about a real phobia? It can be your own phobia (if you feel comfortable talking about it) or that of somebody you know.
- Will you invent a story? Use the list of phobias opposite or your own ideas.
- What exactly is the phobia? What does it mean in practice? Can you tell a story of a specific event?
- What (probably) caused the phobia? If it was a specific event, what happened?
- What are some symptoms and implications of the phobia?
- What (if anything) can be done to deal with/treat the phobia? What happens/happened when the sufferer does/did this?

claustrophobia: fear of enclosed spaces
aulophobia: fear of flutes
arachibutyrophobia: fear of peanut butter
chorophobia: fear of dancing
koumpounophobia: fear of buttons
acrophobia: fear of heights
atelophobia: fear of imperfection
glossophobia: fear of public speaking
arachnophobia: fear of spiders
didaskaleinophobia: fear of school
agoraphobia: fear of open/crowded spaces

Lesson 4D English in action

Exercise 9a

Student A

Read the information on your role cards and invent any other information you need.

Situation 1

You work in the same office as Student B. You have noticed that somebody has been eating your food from the office fridge, drinking your tea and coffee, and even using your favourite mug. To make matters worse, he/she never clears up after himself/herself, so you usually end up doing it every evening.

Today you are especially angry because your delicious homemade meal has disappeared from the fridge and you're hungry! You notice Student B eating it. Start a conversation with Student B to express your anger/frustration. You're quite emotional at first – you can threaten to cause trouble for him/her with the senior managers. Later in the conversation, if Student B manages to calm you down, be prepared to de-escalate your conflict.

Situation 2

You are Student B's neighbour, living in a small block of flats. You moved into the upstairs flat because the rent is cheap and you don't have much money at the moment. You work from home, so you often have long phone calls and online meetings with clients and colleagues. You eat a lot of takeaway food because you're too busy to cook. There wasn't a washing machine in the flat when you moved in, so you bought a cheap second-hand one ... which you now regret, because it often leaks water all over your bathroom floor. You need to get a new one as soon as you can afford it.

When Student B (your downstairs neighbour) approaches you, do your best to de-escalate the conflict from the beginning.

Lesson 4C

Exercise 11

Student B

Read the following script to your partner, pausing and waiting for his/her responses.

OK, I want you to imagine you're in a field in summer. What can you see? What can you feel? What can you smell? What can you taste? What can you hear?
You see a traveling circus approaching. What can you see? What can you smell or hear? How do you feel?

Lesson 4D English in action

Exercise 9a

Student B

Read the information on your role cards and invent any other information you need.

Situation 1

You work in the same office as Student A. You have recently started working in the new office. In your previous office, the cleaners always kept the kitchen spotlessly clean all day long, but the cleaners in your new office only seem to come in the evenings (after you've gone home) ... and they don't do a great job!

Also, in your previous office, the kitchen was always well stocked with free snacks and drinks for employees, but you've been slightly disappointed with the quality of snacks available in your new office. However, today you've found a delicious meal in the fridge, which you're eating now. When Student A approaches you, do your best to de-escalate the conflict from the beginning.

Situation 2

You are Student A's neighbour, living in a small block of flats. You've lived in the downstairs flat for a few years. Your previous upstairs neighbour was lovely and quiet, but the new tenant is terrible. He/She seems to spend the whole day chatting noisily on the phone – including a very annoying habit of laughing out loud all the time. To make matters worse, he/she orders a lot of takeaway food, but never gives the right address to the delivery driver, who always seems to knock on your door by mistake in the middle of your favourite TV programme. Today you came home to find water dripping from your bathroom ceiling, and your bathroom carpet soaking wet.

Go upstairs to complain to your neighbour, Student A. You're quite emotional at first – you can threaten to contact his/her landlord/landlady. Later in the conversation, if Student A manages to calm you down, be prepared to de-escalate your conflict.

Master your reading 4A

Exercise 8b

Events that are foreshadowed

1 Apple used Feynman's image in a commercial in the 1990s, more than ten years after his death.

2 Feynman's last words were 'I would hate to die twice. This dying business is boring.'

Lesson 5D English in action

Exercise 10

Student A

Roleplay the situations with Student B, using language and techniques from this lesson. Try to stay polite and positive!

Situation 1

Your car has broken down after dark in the middle of nowhere. Your phone battery is dead and you don't have any cash or credit cards on you. You flag down a passing motorist (Student B) to ask for help.

Situation 2

You're walking through a strange neighbourhood, feeling slightly apprehensive and desperate to go home, when you're stopped by a stranger with two noisy, scary dogs, outside a chemist's shop. There's a huge queue inside the shop.

Lesson 6A

Exercise 10

Short summaries

***The City and the City* by China Miéville (2009)**

This story takes place against the backdrop of a fictional twin-city state. The residents of each half of the city's population must 'unsee' or not pay attention to or integrate with the other half of the population, even though they live among each other.

***Black Mirror*, Series 2, Episode 1: Be Right Back (2013)**

A young man who is an active social media user is brought back to life after a car accident. His personality is devised of his social media activity. However, the 'new man' reflects only his social media personality, not his real personality.

***Logan's Run* by William F. Nolan and George Clayton Johnson (1967)**

This novel explores a dystopian future society where society is maintained at an optimum by enforcing the death of everyone when they reach the age of 21.

***Blind Faith* by Ben Elton (2007)**

This story takes place in a world which has been engulfed in water as a result of climate change. Everyone is required by law to share every aspect of their life on social media. 'Privacy' is considered a crime.

***Black Mirror*, Series 2, Episode 3: *The Waldo Moment* (2013)**

A computer-animated bear called Waldo is popular on a late-night TV show. He mocks politicians in an election and the creator is persuaded to enter Waldo into the election, despite having no real policies. He gains popularity and eventually wins.

***Idiocracy* (2005)**

This film explores a future society which has been taken over by anti-intellectualism and commercialism. A soldier who has been part of an experiment to 'freeze' his living body wakes to find a dystopian nightmare ruled by stupidity.

Lesson 5D English in action

Exercise 10

Student B

Roleplay the situations with Student A, using language and techniques from this lesson. Try to stay polite and positive!

Situation 1

You're driving to an important event one evening when you see a broken-down car by the side of the road. You pull in to help, but you're reluctant to make yourself late for your event and you're far from sure the other driver isn't simply a scammer trying to take your money.

Situation 2

You're taking your two big dogs for a walk when you start to feel weak and ill. You're a long way from home. You find a chemist's shop where you can buy something to make yourself feel better (and ideally have a sit-down for half an hour), but there's nowhere to leave your dogs while you're inside. You stop a passing stranger (Student A) to ask for help.

Lesson 7D English in action

Exercise 10b

Student A

Use the procedure below to chair the first part of the debate. Spend a few minutes planning what to say.

1 Student A: Chairs introduction – explaining the procedure and rules (1 min)
2 Student/Team B: Three arguments in favour (3 mins)
3 Student/Team C: Three arguments against (3 mins)

Tell the speakers they have five minutes to plan their counterarguments.
Use the procedure below to chair the rest of the debate.

4 Student/Team C: Counterarguments (2 mins)
5 Student/Team B: Counterarguments (2 mins)
6 Student A: Organise voting (if there's an audience) or choose a winner based on the speakers' skills rather than the merits of their arguments.

Lesson 6C

Exercise 12

Name for a café

- One more café
- Whole Latte Love
- The Delicafé
- Brighten your eyes
- Coffee
  And
  Fabulous
  Eats

A soft drink slogan

- Cooler than the rest
- Busy Fizziness
- Prince
  Of
  Pop
- The best mini soda from Minnesota.
- Because all other soft drinks are soda pressing.
- We put the fizzics into fizzy drinks.

A sign to encourage people to pick up litter

- Bin
  It
  Now
- Sue Clean says, 'Keep it so clean!'
- Every litter bit counts. Take it with you.
- If you can't, trash can!
- Don't be a bitter Lin, use a litter bin.

Name for a hairdresser's

- Hairway to heaven
- Cuts for cats
- The Metamorphosis
- Million Hairs Cuts
- Basic looks

Lesson 8A

Exercise 11

Student A

Choose four of these things that you do, or think of your own ideas, or a combination of both.

- When cutting wrapping paper to wrap a present, you don't cut with the scissors, but slide them like a knife.
- Pretending not to see someone you recognise.
- Testing if something is hot by touching it with your fingers.
- Reading the directions for cooking food on a packet, then throwing it away. Then forgetting and having to fish it out of the bin again.
- Hitting the call button for a lift several times, even when the light is on.
- Putting your music on shuffle, then pressing 'next' until you find a song you want to listen to.
- Making up words to parts of songs you don't know the words to.

Lesson 8A

Exercise 11

Student B

Choose four of these things that you do, or think of your own ideas, or a combination of both.

- After making a slice of toast, you leave the knife you used to spread butter on it hanging half-way over the sink, in case you want to make more.
- Reading an email and checking it's OK after you've hit 'send'.
- You hear someone laugh near you and think they're laughing at you.
- Keeping your headphones on after you've finished listening to something without realising.
- Forgetting someone's name, but then leaving it too long to check and then having to avoid them.
- Thinking of an amazing thing to say, hours after a conversation.
- Speaking to pets like they're babies.

Lesson 8D English in action

Exercise 11

Student A

Situation 1

You receive a call from a family member who really likes to talk at length. Listen to what they have to say but then try to end the conversation.

Student B starts the call.

Situation 2

You call your friend in the UK to find out if you can stay with them when you visit next month. However, you don't want to appear rude by just asking them, so make a lot of small talk.

You start the call.

Lesson 9A

Exercise 8

Story ideas

- You're in a high-stress situation (e.g. an exam/a job interview) when something goes wrong (e.g. you spill coffee/there's a power cut).
- You're on your way somewhere when you see an animal (e.g. a cat/a crow) that seems to be leading you somewhere.
- You're trying to explain something complicated from your area of studies/expertise. You decide to use a story to 'explain' it.

Master your writing 6A

Exercise 4b

1 30%

2 5%

Lesson 9C

Exercise 10

Read the information and briefly discuss the questions.

A local entrepreneur has contacted the council planning committee with a proposal to buy a huge expanse of farmland/wasteland in your region and to rewild it – including re-introducing large wild animals.

1 Where in your region will the rewilding site be?
2 What is the land currently used for?
3 How will it be rewilded?

Divide your group into two teams to prepare for your meeting.

Team A: You are members of the council planning committee. Prepare for your meeting with the entrepreneur and his/her colleagues, by thinking of concerns and objections to the proposal. What questions do you need to ask?

Team B: You are the entrepreneur plus his/her colleagues. Prepare to explain your proposal in some detail. Try to predict what objections might arise in the meeting. Plan how you could allay those concerns.

Lesson 9B

Exercise 9

Student A

Roleplay 1

You and your partner both love gossiping. Share the following gossip about two of your work colleagues.

- Fiona hardly made any effort in the recent team project, but she was happy to take her share of the credit. Perhaps she is selfish and not a team player.
- George is extremely secretive, and often disappears from the office for hours and gives a clearly invented explanation. Perhaps he is planning to leave the company.

Be prepared to add details and examples to make the gossip as juicy as possible. When your partner is sharing his/her own gossip, use phrases from this lesson to manage any undercurrents.

Roleplay 2

You are the same gossipy character as in Roleplay 1, but your partner is now playing a different character – one of the targets of the gossip from Roleplay 1. Share the gossip you heard/spread in the earlier conversation. ('A little bird told me …'/'It's rumoured that …')

Roleplay 3

You are one of the targets of the gossip from roleplays 1 and 2. Choose one of these characters:

- You are Harry. You have excellent qualifications, but you don't like to talk about them to colleagues because it feels like showing off. You recently got a big promotion because the job is closely connected with your earlier academic research.
- You are Irena. You have been asked to develop new products/services for your company, but because the office is so full of gossipers and your work is confidential, you've had to do that work from home and keep it a secret.

Listen to the gossip about you. Then reveal the truth about yourself.

Lesson 8A

Exercise 11

Student C

Choose four of these things that you do, or think of your own ideas, or a combination of both.

- Believing you have enough time to watch the next episode of a TV show, when you clearly don't have enough time. For example, the show is forty minutes long and you have to go out in twenty minutes.
- Taking your phone out of your pocket or bag to check the time, then putting it back. Two seconds later you've forgotten what the time is and you take it out again.
- Feeling personally victimised by inanimate objects.
- Checking your symptoms when you're ill on the internet and worrying you're about to die.
- Forgetting why you walked into a room.
- Pacing up and down while talking on the phone.
- Counting down the hours, minutes and seconds until you have to wake up when you can't sleep and have work or school in the morning.

Lesson 8D English in action

Exercise 11

Student B

Situation 1

You're student A's family member (decide which) and you have some news for them. You've got a new job and you want to tell them all about it (decide what it is). You're very proud of getting this job and want to talk to them for as long as possible about it.

You start the call.

Situation 2

You're on a five minute break at work and you're really busy. You know your boss is watching you carefully as you were late for work this morning. Unexpectedly, your friend from overseas calls you. You only have five minutes to speak to them, and you don't want to appear rude. Find out why they're calling and try to get off the phone as quickly as possible.

Student A starts the call.

Lesson 10C

Exercise 9

Student A

Mobile learning

This involves using apps and mobile devices both inside and outside the classroom. For example, a teacher might ask learners to look up new words on their mobile phones, while reading. Alternatively, learners can play games outside the classroom which help practise specific language points.

Dogme

This approach advocates a 'materials-light' approach to learning a language. Lessons begin without a structured plan. The teacher introduces a topic for discussion, and the lesson moves forward according to which way the discussion goes. Along the way, the teacher picks up on 'emerging' language and uses this as the basis for teaching new language.

Lesson 9B

Exercise 9

Student B

Roleplay 1

You and your partner both love gossiping. Share the following gossip about some of your work colleagues.

- Harry recently got a big promotion, despite having much less experience and worse qualifications than many colleagues. Perhaps he cheated in some way to get the job.
- Irena often works from home, but never seems to achieve much when she is out of the office. Perhaps she's lazy, or even working for somebody else during company time.

Be prepared to add details and examples to make the gossip as juicy as possible. When your partner is sharing his/her own gossip, use phrases from this lesson to manage any undercurrents.

Roleplay 2

You are one of the targets of the gossip from Roleplay 1. Choose one of these characters:

- You are Fiona. You have a tendency to dominate group projects and do everything yourself. For the most recent project, your manager instructed you to take more of a back seat to give others a chance to show leadership, etc.
- You are George. You've been asked to plan a team-building event for your colleagues in an exotic location. It's supposed to be a secret/surprise, so you've had to work on it away from the office and invent excuses for your regular absences.

Listen to the gossip about you. Then reveal the truth about yourself.

Roleplay 3

You are the same gossipy character as in Roleplay 1, but your partner is now playing a different character – one of the targets of the gossip from Roleplay 1. Share the gossip you heard/spread in the earlier conversation. ('A little bird told me …'/'It's rumoured that …'

Master your writing 6A

Exercise 1a

Student A

Study the words for exactly one minute and try to remember them in order. Do not write anything down. After one minute, return to Exercise 1b on page 136.

1 **purple**	4 **brown**	7 **reddish brown**
2 **green**	5 **turquoise**	8 **orange**
3 **bright white**	6 **pale yellow**	9 **pitch black**

Master your reading 4A

Exercise 5b

The letter that Feynman wrote was never seen by his wife because he wrote it two years after she died. Rereading the letter, we realise that one of the great scientific minds of the century found it necessary to do something deeply irrational: to write a letter to someone who would never read it. 'You dead,' he wrote, 'are so much better than anyone else alive'. It's a profound comment on what it means to be human. The letter remained unopened until Richard's death.

Lesson 10A

Exercise 10a

Inventions

- An app to determine the nutrition information (calories, protein, etc.) of food from a photo.
- An app which lets you know what someone wants to speak about when they're calling you.
- A holder for a coffee cup or mobile phone on an umbrella so you can use and carry it when it's raining.
- An app to help you remember people's names.
- A portable, wireless phone charger which is built into your pocket.

Lesson 10C

Exercise 9

Student B

Translanguaging

This is concerned with exploiting the different languages present in the language classroom, instead of insisting on using English only. The teacher might encourage translation, or encourage learners to use their knowledge of other languages to help with English. For example, a Spanish speaker meeting the word *encounter* for the first time might refer to the Spanish verb *encontrar*, in order to help remember it.

Language Play

This approach to language learning has many aspects. One of these refers to the contexts in which the teacher might introduce new language. Rather than trying to create a 'real-life' scenario in the classroom, such as a job interview, the context used is an imaginary, unreal world, such as an interview with an alien about life on their planet. It is suggested that the use of imaginary contexts like this makes them more memorable.

Master your reading 6B

Exercise 1b

Answer

XYZ Bank is better.

After **one year** you end up with the following amounts:

ABC bank: £5070

XYZ bank: £5100

After **two years** you end up with the following amounts:

ABC Bank: £5140.35

XYZ Bank: £5202

Master your writing 6A

Exercise 1a

Student B

Study the words for exactly one minute and try to remember them in order. Do not write anything down. After one minute, return to Exercise 1b on page 136.

1 **purple**	4 **brown**	7 **reddish brown**
2 **green**	5 **turquoise**	8 **orange**
3 **bright white**	6 **pale yellow**	9 **pitch black**

Pearson Education Limited
KAO TWO
KAO Park
Hockham Way
Harlow, Essex
CM17 9SR
England
and Associated Companies throughout the world.

english.com/roadmap

First published 2021
Third impression 2022

ISBN: 9781292391533

Set in Soho Gothic Pro

Printed in Slovakia by Neografia

Acknowledgements

The Publishers would like to thank the following people for their feedback and comments during the development of the material:

Peter Mason, Inigo Casis, Gordon Semple, Konrad Djeko, Agnieszka Tyszkiewicz-Zora, Katie Crawford, Mirta Bugacoff, Kate Brown, Jasper Luke Stein, Alexandra Warden, Bruna Mora Bastos, Susana Royo

Non-Prominent Text Credit(s):

108-109, Guardian News and Media Limited: Elle Hunt, Is it possible to work 22-hour days? Danielle Steel says it is the secret of her success, 13th May 2019. © 2019; 124, Guardian News and Media Limited: David Shariatmadari, Language wars: the 19 greatest linguistic spats of all time, 17th June 2018. © 2017.

Illustration acknowledgements

Daniel Limon (Beehive illustration agency) Pages: 8, 26, 48, 49, 50, 52, 54, 68, 72, 124, 126, 128, 129, 137, 141, 145 Lauren Radley Pages: 24, 38 Ash Jin Pages: 36, 84, 136 Tony Richardson Pages: 86, 144, 115

Photo acknowledgements

The publisher would like to thank the following for their kind permission to reproduce their photographs:

123RF.com: Anastasiya Aleksandrenko 18, Ann Dudko 122, Anyaberkut 118, Belchonock 135, Luca Bertolli 42, Mathisa 14, Milan Gonda 178, Ozgur Coskun 31, Racorn 64, Ryan DeBerardinis 117, Viktoriya Malova 78, Zulhijrah 89; **Alamy Stock Photo**: Banda Aceh 10, Deborah Vernon 83, DPA picture alliance 47, IanDagnall Computing 93, Matteo Omied 90; **Getty Images**: 10'000 Hours 74, Abel Mitjà Varela 38, Allison Michael Orenstein 132, Arpad Benedek 2017/Twilightcolors 19, Azem Ramadani 61, Benoitb 70, Buena Vista Images 37, Cavan Images 60, Colin Anderson Productions pty ltd 102, Cultura RF 7, DEA PICTURE LIBRARY 92, Denver Post 70, Diana Walker 113, Digital Vision 12, Dorling Kindersley RF 28, Dougal Waters 108, E+ 91, 140, FangXiaNuo 19, FLYFILM 60, Francis Miller 96, Gary Burchell 80, Hill Street Studios 5, 57, 101, Hiraman 56, Ika84 65, Irina Marwan 109, iStockphoto 3, 32, JOHANNES EISELE 142, Jonathan Perugia 123, JW LTD 81, Katya_Havok 120, Kevin Schafer 107, Keystone 112, Marc Dozier 88, Maskot 19, 20, Michael Duerinckx 143, Monty Rakusen 132, Mustafagull 62, Noel Hendrickson 110, Paul Bradbury 3, 29, PeopleImages 5, PeopleImages 64, Peter Cade 102, RapidEye 103, REDA&CO 70, Richard Drury 74, Robert Kneschke 6, Robert Kühne 120, Sanjeri 56, Sean_Warren 33, South_agency 35, Spencer Platt 130-131, Studio-fi 18, Sylvain Gaboury/FilmMagic 108, Tetra images 5, 70, Thomas Barwick 21, 44, Thomas M Barwick INC 5, 13, 90, ThomasVogel 14, Tim Robberts 11, Visual China Group 100, Westend61 81, WILLIAM WEST/AFP 98, Yuri_Arcurs 105, Zave Smith 79; **Shutterstock**: Adrian Bradshaw/EPA 99, AlekseyIvanov 3, 7, Basyn 16, Daily Mail 121, David Tadevosian 34, Diego Fiore 107, Dmitry Kalinovsky 42, Elnur 88, ESB Essentials 20, FER737NG 106, Fizkes 74, Gorodenkoff 90, Hanohiki 67, Howard Sandler 44, Htneim 16, Immersion Imagery 178, Ivan Bondarenko 31, Ivan_Kislitsin 97, IxMaster 29, John Wollwerth 122, Juan Ci 116, Kaspars Grinvalds 139, Kiattisak Anoochitarom 93, Leonid Ikan 5, 82, LightField Studios 104, Mar1kOFF 121, Michaeljung 16, Natthawon Chaosakun 7, Oliver Foerstner 89, Peter Stuckings 15, Pressmaster 29, QQ7 66, Rawpixel.com 3, 17, REDPIXEL.PL 25, Rich Carey 3, 47, 134, Roman Kosolapov 46, 56, Ruta Saulyte-Laurinaviciene 14, Ryan Sault Photography 33, Singkham 63, SizeSquare's 138, SpeedKingz 35, Svetlana Lazarenka 44, Syda Productions 117, Tyler Olson 78, View Apart 83, Volkovslava 78, Wavebreakmedia 31.

Cover Image: *Front*: **Getty Images**: Buena Vista Images

Every effort has been made to trace the copyright holders and we apologise in advance for any unintentional omissions. We would be pleased to insert the appropriate acknowledgement in any subsequent edition of this publication.

FSC www.fsc.org MIX Paper from responsible sources FSC™ C128612